T0366323

THE MEANINGS OF GENEALOGY FOR SCIENCE AND RELIGION

Science as Prose, Religion as Poetry

JAMES S. TOMES

AuthorHouse™ LLC
1663 Liberty Drive
Bloomington, IN 47403
www.authorhouse.com
Phone: 1-800-839-8640

© 2014 James S. Tomes. All rights reserved.

*No part of this book may be reproduced, stored in a retrieval system, or transmitted
by any means without the written permission of the author.*

Published by AuthorHouse 08/01/2014

ISBN: 978-1-4969-3212-9 (sc)
ISBN: 978-1-4969-3211-2 (e)

*Any people depicted in stock imagery provided by Thinkstock are models,
and such images are being used for illustrative purposes only.
Certain stock imagery © Thinkstock.*

This book is printed on acid-free paper.

*Because of the dynamic nature of the Internet, any web addresses or links contained in this book may have changed
since publication and may no longer be valid. The views expressed in this work are solely those of the author and do
not necessarily reflect the views of the publisher, and the publisher hereby disclaims any responsibility for them.*

THE MEANINGS OF GENEALOGY FOR SCIENCE AND RELIGION

Science as Prose, Religion as Poetry

JAMES S. TOMES

CONTENTS

PREFACE

This book and its companion, Serendipity, was stimulated in large part by having discovered, transcribed and privately published the memoirs and journals of my great-grandfather, Robert Tomes, and my great-great-grandfather, Francis Tomes. Their memoirs and journals were also not written for commercial publication, but simply as a record of their lives for reading by their children and grandchildren. Reading their memoirs and writing about their lives has given us an insight into our inheritance that we believe is worth passing on to our descendants.

These books are an attempt to follow in their tradition. They are not scholarly treatises, even though they have been carefully researched and written. This book, in particular, covers vast categories of knowledge so it can only be my necessarily amateur summary of what we have learned. We don't apologize for this because we all must make our minds up about our views of the world, and none of us can ever know everything. It is simply our attempt to tell the truth about the world, and ourselves, as we see it. It is certainly the best we can do to record and comment on our long lives of work and study.

Josie and I hope it is of some interest and use to our children and grandchildren.

ACKNOWLEDGEMENTS

THE MEANINGS OF GENEALOGY FOR SCIENCE AND RELIGION

This book is the culmination of a life-long interest I have had in religion and science - how they differ and how they relate to each other. My interest began with a Confirmation class I was enrolled in when my family moved to Northbrook, Illinois in the summer of 1940, sixty-eight years ago when I was thirteen years old. We moved to town late in the summer so I couldn't join the regular class and took independent instruction from the minister of the local Protestant Village Church. He was a Presbyterian trained minister whom I learned later was simply a "conservative" theologian.

I did the homework assigned to me and showed up at the minister's house one afternoon for a discussion. During the discussion I innocently said I didn't understand Divinity and asked if Jesus could have just been a very good man and was not a God. Well, I immediately learned that the minister had a quick temper and was not going to be challenged about the fundamentals of Christianity. I didn't mean to be challenging, but I honestly couldn't understand what was being claimed and merely asked the questions which seemed to me to be obvious. The minister's stern admonition to never question Jesus' Divinity taught me mainly that I was not going to have a reasonable discussion with him. But it also served to peak my curiosity, which has, since then, never ceased. (I had no idea then that the same question had been asked, and much more profoundly, since the very beginning of Christianity and through the ages by people such as Baruch Spinoza, Thomas Paine, Thomas Jefferson, Albert Schweitzer, Albert Einstein, and many other well-known theologians, scientists and philosophers.)

The idea that some subjects were beyond the pale of reasonable discussion just seemed to me to be unacceptable - to be, in effect, what I have later come to call "intentional ignorance". So, the first person I must acknowledge as a source for this book is that minister. The experience was, in fact, a very good lesson about the difference between science and religion. If science is "organized uncertainty", and religion is "organized certainty", the contrast could not have been more clearly illustrated.

The most significant contributor to my later education about these subjects is Rev. Philip Blackwell whom I met in 1985 when he was the pastor of the Trinity United Methodist Church of Wilmette, Illinois. My wife Josie and I became members of Phil's church; he performed the wedding ceremonies for each of our four children, and we continue to be friends with Phil and his wife Sally, even though Phil is now the Senior Pastor of the downtown Chicago United Methodist Church and we are no longer members of the Methodist Church. However, while we were members of Trinity Phil and I organized a book reading group designated "Science and Religion" and met with the group every month for fifteen years.

The group was attended by members of the church and others from other churches and synagogues in the local area. They had diverse backgrounds, in science, religion, business, law, and homemakers. We selected books on the recommendation of any member of the group and covered a very wide range of scientific and religious subject matter during the fifteen years. I bought all the books for myself, plus many other related books, and ultimately gave the entire collection of over 1,000 books to Phil's present church where they are available for reading by the public. Many of those books are referred to here.

For the past four years I have also been privileged to be a member of another stimulating book reading group, self designated as "Phoenix" which meets four to six times each year at the downtown Chicago United Methodist Church. Phoenix is chaired by the Rev. Dr. Robin Lovin, University Professor of Ethics at Southern Methodist University, Dallas, Texas. The Phoenix group includes the Rev. Philip Blackwell, senior lawyers Richard Hoskins and Bob Hoogendorn, Federal District Court Judge Joann Gottshall, County Judge and Professor Tom Donnelly, trial lawyer John Rushing, other State of Illinois men and women officials, and a few Chicago seminary school academics.

Other significant contributors to my education in science and religion are, first, Dr. Robert Dentler, a college roommate at Northwestern University who later became a PhD Sociologist who authored many well-known texts and other books, and who also just recently completed a distinguished career as a professor and academic scholar in the field of Sociology. Bob and his wife Helen have remained our good friends since college and we continue to discuss and critique the subjects in this book. Sadly, Bob died in March, 2008.

Second, and another excellent scholar and good friend, is Dr. Robin Goldsmith. Robin and Josie met early in their careers in the fashion industry, which Robin left to pursue a career as an academic and teacher. Robin earned her masters and PhD in religious history at Northwestern University where she wrote her dissertation on Rheinhold Niebuhr and Martin Buber and also converted from Christianity to Judaism. Robin was married to a wonderful and very accomplished architect, Myron Goldsmith, who died ten years ago. For all of his creative brilliance Myron was always a kindly, gentle and thoughtful man. Robin and Myron moved to Wilmette, Illinois and were neighbors for many years while their children and ours were growing up together through high school. Their daughter Chandra was a particularly close friend of our daughter Julia. Myron (1918-1996) was a Fulbright Scholar in Italy under Pier Luigi Nervi and then studied at the Illinois Institute of Technology where his thesis was advised by his mentor and friend Ludwig Mies Van Der Rohe. From 1955 through 1983 Myron was the Chief Engineer of Structures and a Principal at Skidmore, Owings and Merrill, world-renowned architects. Myron began his teaching career at IIT in 1961 and continued teaching and consulting throughout his life, creating a cadre of many admiring students and clients. Robin has been one of our closest friends all our adult lives and has also served as a serious and most helpful critic of this book during its writing.

Many friends in The Caxton Club, a wonderful gathering of Chicago bibliophiles , including, but not limited to: Edward Quattrocchi, the late Truman Metzel, and Dr. Frederic Kittle, and each of their respective spouses, and many others. And, overlapping the Caxton Club membership are the Chicago Literary Club, the University of Chicago Library Society, the Cliffdwellers Club, and The Newberry Library each of which has a creative and stimulating membership that challenges and informs my wife Josie's and my lives. Specifically at The Newberry, Dr. Robert W. Karrow, Curator of Special Collections and Maps, and Jack Simpson, Curator of Genealogy and Family History, have been very helpful.

Significant thanks are also due to the founders, editors and contributors to Zygon, the premier Journal of Religion and Science, and to one of its long time Life-Guarantors, the late Sir John M. Templeton, who himself contributed much to enhancing communication among these realms of thought.

Many thanks also to Joyce and Bruce Chelberg, a remarkable couple whom we came to know through their support of the Japan America Society of America of Chicago. Their generous support of other Chicago cultural institutions, such as The Field Museum, Steppenwolf Theatre, The Japan-America Society, The Art Institute of Chicago, and others, sets an exceptional example of enlightened citizenship. They are also energetic and intrepid world travelers who continue to enrich and inform our lives with their "Marco-Polo-like" reports from, for instance; Mongolia, China, the Arctic and the Middle East.

There are also many other friends and scholars who have given me wise counsel during the years this book has been in preparation. For instance, members of the Trinity book group; such as Dr. Corbin Covault, Larry and Joann Aggens, Bob and his late wife, Helen Piros, Reverend Bill Hensley, and Dr. Cliff Matthews each taught me their insights during each discussion. Our close friends, Dick and Jackie Higgins have done yeoman's duty on both copy editing and critiques of the content if this book. There are, unfortunately, too many other people to catalog here. Suffice it to say that I appreciate all the help I have received from so many people. The subjects of science and religion touch everyone's lives and almost everyone will readily engage in their discussion.

Most important is the help I have received for so many years from my wife Josie. She is a very astute, independent and honest critic and has significantly influenced this book and everything else I have written.

INTRODUCTION

A view from the Concorde

Just as the first book, "Serendipity", the genealogy and history of our families, this second book is written for our children and grandchildren, intended to help them find their own ways in the world. It is not a prescription, or even a proposal, for a way of life. It is instead a story of how Josie and I understand the different ways mankind has chosen to see itself; who we are as human beings, and where we come from. Our children and grandchildren must each decide for themselves how they view the world, but we at least want to record and pass on to them what we understand.

When I was a young man I found myself frequently perplexed by observing both ignorant and educated people making quite self-confident, but apparently irrational judgments about one course of action or another. What was going on? How could they be so self-confident? What was I missing? What might they know that I didn't? My parents weren't much help since my father hadn't finished high school and my loving mother had studied home economics. Our home "library" consisted mainly of The Reader's Digest, Time and Life magazines and the Bible. What I have learned later in life is that: (1) most people aren't as self-confident as they pretend, and (2) most people don't really think very hard or carefully about what, or why, they are doing what they do. In other words, they didn't really know what was going on either, but they didn't worry about it. Unfortunately, ignorance, or careless indifference, or both, are handmaidens to much self-confidence. (Incidentally, I have learned later in life that there are also many good people who do know "What is going on" and have a valid basis for their self-confidence.)

My youthful feelings of inadequacy led me early on to try to learn as much as I could about what is really going in this world. I began to inquire as broadly as I could about as many subjects as I could, and I have continued to do so all my life. I became a serious student of science, law, business, history, comparative religion, philosophy, psychology, and the arts; I also learned that such a general pursuit of knowledge can only be done as an amateur. I became proficient as a science student in biology and chemistry, and later as a practicing lawyer, and then as a successful international businessman, but in every other field I have always been just a serious amateur. It could not be otherwise - there is too much to learn.

But saying one is an amateur is not to apologize, quite the contrary. To be a serious amateur is to love what one is doing or learning. And I have certainly loved learning all my life. One of the benefits of living a long life of learning is the possibility of gaining a broad perspective, of seeing the interrelationship between many things and experiences. It is as if you have flown very high and so can see very far. I flew on occasion as a business passenger on the Concorde, the French-British supersonic airplane that crossed the Atlantic in 3 $\frac{1}{2}$ hours by climbing almost to the stratosphere. It was an exciting experience, but the most surprising fact of the trip was that sitting in a Concorde window seat you could actually see the curvature of the earth from that very high altitude. Just as we have all seen photographs taken from the moon of our "space ship earth" floating in space, I will always have these images in my mind as metaphors for learning. If we can climb high enough in learning we can see the whole perspective of a subject. We may not be able to know all the details, but we can see the boundaries, and the major elements, and how each subject relates to others. Now that we are over 80 years old we want to pass on that perspective, particularly to our children and our still very young grandchildren.

PREFACE TO GENEALOGY

Why bother with genealogies at all? Although I am still an amateur genealogist, I have found that searching for one's family roots can be a surprisingly rewarding experience. When I started my search over forty-nine years ago I was simply curious about the ancestors my father never discussed. I have discovered much more.

Why bother with genealogies at all? Who cares? Isn't it just an impractical and useless conceit? Particularly in America, where who you are now is much more important than who your ancestors were. Well, yes, it is certainly impractical, but it can also be source of profound knowledge. Knowing, and being able to tell your children and grandchildren about their ancestry is a very personal way to relate their lives to history. History becomes part of your family history and is unforgettable. Also, if you are as lucky as we were, finding memoirs and journals and books written by our ancestors, they come alive as real people. To read now what they thought over 150 years ago can be quite moving. Our historically still quite young American society is so future oriented that it is quite easy for us to forget the sacrifices made by our many hardworking deceased ancestors to make our lives so blessed. Knowing about their lives gives us a worthy reputation to maintain, and pass on.

Mortality
It is also profound in the sense that seeing your own ancestral tree is a personal reminder that none of us lives forever. Seeing your own name at the bottom of a long, ten-generation ancestral chart makes it very clear that we are each marching in an inexorable column of mortal beings. As one of our children said after seeing our ten-generation chart:

"Gee, Dad, we seem to come from a long line of people who have all died!"

Very true, and a dramatic way of teaching the lesson of every human being's inevitable mortality.

The extraordinary affluence and freedom afforded many Americans, unprecedented in all of human history, has made some of our citizens incredibly self-absorbed and living only in the immediate, entertainment-drugged present. We have gone to extreme lengths to idolize and sell products to the "youth market", with "ever-more-youthful" and mostly mindless celebrities who behave as if they think they are immortal; we try to delay our normal ageing processes with medical treatments and cosmetic surgery, and we deny or prettify death. Funeral practitioners are considered successful if the deceased "looks so natural" and, with cremation, the deceased simply disappears.

We instinctively fear and fight against death as part of our survival instinct. The loss of close relatives and friends cause us profound grief and we mourn our losses as if we are personally wounded. Other primates and other mammals also show grief and mourning over the death of close relatives. Most religions offer some form of "life after death" as a way of coping with the loss of one's own life and other's lives. They engender the hope that a "spiritual life" can continue after physical death and that a spiritual life can continue in "heaven". Belief in a life after death lets us keep in "spiritual" touch with our deceased loved ones and provides hope for our own continued life after death. There will of course be obvious confusion if the belief is asserted as literally, or scientifically, true. It is a poetic truth, but not a scientific truth. It is important to know the distinction between these two different kinds of truth.

Paraphrasing the words of the Roman Catholic author, John Dominic Crossan*, commenting on whether Jesus could have been physically resurrected to reappear on the road to Emmaus; "Emmaus never happened!" Crossan continues, "But Emmaus will always happen when people refuse to accept the death of a loved one. No one can come back from the dead physically, but our loved ones live in our hearts forever. The people who loved and believed in Jesus would simply not let him die in their hearts and they expressed their love in the language of a physical resurrection."

So it is with us all as individuals. As much as we try to rationalize death, we all grieve when a loved one dies. This common experience is a perfect metaphor for the difference between religion and science. We know that it is scientifically impossible to bring a dead person back to life, but we also don't want to accept their death, so we think of them as continuing in life. Our poetic hearts keep them alive even though our prosaic brains know that they are physically dead.

We are all therefore, simultaneously, scientific and religious. This may seem self-contradictory, and too complex, but then as human beings we are self-contradictory and complex. We have "poetic hearts" and "rational brains". We cannot be just purely scientific OR purely religious, we are each both, even though we proclaim to be one or the other. Even though we may not belong to any organized religious institution we have religious feelings. And even if we may disagree with some scientific findings, we are also scientific to the extent that we function in a largely scientific and technological world.

It is interesting to note in this regard that the 2007 study by the National Opinion Research Center at the University of Chicago shows that since 1973 between 70% and 75% of American adults state in a formal interview that they believe in life after death. (Schott's Almanac 2007)

*See later pages of this book for a more complete description of Crossan's work.

But a culture that denies human mortality is like Emelia, the 300-year-old heroine in Leos Janacek's great opera, "The Makropolis Affair", who could not love anyone until she was released from the elixir and curse of immortality. Her deal with the devil to give her the elixir of immortality had cursed her with an inability to love anyone. Her release from the curse finally allows her love someone, but also requires that she die. The knowledge and fact of mortality makes life valuable, and love possible.

I am not arguing for a "culture of the dead", but I am saying that people who have knowledge of their past, and their own mortality, are more likely to be conscious of the value of life and the common humanity they share with everyone else. Personal knowledge of one's own ancestry, and mortality, is fundamental to the appreciation of life.

The Biology of Mortality is Genetically Beneficial
It is a biological fact for all living organisms that reproduce sexually, by combining the genes of a female and male parent; a new generation is created with a new genetic make-up. Such new genetically different generations are critical to the long-term survival of each species, through the natural selection of its most fit offspring. It is the only way the species can keep generating new genetic strength. Such surviving new generations can be created only if each prior generation is born, matures,

reproduces and dies. Thus, each generation's death is a necessary step in the survival of each species. In other words, death is a biological necessity of life.

Or, from a biological, and philosophical, point of view - one can say we have each actually "experienced death", to the extent that none of us know anything of "who we were", or "where we were" before we were born. If death is merely ceasing to exist as a biological organism, then each of us has had the "experience of non-existence" before we were born. So, if one thinks of death as simply returning to the state of our pre-birth "non-existence", it is not something to be afraid of - we have all "been there and done that".

**Some Genealogical
Conceits and Perspectives**
One of the not so obvious conceits of genealogy is the choice we all usually make to trace only the line of ancestry carried by our paternal or maternal surnames - Tomes and Steel for me, and Raymaley, Schaeffer, Witmeyer and Burger for Josie. The conceit is, however, necessary because the geometric expansion of the number of each of our ancestors would quickly make our searches impossibly unwieldy if we didn't limit them to just a few names.

For example; since we all have two parents, and each of them has two parents, etc., the arithmetic illustrates the problem in just ten generations. The geometric progression of 2, 4, 8, 16, 32, 64, 128, 256, 512, and 1,024 shows that each of them has 1,024 ancestors in just ten generations! An impossibly huge chart. So for practical reasons we must limit our searches. It is however important to remember that if we trace only one surname back ten generations we are seeing only 1/1,024th of our genetic heritage at the tenth generation.

Counting backwards in history is also instructive. If each generation takes twenty years, ten generations is only 200 years. Our own family's ancestry has actually averaged 35 years per generation for ten generations, so our ancestry goes back 325 years to the 1600's (from our grandson Alex Tomes, born 1995 back to Benjamin Tomes, born 1680). Our indirect, collateral Tomes surname ancestry goes back to the 1300's in England, another fifteen to twenty generations, give or take a few. Since surnames were rarely used by ordinary people before the 1300's, it is extremely unlikely to find genealogies that go back further in time. We are each the product of an enormous gene pool. The recent developments in the science of population genetics, using DNA science, shows how all mankind is closely related and has left a traceable trail of its migrations covering the earth.

Counting backwards in history will also quickly illustrate how short a 10, 25 or 30-generation span of genealogy is compared to the total number of hundreds and thousands of human generations who have lived on earth.

And we will discuss mythology from prehistoric time, through the Axial Age (800 - 200 BCE) when most of today's religions were created. As a part of this discussion we will consider the origins of language and how it grew from simple gestures and naming of concrete objects and actions, to a complex system of naming categories of things and events, and finally to a very complex system of identifying and naming abstractions, such as "gods", "souls", "spirits", "heaven" and "hell", and "life after death". Once human language became very complex and such abstractions were given names and woven into stories populated with virtual Beings (per Alfred North Whitehead's "misplaced concreteness of the abstract"), the distinction between the natural and the supernatural, the real and the unreal, was lost. The result was, and still is, a monumental confusion between the real and the unreal, the natural and the supernatural.

Mankind's incredibly fertile imagination, and capacity for experiencing (or inducing) a variety of mental states, has created a massive variety and confusion of gods and other illusions, which confound us at every turn.

Gods, whom we created and claimed to be exclusive, omniscient and omnipotent, are now obviously not (There have been over 2500 gods throughout human history). And the same is true for "life after death", "souls" and "spirits", for which there is no scientific evidence. They are however, powerful and useful myths or illusions. When the world became a global community, and is now an electronic global community, the contradictions and impossibilities of all of these myths or illusions has become obvious to some, but not all people.

One of the results of this self-created confusion is a cacophony of so-called "Theologies", attempting to make logical sense are of our disparate imaginings and "misplaced concreteness of the abstract". Questions of whether or not specific gods, or other illusions, continue to live, or have died, or what they mean, can become quite absurd when in fact they are simply products of our fertile imaginations. Like trying to make sense of our dreams.

It is also true, however, that when most people in a given culture believe in such imagined gods, or life after death, or souls or spirits; it is AS IF they are actually real and not illusions. And, when different cultures believe in different gods, or even different rituals, and consider their beliefs to be fundamental to their Being, so much so that they will go to War on their account, THEY MIGHT AS WELL BE REAL, and not illusory.

By saying that our Gods and Life After Death, etc. are illusions is not to demean them, but rather to call them what they are; grand, fearful, hopeful, poetic and sacred illusions. To subject such ideas to the prosaic tests of scientific evidence is to demean them. They were never conceived as scientific truths, they were sacred. They were the products of our heartfelt emotions and not our merely rational brains.

And, even though such gods or other illusions may not be "real" in the scientific sense, they are expressions of very real human hopes and fears and desires, thus adding urgency to their beliefs. None of us wants to die so it is comforting to believe in "life after death" where our "souls" and "spirits" continue on after our biological bodies die.

The Contents of this Book

This book will also cover the following subjects:

1. Our mortality. The fact that makes us all amateur philosophers.

2. The major worldviews held by the many various people on earth. What people believe as their fundamental world view has real consequences in their and other's, daily lives. It is therefore very important to know, as pop-culture says, "Where you're coming from". There are at least five different major categories of world views; three religious, one political, and one scientific; (1) Polytheistic religions, (2) Abrahamic monotheistic religions, (3) Buddhism – Confucianism - Taoist "religions", (4) 20th Century Utopian political systems - Communism - Naziism and Maoism, and, lastly (5) Scientific Humanism and Religious Humanism.

3. What are the conflicts between religion and science?

4. The differences between scientific, legal, academic and religious evidence.

5. What are the differences between belief and knowledge?

6. What is the history of mankind's ancient religions and their genealogies?

7. What is modern science, from the Big Bang to the present? What is the scientific view of the Universe?

8. How has mankind's behavior evolved biologically, and culturally?

9. What about brain science?

10. How have we created supernatural Gods and Goddesses?

11. What about Biblical interpretation, and Fundamentalism?

12. How and when does knowledge become belief?

13. The history of the Christian Reformation to Humanism

14. What about the Dark Side of Religion?

15. How can anybody be religious and rational? The Poetry - Prose Metaphor.

We will therefore also discuss the biology of belief and its relationship to knowledge. When and how does an imaginative and comforting possibility become a certainty to some people?

We will also consider our biological capacity to observe and analyze the world round us, and our apparent compulsion to make sense out of what we observe - to relate causes and effects has led us to both religion and science.

And, finally, we will discuss some famous scientists as Humanists and Poets, and some remarkable religious people we have known, and many sacred places we have visited. We will consider regarding Science as Prose and Religion as Poetry, both readily accessible to each of us.

WHERE DO WE COME FROM?

There is a remarkable and evocative painting, a true masterpiece, by Paul Gauguin, which hangs in the Boston Museum of Fine Arts, illustrating mankind's most fundamental questions. It was painted in 1898 in Tahiti and shows a number of Tahitian women, children, men, and a religious idol, all-standing or sitting in ambiguous poses, in a South Sea Island tropical landscape. Its title, translated from the French, is:

"Where Do We Come From?
What Are We?
Where Are We Going?"

Answers to these questions have been offered from prehistoric times and throughout human history to the present, first by all of mankind's religions, and more recently by science.

Most religions base their teachings on a statement of belief about how the universe, earth and mankind have been created, and what the rules are for their morality. Many religions have very specific genealogies describing the descent of their people from their gods and ancestors, usually described in supernatural terms. Most religions have what can be called "transactional gods", whose adherents believe have created the universe and mankind, are aware of and care about human needs, can intervene in human affairs to either reward or punish, and provide life after death. People have always sought gods and have always found them, and hold onto them tenaciously. Believing in gods is a pervasive and persistent human trait. As one author said, "God didn't go away after the Enlightenment."

The Dictionary of Gods and Goddesses identifies over 2,500 major Gods in human history. Although many religions claim to be "exclusively true" by their adherents, there

"Where Do We Come From? What Are We? Where Are We Going?" Paul Gauguin 1897-98.

Museum of Fine Arts, Boston.

is no one religion believed to be "exclusively true" by everyone. It seems obvious to me that the only possible explanation for so many Gods is that they are products of the endless variety of creative human imaginations.

Answers to the questions of, What Are We? And Where Do We Come From? Depending upon one's fundamental frame of reference, one's basic "world view". We will therefore consider the major categories of "world views" religions, or belief systems, each one of which defines the origins, destiny and the characteristics of its people. It is very important for each of us to understand our own basic worldview, because it determines what we think about "Where We Come From, and What We Are. There are, in other words, real-life consequences to what we believe.

Are we part of Nature, or separate from it? Are we in God's care as a chosen people, or are we on our own? Should we expect the Gods to fix our problems or should we try to fix them ourselves? Should we read our sacred texts as metaphorical parables, or poetic myths, or literally, as if they are scientifically true? Should we acknowledge our evolutionary behavioral traits and try to manage them or should we accept

mythical definitions of what we are? Are we condemned by "Original Sin", or are we simply evolutionary primates, blessed with an extraordinary intelligence, but still bearing an "original ignorance" and "the indelible stamp of our lowly origins", as Darwin said. Each of these questions is concerned with who has the responsibility for managing human affairs. Gods, or mankind?

MAJOR WORLD VIEWS

Let us compare the various major religions or worldviews: First, the polytheistic religions, such as Hinduism and the Greek and Roman pantheon, and the animistic "spirit" religions, such as Japanese Shinto, Australian and South Pacific Aboriginal and South and North American Indian, and others which also have multiple gods who are believed to have designed the universe and humanity and can be entreated to intervene in human affairs.

Second, the Abrahamic monotheistic religions of Judaism, Christianity and Islam which see humanity as a creation of a single supernatural God, who brought mankind into being and guides it as father, judge and friend. Their God claims exclusivity as the only God, and is believed to intervene in human affairs, rewarding and punishing its adherents, and providing life after death. The Creation Myths of these religions teach that mankind was specially created, separately from the rest of Nature, and given the right of dominion over nature. However, many modern Christian and Jewish theologians are quite comfortable with maintaining their supernatural religious beliefs and also accepting the teachings of modern physics and biological science.

"Deism", Unitarianism and Quakerism descend historically from Judeo-Christianity as ethical systems, but do not accept the teachings of the supernatural or divinity.

Third, Buddhism, which, strictly speaking, is not a "revealed" religion because it was originally without supernatural gods or a supernatural cosmology. Buddha described himself as a mortal man. Buddhism prescribes a "self-taught" "enlightenment" and a code of behavior to relieve human suffering, and teaches that mankind is a part of nature, which it is obligated to conserve and protect. Confucianism, founded about the same time as Buddhism is also not a religion, but a system of ethical rules designed to create a model state, founded on " The Golden Rule". Confucius has also been referred to as the "Teacher of 10,000 generations". Taoism, also founded during the "axial age", by Lao-Tsu is a mystical system of thought intended to bring its adherents to a simple quiet life, close to nature. Although neither Buddhism, Confucianism or Taoism were founded as religions, their adherents have given them religious attributes with temples, priests and prayers, etc.

Fourth, the 20th century utopian political systems of the rapidly fading and mostly dysfunctional "Marxist-Leninist", Communist states, which see humanity as a blank-slate, molded by a Communistic political system. Some modern historians have identified Communism as a "pseudo-religion", and the totalitarian police states of Soviet Communism, German Naziism, Chinese Maoism and North Korean fascism, mimicking the functions of religion, as secular or "surrogate" religions, worshiping nation, class, race, or national leaders. These systems are marked by extreme violence. They are example of mankind's capacity, as compulsive believers, to believe in, or at least accept, secular as well as supernatural gods. Communism, Naziism and Maoism have each prescribed and enforced the desired characteristics of their people. Neither Russian or Chinese "Capitalism" seems to be creating true democracy. They are still police states.

And, fifth, a more radical and small minority world view, Scientific Humanism which "considers humanity to be a biological species that evolved over millions of years in a biological world, acquiring unprecedented intelligence yet still guided by complex inherited emotions and biased channels of learning. Human nature exists, and it was self assembled within Nature. It is the combination of hereditary responses and propensities that define our species. Having arisen by evolution during the far simpler conditions in which humanity lived during more than 99 percent of its existence, it forms the behavioral part of what Darwin called, in his the "Descent of Man", '"the indelible stamp of our lowly origin". Quotes here are from the "Afterward, Evolution and Religion, pp. 1479-1483 of "So Simple a

Beginning" edited by E.O. Wilson (Norton, 2005). Scientific Humanism can only thrive in a society where democracy, individual responsibility, freedom of thought and speech and inquiry thrive. Science, as the language of skepticism, is the language of freedom.

My Personal World View

Personally, I see "Scientific/Religious Humanism" as an extension of Scientific Humanism, and, as such, it sees that religion is one of the important evolutionary and present-day characteristics of human nature. Religious beliefs can confer strong survival benefits, and can also generate great destruction. Most of humanity needs and has always had "sacred" gods, "transcendence", "life after death", places, rituals and sacraments, tribes and communities, and rules of morality and law. Religious Humanism includes recognition of all of these. In this sense, I consider myself a "Scientific/ Religious Humanist". To me, the highest and best expression of our humanity is to live an ethical life. In my view all supernatural gods and many other elements of religious belief and practice are the creation of mankind's fertile imagination. This is not to demean religious belief. Quite to the contrary, religious beliefs and practices are usually the expression of mankind's highest hopes and aspirations, and his greatest fears - the poetic, hopeful and emotional side of humanity. But in the view of Scientific/Religious Humanism they are the expressions of human beings, and not of supernatural origin.

I see Scientific/Religious Humanism as a much more positive and enriching worldview than "atheism" or "agnosticism", both of which are rather empty and negative characterizations. They only express the non-belief in the supernatural; gods, life after death, etc. And they imply or expressly demean religion, overlooking its pervasive and persistent hold on the human psyche and culture. Scientific/Religious Humanism combines the best of science and humanism into a credible and wonderful story of humanity.

CONFLICTS BETWEEN
SCIENCE AND RELIGION

Beginning with Aristotle and the other Greeks in 350 B.C.E., through Copernicus in the 1500's, Galileo in the 1600's, Newton in the1700's, Hutton and Lyell in the late 1700's and early 1800's, Wallace and Darwin in 1859 with his "On the Origin of Species" and "Descent of Man" in 1871, Einstein's Special Theory of Relativity in 1905, Watson and Crick's discovery of DNA in 1953, and the paleo-archeologists, primatologists, evolutionary, behavioral and neuro-scientists of the 20th and now 21st centuries, scientists have offered alternative answers to the questions of what we are and where we come from. This book is not the place for a comprehensive history of science, but there are plenty of good histories of science available in most libraries.

Scientific/Religious Humanism does not purport to explain all of humanity's characteristics, or to answer the most profound questions of "why there is something, rather than nothing", in other words, the mysteries of Being and Time. Thus Scientific/Religious Humanism is not "Scientism", nor is it metaphysics, or a philosophy. When asked, "What was there before the Big Bang?" the scientific answer is "We don't know". Science is concerned only with meas-urable natural phenomena and not with the supernatural. It is, rather, an attempt to explain scientifically who we humans are within the context of our lives here on earth. It includes an attempt to understand and explain the processes by which humanity expresses its needs for and practices of religion. This essay is an attempt to interpolate and communicate between the worlds of science and religion.

Conflicts between religion and science usually arise when a new scientific discovery contradicts a nat-ural phenomenon described in a sacred religious text or dogma. For instance, the first serious "modern" conflict between religion and science didn't occur until the 1500's when Copernicus asserted that the Earth revolved around the Sun, contrary to the Biblical and Aristotelian view that the Earth was the center of the Universe. While Copernicus died shortly after the publication of his "De Revolution bus", his discovery was confirmed in the 1600's by Galileo, who was made to recant by the Church and its Aristotelian Academy and kept under house arrest until his death. The Church finally "acquitted" Galileo in 2000, almost 400 years after he was forced to recant.

The next major conflict occurred between science and religion beginning in 1859 with the simultaneous publication of Wallace and Darwin's theory of evolution by natural selection. The problem of course was that the theory of evolution contradicted the literal Biblical assertions about the origins of mankind. The ideas and facts of evolution presented a much more fundamental challenge to religion than did the cosmology of Copernicus and Galileo. The Roman Catholic Church has long since accepted the teaching of evolution in its church schools as well-founded science, reserving for its theology only the origin of man's "soul". Judaism and most Protestant churches also accept the scientific teachings of evolution.

But some very vociferous American Fundamentalist Protestant churches still deny evolution and propose "Creationism" or "Intelligent Design" as alternative "theories". However, American courts have repeatedly ruled that such alternatives are simply not science and therefore cannot be taught in public school science classes. However, the debate continues, particularly in America, where over one-half of the adult population still believes in the Biblical version of the origin of mankind. An amazing example of how religious belief can trump rational, scientific evidence.

The conflicts, in short, have arisen because the natural phenomena previously described as part of a religious belief system, based upon supernatural premises, have been challenged by subsequently discovered scientific evidence. The continuing problem is that even though the evidence is clear, some Fundamentalist religious institutions, and a poorly science-educated population, still deny the clear scientific evidence.

Worse yet is when governments base their policies and enforcement actions on religious beliefs that are contrary to scientific facts. The present, 2000 - 2008 American political administration and congress, led by president George W. Bush, is under the sway and leadership of many Fundamentalist Christians, including the president, who have repeatedly and persistently legislated, ruled and spoken out against scientific findings, such as global warming, evolution and stem-cell research. The most significant long term conflict in this regard has to do with global warming, which virtually all scientific observers agree is a serious and threatening fact, a clear and present danger, affecting the lives of all human beings, but which is denied by the religious Fundamentalists and their political supporters. This issue can have more profound consequences than either the Galileo's cosmology or Darwin's evolution.

As Mark Twain once said: "It ain't what you don't know that gets you into trouble. It's what you know for sure, but just ain't so."

The Fundamentalist's denial of the scientific facts of Global Warming can lead the whole human race into serious, long-lasting trouble. However, one hopeful recent development is that a large group of American Evangelist churches have spoken out in agreement with traditional environmentalists on behalf of energy conservation and other actions to mediate global warming. They now profess to believe that the Bible declares that the earth "belongs to God" and that "mankind has a responsibility to care for it." (For a recent attempt by a renowned scientific humanist,

Professor E. O. Wilson, to bridge the gap between science and religion on the subject of environmental conservation, see his "Letter to the Baptist Church", 2006. It is, as usual, Wilson's heartfelt and thoughtful plea to help save our earth from destruction.)

So, we must talk about religion and science in any serious discussion of genealogy - What We Are and Where We Come From. These basic subjects are huge, and even this necessarily brief and summary discussion is itself rather long and sometimes complicated. My hope is that this kind of discussion will reduce the barriers between religion and science and allow each to thrive in its own domain, without conflict. Later in the discussion I will try to develop and illustrate the metaphor of religion as POETRY, and science as PROSE, as a way of making both subjects accessible to everyone without conflict.

As our good friend Mary Swope, herself a published poet, says, Poetry has a way of "plumbing the depths" at its best, of uncovering Truth in the largest sense of the word - truths of the human heart and truths of a more existential sort."

EVIDENCE: SCIENTIFIC, LEGAL, ACADEMIC AND "RELIGIOUS"

First what is the nature of the evidence for these different views of the origin of the universe and mankind's place in it? We must begin by examining the differences between scientific, legal and "religious" evidence. These differences directly affect our interpretation of genealogy.

a. The Author's Educational and Religious Background

But, before I begin the discussion, I will recite here briefly my educational and religious background so the reader will be able to put my points of view in perspective. (This detailed personal information is provided primarily for our grandchildren who are so young that we will probably never know them as adults. The general reader is certainly welcome to skip these details.)

My Educational Background:
After high school and military service from 1944 to 1947 I began college on the GI Bill at Northwestern University in Evanston, Illinois where I earned a degree in biology, with minors in chemistry, sociology and psychology. Courses in comparative anatomy, taxonomy, botany, embryology, histology, physiology, genetics, evolution, organic and inorganic chemistry, physical chemistry, physics, and mathematics through calculus, were the science ABC's of my college education.

I graduated with the class of 1952 with a Bachelor of Science, while home on leave because I was recalled into military service during the Korean War in 1950 - 53. After college I also earned a Juris Doctor from Chicago Kent College of Law in 1957.

I practiced law for a few years and then became a businessman and president and CEO of various manufacturing and publishing businesses until I retired at age 70 in 1997. Since college and law school I have also been a serious (but necessarily amateur) student of science, philosophy, history, prehistoric man, the arts and comparative religion. In this life-long pursuit of knowledge I have been professionally involved with legal, scientific and religious evidence, and acquired a significant library in each of these areas of study.

I recently donated my approximately one thousand volume, science and religion part of this library to the First United Methodist Church, "The Temple", at Clark and Washington streets in downtown Chicago (60602) Illinois. The church's senior pastor is Reverend Philip L. Blackwell, with whose help and guidance I developed the library while he was pastor and I was a member of Trinity United Methodist Church in Wilmette, Illinois from 1984 to 1997. (More about Rev. Blackwell later) The library is open to the public, but is not a lending library.

My Religious Background

My religious background began with my baptism as an infant in a Presbyterian church in Milwaukee, Wisconsin. My mother was a Scotch-Presbyterian and my father was an Episcopalian. One of my great-grand-

fathers, Alexander Wilson was a Congregationalist minister in Paisley, Scotland for 43 years. I attended protestant churches with my parents as we moved to various communities in the Midwest during the 1930's. I was confirmed as a member of the Village Church in Northbrook, Illinois by its then Presbyterian minister in 1940. The church was very small at that time, with less than 150 members. During my confirmation class at age 13, I was admonished by that minister for merely saying that I could not understand Divinity and asking if Jesus could not have simply been an extremely moral and brave man. (I had no idea as a 13 year old boy in 1940 that this same question bad been asked by many, many people before me, including Baruch Spinoza, David Hume, Thomas Jefferson, Thomas Paine, William James and Dr. Albert Schweitzer, among many others) I attended the Village Church, without asking the minister any more questions, until 1944 when I joined the army at age 17.

I did not attend any regular church services during my two periods of military service from 1944 - 1946 and 1950 - 1953. Nor did I attend any regular church services during college or law school. My wife and I were married in 1954 in Howes Memorial Chapel, a Methodist Chapel attached to Garrett Theological Seminary on the campus of Northwestern University. We did not attend any regular church services until we joined the Unitarian Church in Evanston, Illinois after the birth of our first child in 1960. Our first three children were "dedicated" as infants in that Unitarian Church, which we attended until we moved to Wilmette in 1963. We joined Trinity United Methodist Church in Wilmette in 1984 where we participated actively until 1997 when we resigned because we disagreed strongly with the Methodist Church's Judicial Council's ruling discriminating against some church members and clergy. In our view their ruling was both theologically wrong and contrary to the inclusive and loving spirit of Reverend John Wesley, the principal founder of Methodism. So, we have not been a member of any church since 1997, but we do support Rev. Phil Blackwell's church in Chicago.

Where I stand now:
Since leaving the Methodist Church I realized that I have become, over the course of many years of study and thought, a humanist with a serious interest in both science and religion.I have great respect, and love, for many Christian friends (as well as many Jewish, Buddhist, atheistic and other friends), and also for some aspects of Christian and other religious institutions, and some of their teachings, their sacred places music

and poetry. But I simply cannot honestly accept, or recite, or believe in, Christian dogma and therefore cannot, and should not, profess that I am a Christian.

b. Scientific Evidence
Science is primarily concerned with physical evidence of natural phenomena. Science is not concerned with supernatural phenomena. Stars, planets; rocks, fossils, archeological remains, living organisms, and DNA are scientists principal tools and evidence for the physical nature of the universe and mankind's place in it. Scientific evidence is, by definition, objectively measurable and repeatable in a public forum. Science, also by definition, is always subject to modification, depending upon the most recent discoveries.

In a 1982 court case, McLean vs. Arkansas Board of Education, which invalidated a statute mandating the teaching of creation science in public schools, Judge Overton's opinion declared in part, "The essential characteristics of science are: (1) it is guided by natural law; (2) it has to be explanatory by reference to natural law; (3) it is testable against the empirical world; (4) its conclusions are tentative, i.e., not necessarily the final word; and (5) it is falsifiable." Creationism failed to meet these criteria, Overton concluded; and therefore could not be taught as science.

It should be noted here that Buddhism, while known as a religion, is fundamentally different that Abrahamic monotheistic religions (Judaism, Christianity and Islam) because it is not God - centered, is not "revealed by any supernatural being", and does not have a creation myth, or metaphysics. Buddha himself was a mortal man who taught the students of Buddhism to follow a system of self-taught enlightenment. The central concern of Buddhism is the alleviation of suffering, similar to the goals of Abrahamic monotheistic religions, but it prescribes the reduction of desire as the means to alleviate suffering, by rational thought and meditation, and not by sacrifice, prayer, or divine intervention. For these reasons Buddhism should be considered as "science" in this discussion of evidence.

c. Science as "Organized Skepticism"

An excellent statement about science, from the recently published "Origins", by Tyson and Goldsmith (W.W. Norton, 2004), after commenting on page 17 about the "sixteenth and seventeenth century's spread of books and improvements in travel allowing individuals to communicate more quickly and effectively, had led to a new way of acquiring knowledge, based on the principle that the most

effective means of understanding the cosmos relies on careful observations, coupled with attempts to specify broad and basic principles that explain a set of these observations."

"One more concept gave birth to science. Science depends on "organized skepticism", that is, on continual, methodological doubting. Few of us doubt our own conclusions, so science embraces its skeptical approach by rewarding those who doubt someone else's. We may rightly call this approach unnatural; not so much because it calls for distrusting someone else's thoughts, "but because science encourages and rewards those who can demonstrate that another scientist's conclusions are just plain wrong. To other scientists, the scientist who corrects a colleagues error, or cites good reasons for seriously doubting his or her conclusions, performs a noble deed, like a Zen master who boxes the ears of a novice straying from the meditative path, although scientists correct one another more as equals than as master and student. By rewarding a "scientist who spots another's errors, a task that human nature makes much easier than discerning one's own mistakes, scientists have created an inborn system of self-correction. Scientists have collectively created our most efficient and effective tool for analyzing nature, because they seek to disprove other scientists' theories even as they support their earnest attempts to advance human knowledge. Science thus amounts to a collective pursuit, but a mutual admiration society it is not, nor was it meant to be."

d. Legal Evidence and Academic Evidence

American laws of evidence, generally based on English Common Law, also attempt to achieve objectivity, and require presentation in a public forum. The well-known human capacity for deceit, plus the unreliability of memory, and of "eye witness" testimony, has generated an Anglo American adversary system of law designed to overcome human frailty and bias. (See "Seven Sins of Memory", Daniel Schacter, 2001) The rules of evidence therefore give most credence to "direct evidence" as shown by relevant documents and to witnesses who have observed relevant events directly. Strong credence is also given to corroborating witnesses, "dying declarations" and "statements against interest".

On the other hand, "Hearsay" evidence, that is, testimony by one person about the content of what was said by another, is usually excluded. Also excluded are "self-serving statements", statements made by litigants obviously intended to support their contentions.

Where no direct evidence is available most American courts will allow "circumstantial evidence", i.e.; evidence of circumstances, which logically infer the events or facts for which there is no direct evidence. Also, in criminal cases, the presumption is that the accused is innocent until proven guilty, and the prosecution must prove its case "beyond a reasonable doubt". The proof of the accuser's "intent" to commit the prohibited act is frequently required. In civil cases there need only be "preponderance of evidence" in favor of the alleged fact. So, in criminal cases where the penalty can be imprisonment, or even death, the level of proof required is much higher than in civil cases where the penalty is usually just monetary.

However, the attempt behind each of these rules is to arrive at an objective, publicly stated, measure of disputed events. The Anglo-American tradition of adversary proceedings is also an attempt to get at an objective "truth" by allowing the expression of contrary views via the cross-examination of direct witness testimony. This is even the method in the case of "expert testimony" where each side is permitted the right to present his own "expert". Further, where testimony is taken in the presence of a jury, the demeanor of the witnesses is usually a particularly important factor in the jury's assessment of the truth of the testimony.

Academic evidence is another version of legal evidence, trying to achieve objectivity, although its challenges are much more difficult. The "Historical-Critical" method of academic inquiry usually requires: (1) that two or more corroborating sources are presented, and (2) that the event described is consonant with other contemporary events, and, (3) that the historical natural phenomena are consonant with modern science. For example, that the sun could not have "stood still", or that dead people could not have come back to life. Some theologians attempt to explain Biblical hermeneutics and exegesis (interpretation) on the basis of the historical-critical method (See later in this book the Jesus Seminar and the Vatican Rule on Biblical Interpretation.) The obvious difficulty with academic evidence is the wide latitude that must be given to interpretation of events that happened long ago for which there are no living witnesses who can be examined, or cross-examined.

Thus, in scientific, legal and academic evidence the attempt is always to arrive at an objective truth. Conclusions are based upon the most current, publicly available, objective evidence.

If the evidence changes, the conclusions change.

In our "post modern' world the very idea of an "objective truth" has come under serious attack with "deconstructionism", and the misapplication of the "Heisenberg uncertainty principle" of nuclear physics. But most reasonable people have found a common sense, practical confirmation of the fact that many events and things can be agreed to be objectively either true or false. For excellent discussions of this subject see: "Truth, A Guide", by Simon Blackburn (Oxford U. Press, 2005), and "True To Life, Why Truth Matters", by Michael P. Lynch. (The MIT Press, 2004)

e. Religious Evidence as "Organized Certainty"

In contrast, evidence of religious phenomena is typically observed and measured subjectively. Dreams, visions, and voices, are usually experienced by individuals in private, but sometimes induced by communal worship, music, dancing, or hallucinatory drug induced ecstasy or trances, or fasting, or meditation. Many such altered states of consciousness can create a variety of "anomalous", "out-of-body", or even "near-death" experiences, which can be more vivid to the one having the experience than the normal everyday experiences of life. These "experiences" however occur inside the brains of individuals and are therefore not subject to external verification. The fact that the person having such "experiences" can believe they have actually occurred "in the real world", or "supernaturally", further complicates the question of their validity as evidence. (See "Varieties of Anomalous Experience: Examining the Scientific Evidence, by Cardena Lynn & Krippner, 2000, American Psychological Assn.)

Religious phenomena are also concerned many times with perceived supernatural events. Other important elements of religious evidence are sacred texts written by ancient, long dead authors, now unavailable for examination. Communal religious worship and ritual are of course well-known and common experiences throughout human history.

Religious beliefs are certain, simple and unchanging – such is their purpose. Scientific knowledge is uncertain, complex and changes often, requiring work and flexibility to keep current. If one definition of science is that it is "organized skepticism" then religion is, in contrast, " organized certainty".

It seems obvious that there is a human compulsion to believe and to tell stories. My own extensive reading of human history tells me that we are, among other things, the "believing species". We seem compelled to ask questions - to find out how the universe and the world works - giving us a powerful competitive advantage - and we also seem compelled to provide answers, no matter how questionable the objectivity of the evidence. Our religions and our sciences are both attempts to explain who we are, with quite different evidentiary bases. In this way religion can be viewed as humanity's "first science".

We are storytellers and our stories must have beginnings and endings. We demand answers – and we are averse to uncertainty – it makes us anxious. We seek to relieve our anxiety by finding answers. We are believing organisms and, if necessary, we will create or believe in answers to our most important questions, without careful regard to the nature of the evidence. It is also a biological fact that our emotional response is usually quicker and more powerful than our rational response, which can then be just a rationalization of the emotional. And there does not appear to be any "rational editor" in our brains. In many cases the reverse is true; our beliefs, based on emotional evidence, can trump our rational mind. No "fuses blow" when there are inconsistencies in our minds. We can easily hold to beliefs that are contradicted by our "rational minds". Or, for that matter, our "ethical" minds.

Given this hierarchy of evidence it should be no surprise why religious beliefs about the origins of the universe, the creation of the earth and mankind's place on it have prevailed for so long.

A recent book by Michael Gazzaniga, "The Science Behind What Makes Us Unique" sheds important empirical light on the question of belief. Gazzaniga begins by reminding us of the complexity of the human brain: "The human brain has approximately 100 billion neurons, and each, on average, connects to about 1,000 other neurons. A quick multiplication reveals that there are 100 trillion (!) syntaptical connections. So, how is all this input getting spliced and integrated into a coherent package? How do we get order out of this chaos of connections?" Gazzaniga's empirical work focused on "split brain" phenomena that illustrates the theory that the "right brain" specializes as the data collector while the "left brain" specializes as the interpreter of the data. Gazzaniga observes, "The left brain interpreter makes sense out of all the other processes. It takes all the input that is coming in and puts it together in a make-sense story, even though it may be completely wrong! The answer may lie in the left-hemisphere interpreter and its drive to seek explanations for why events occur." ... "This finding illustrates the human tendency to generate explanations for events. When aroused, we are driven to explain why. If there is an obvious explanation, we accept it,…When there is not an obvious explanation, the left brain generates one. This is a powerful mechanism, once seen, it makes one wonder how often we are victims of spurious emotional-cognitive correlations." ….The interpreter is driven to generate explanations and hypotheses regardless of circumstances."

Thus,"crazy" and "illogical" dreams are probably our interpreter left-brains trying to make sense out of the randomly input visions and thoughts dredged up by our right-brains while we sleep. And, similarly, when we are confronted by an otherwise inexplicable natural even our interpreter left-brain will supply us with an answer, now matter how spurious the evidence.

All of which leads us into our next subject, belief and knowledge. There are many excellent books about belief, such as: "Six Impossible Things Before Breakfast", by Lewis Wolpert (2006), and "How We Believe", Michael Shermer (2006). These two books also have extensive bibliographies of many other books about belief.

BELIEF AND KNOWLEDGE

As Edward O. Wilson, Professor Emeritus of biology at Harvard, once said; "People would rather believe than know". The certainty of adherence to unchanging "infallible" religious beliefs is regarded by believers as a strength. Religious institutions, like most institutions, have an authoritarian hierarchy, compelling adherence to its teachings. Religious evidence is obedient to such authority.

The expression of religious belief is usually expressed in the form of emotionally affective activities: ritual, sacrifice, music, dance, theater, painting, sculpture, and poetry. Religions typically provide simple answers to complex and vexing questions. Religious systems of thought also provide hope to the otherwise hopeless, and solace to the otherwise inconsolable. Strong religious belief has sustained many people through difficult, life-threatening circumstances. Community worship and support systems also provide strength. And prayer is an important part of many religions. Belief in the possibility of communicating with one's God provides hope, even though the rational evidence for the efficacy for prayer is slim, at best. But, if prayer strengthens the resolve and hope of the one offering the prayer, it is certainly conferring a powerful and real benefit here on earth. Christianity and Judaism stress the healing, confessional and atonement power of prayer, and Islam mandates prayer five times each day

The late, great, Primo Levi, a Jewish, but agnostic Holocaust survivor, and author of "Survival at Auschwitz" (1947) stated from his own personal experience that those who had a religious belief, even those who had a "religious belief" in Communism, had a much better chance of survival in a concentration camp. Belief in a "cause" or a caring God, and life after death can provide strength in the face of severe adversity here on earth.

Most religions include prayer as a way of communicating one's wishes or hopes to their deities. Many true believers have steadfastly held onto their beliefs during relentless torture under threat of death, and then horrible death as martyrs by drowning, burning at the stake, or mutilation, even professing their beliefs while being tortured and killed. (See "Mirror of the Martyrs", the stories of medieval Mennonite martyrs tortured by the ruling church and state, by Oyer and Kreider (1973)

The certainty offered by most religions makes most people prefer to settle on unchanging beliefs instead of trying to stay current with constantly changing information. The global pervasiveness and strong persistence of many different religions throughout human history illustrates clearly that the certainty of religious belief is necessary and important to most people.

a. Science is not "Scientism"

Most religious concepts and practices are outside the scope of science. Scientists do, however, study mankind's religious practices in anthropology, archeology, psychology and neurobiology. Science, based as it is upon the premise of dealing only with the natural world, does not and cannot deal with the supernatural. Science takes natural phenomena as it finds them and does its best to analyze and understand how the phenomena work and relate to other phenomena.

There are some people who advocate "Scientism", asserting that science can explain everything and become a substitute for religion. Most scientists do not assert such a claim, recognizing that science cannot explain profound philosophical questions, such as; "Why is there something, rather than nothing?", or "Is there life after death?", or "What is the "intent" of the creator of the universe?", or "What was there before the Big Bang?" Most scientists recognize that there are many such questions, even beyond the mystery of "waves or protons?" in quantum physics, that science cannot answer, simply because they are not measurable natural phenomena. The appropriate scientific answer to these kinds of questions is simply, "We don't know." However, for those people who demand an answer to every question, "don't know" is not enough.

The scientific view of the Universe and Nature is so infinite, complex and mysterious that it greatly surpasses any of the Universes contemplated by the pre-scientific era religions. Most modern science has been created since the 16th century, so it didn't even exist when most religions were being formed. Our known Universe is so vast, with at least 100 million galaxies, that the gods of pre-scientific religions now seem embarrassingly mundane and demeaning of the power and enormity of the scientific epic of creation. (Our earth is, after all, just a small planet in a minor solar system at the perimeter of a small galaxy.) Many find this alternative scientific view a compellingly profound basis for living a creative, moral, productive, loving, joyous and tolerant life, and work hard to alleviate suffering and advance mankind's happiness here on earth.

However, all of us, scientists and religious believers alike, exist inside of and are part of the enormous mystery of Being and Time - the essence of which we do not understand, probably because we cannot stand outside of it and observe it. It is this awesome mystery within which we all live, and before which we must all stand in reverence, whether we call it God, or simply admit our ignorance. From mankind's earliest sentient beginnings we have tried to understand these fundamental secrets of the universe. Our religions are attempts to understand, just as out sciences are our more recent attempts to understand. Both religion and science see the universe through different lenses; religion with many profound and poetic truths, and science with many brilliant rational truths, but both are looking at the same universe.

b. Humanity as "Homo-Religious"

Wendy Doniger, the Mercia Eliade Professor of Comparative Religion at the University of Chicago says that Eliade "argued that every human is basically religious, whether he knows it or not; humankind is "homo religiousus", and therefore every human has a need to find meaning, to discern patterns, though each culture, indeed each individual, may fill the broad outlines differently. She goes on to say "And though it is surely evident by now that not every "homo" is "religious", it is equally, and painfully, evident at last, even to the positivists who for years scorned religion and looked forward to replacing it with science, that a great deal of the human race finds a deep, and often violent need to ground their lives in religious beliefs."

Science, as man's expression of rational thought does not usually provide hope or solace, or emotionally affective answers to the questions of how to live our lives. Some medical researchers claim to find scientific evidence that people professing religious belief can heal more quickly than those who don't. Other recent studies show that group prayer to help healing has no positive effect, and can be negative if false hopes are raised.

Many scientists are puzzled by the persistence of American Fundamentalist religious beliefs in Creationism and Intelligent Design, in spite of the overwhelming scientific evidence in favor of Evolution, and the repeated American court decisions ruling that such beliefs are not science. As commented earlier the problem lies primarily in the poor quality of American science education, but also in the simple fact that science is not obvious to the uneducated. It is not "common sense" in the normal use of the term. It is "common sense" that the earth is flat and that complex living organisms must be "designed" to someone who hasn't studied science. One must study science and learn to overcome the ordinary "common sense" that one sees from an uneducated and limited perspective is not so. One must do one's homework. Unless and until more Americans do their homework and science becomes the educated "common sense" of the public mind, we will continue to have the difficult conflict between science and religion in America.

It will also require more "homework" for both scientists and religious believers to understand that a rational understanding of the "prose" of science need not conflict with the "poetry" of religious belief.

c. Speaking Out For Science

It will, for instance, take more speaking out by the leaders of responsible religious institutions and others on behalf of science. Pope John Paul II, for example, spoke out strongly on behalf of Evolution as "more than a hypothesis" in 1996 and supported the continued teaching of Evolution in its church schools. The present Pope Benedict VI also spoke out in support of the recent court decision in Dover, Pennsylvania, which decided that "Intelligent Design is not science". Pope Benedict VI also spoke out when he was still Cardinal Ratzinger in 1994 announcing the rule of the Roman Catholic church endorsing the Historical-Critical method of Biblical interpretation, calling literal Biblical Fundamentalism "a kind of intellectual suicide" and contrary to the spirit and teachings of the church.

Some political leaders have also spoken out forcefully on behalf of science, such as Michael Bloomberg, Mayor of New York City, when he spoke at the 2006 Commencement ceremonies of the medical school of Johns Hopkins University, on May 30, 2006 and said that "Today we are seeing hundreds of years of scientific discovery being challenged by people who simply disregard facts that don't happen to agree with their agendas. Some call it "pseudo-science," others call it "faith-based science", but when you notice where this negligence tends to take place, you might as well call it "political science". Bloomberg went on to decry the ideology and short-term economic reason of "political science" recently being used to challenge the near unanimity of the science community on the clear and present danger of global warming; and the attempts to stymie the development of stem-cell research, and the increasingly absurd continued denial of the facts of Evolution. Bloomberg concludes by saying, "Think about it! This not only devalues science, it cheapens theology. As well as condemning these students to an inferior education, it ultimately hurts their professional opportunities."

When such high ranking and courageous religious and political leaders speak out on behalf of science, and against literal Biblical fundamentalism, the path toward compatibility between responsible religion and science is made considerably more secure.

ANCIENT RELIGIONS
AND GENEALOGY

Next, let us turn to a discussion of how science and some religions have dealt with genealogy. I will endeavor to refer in each case to the evidence upon which my comments are based. The world of genealogy is wonderfully complex so it is always important to keep track of the basis for our statements.

A. Prehistoric Man's Religions and Practices

Most religions have genealogies, and now, since the advent DNA, science does too.

For an excellent summary of the evidence for prehistoric man's religious beliefs and practices please read Mircea Eliade's book, "A Guide to World Religions" (1991). Archeological evidence of Paleolithic burials accompanied by jewelry and offerings of food and weapons clearly suggests a belief in an afterlife. Prehistoric sculpture, paintings and other objects also give ample evidence of early man's capacity for realistic and ritualistic art. Other evidence shows footprints of circular group dancing, altars and sanctuaries.

Having personally seen the wall paintings inside the original caves of Lascaux *(16,000 BCE) And many other sites of prehistoric art in south central France, I can attest to the clear impression one gets of their spiritual nature. By spiritual I mean a sense of reverence, beauty and awe. As such, Lascaux is truly a sacred place. The Chauvet caves, in the nearby Ardeche River valley of France, are even more vast and beautiful (only available by color photographs, because no public visitors are allowed), and far more ancient (31,000 BCE). See "The Cave of Lascaux, The Final Photographs", 1986); and "Dawn of Art, The Chauvet Cave", (1996) Sacred experience has obviously been an important part of mankind's earliest Paleolithic hunter-gatherer cultures.

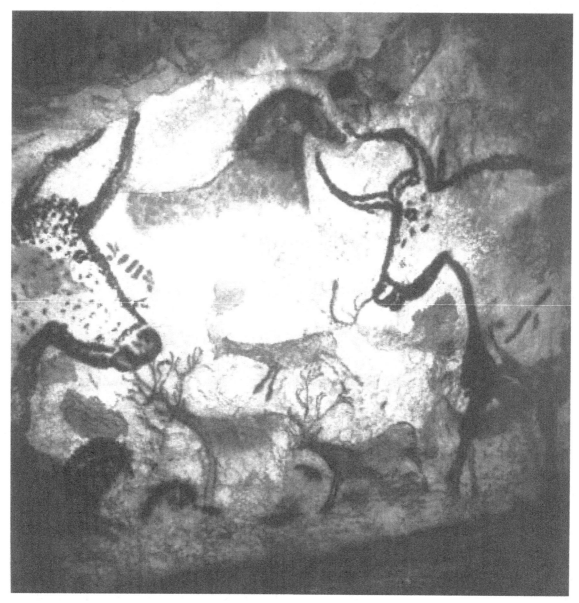

Bulls' Chamber, Lascaux caves.

MARCEL RAVIDAT, DISCOVERER OF LASCAUX

The apprentice mechanic was 18 years old. On 8th September 1940, alerted by Robot, his dog with a long russet-coloured coat, he discovered the entrance to the cave – a mere hole in the ground. The young man was obstinate and adventurous. He wanted to get into the tunnel but it would need to be widened. On 12th September, armed with a knife and torches, he forced his way through the narrow entrance and slid down the sloping floor of the cave. He was dazzled by what he and his three friends (Georges Agniel, Simon Coencas and Jacques Marsal) saw. The lads told the schoolteacher, Léon Laval, about their discovery and he became the cave's first curator. Father Henri Breuil, the "Pope of Prehistory", arrived a short time later. With Jacques Marsal, who came from Montignac like him, Ravidat acted as keeper of the cave which was soon overrun by visitors. A short time later, he became a member of the French Resistance. He went on to fight in Germany. What was his reward? As soon as the cave was opened to the public in 1948, he became one of its guides, with Jacques Marsal, and he remained so until the cave was finally closed in 1963. It was Marcel Ravidat who detected the first signs of the "green disease" in 1957-1958.

Discoverer Marcel Ravidat. Standing guard near his tent, he keeps watch over his discovery during the autumn of 1940 (Laval collection).

Based on average of fifteen years per generation, these Homo Sapiens people living 18,000 and 33,000 years ago at Lascaux and Chauvet would have lived approximately 1,200 and 2,200 generations ago respectively.

One of my favorite writers, Dr. Philip Appleman, Distinguished Professor Emeritus at Indiana University, and the author of the annual Norton Critical Edition of "Darwin", included in the 2001 edition his own poem, "Creation", an ode to prehistoric man's creative art.

* We first visited the Dordogne in France, which has more prehistoric archeological sites than anywhere else in Europe, in 1992, when we met Dr. Christine Desdemaines-Hugon, then a young English woman married to a French artist. Christine was then studying prehistoric archeology at the University of Bordeaux, from which she has subsequently received a PhD. She introduced us to many prehistoric sites and then helped us gain admission to the original Lascaux cave in May of 1994. Christine and her husband Frank continue to live in LeBugue, nearby Les Eyzie de Tayac, "The Capital of Prehistory" in which is also located the extraordinary Musee Nationale de la Prehistoire. The general public has not been admitted to Lascaux since 1963 when it became known that the pollution from public crowds

was deteriorating the art. So, we were very fortunate to be able to be two in a small group of five allowed in to the original Lascaux in 1994.

"Creation"
(For the discover of the Grotte de LaScaux, Marcel Ravidat, 1923 - 1995).

"On all the living walls of this dim cave, soot and ochre, acts of will come down to us to say:

This is who we were.

We foraged here in an age of ice, and, warmed by the fur of wolves, felt the pride of predators going for game.

Here we traced the strength of bulls, the grace of deer, turned life into art, and left this testimony on our walls.

Explorers of the future, see how, when our dreams reach forward, your wonder reaches back, and we embrace.

When we are long since dust, and false prophets come, then don't forget that we were your creators.

So build your days on what you know is real, and remember that nothing will keep your lives alive but art – the black and ochre visions you draw inside your cave will honor your lost tribe when explorers in some far future marvel at the paintings on your walls."

Philip Appleman, 2001

As Eliade says: "There seems to be no reason why the idea of mythical ancestors should not form part of the religious system of the Paleolithics: it is bound up with the mythologies of origins, origin of the world, of game, of man, of death - that is universally disseminated and mythologically fertile, for it has survived in all religions, even the most complex (with the exception of Hinayana Buddhism)…Eliade, "A History of Religion, Part I, page 32.

Also, for an excellent telling and interpretation of the story of what is called "The Big Bang of Human Consciousness" read Richard Klein's "The Dawn of Human Culture" (2002), and, William Calvin's "A Brain for All Seasons" (2002). These books, and many others referred to in their bibliographies, tell of the incredibly significant, and quite recent, scientific discoveries of the evidence of prehistoric man's physical and behavioral development.

B. The Neolithic Revolution
Following the Paleolithic era (Old Stone Age) there occurred what some scholars call the "Neolithic Revolution" (New Stone Age) that took place between 9,000 and 6,000 BCE. Groups of people lived in villages and survived by collecting wild grains and fruits, and domesticating sheep, cattle and pigs. This period of time preceded the discovery and

development of agriculture, which preceded the development of making pottery. Once man produced his food he had a need to calculate time and plan more complex activities concerning agriculture and village life.

For most of humanity's existence we have been totally immersed in nature. The obviously overwhelming and frightening forces of nature have been profound and pervasive throughout most of our specie's time on earth. It is only very recently that we have lived in man-made environments.

This Neolithic Revolution also profoundly affected religious beliefs, increasing the power of feminine and maternal sacrality. Eliade, again: "The fertility of the earth is bound up with feminine; hence women became responsible for the abundance of harvests, for they knew the "mystery" of creation. It is a religious mystery for it governs the origin of life, the food supply, and death"... "The sacrality of sexual life, and first of all feminine sexuality, becomes inseparable from the miraculous enigma of creation.... "The assimilation of human existence to vegetable life finds expression in images and metaphors drawn from the drama of vegetation (life is like the flowers of the field, etc.). This imagery nourished poetry and philosophical reflection for millennia, and it still remains "true" for contemporary man."

C. Ancient Historical Religions and Cultures

Sumerian-Akkadian-Mesopotamian Cultures:

From approximately 5,000 BCE to 2000 BCE these theocratic cultures, described by S.N. Kramer in his book, "History Begins at Sumer" (1981), shows that with man's first written record the Sumerians continued their predecessor's engagement with a variety of religious beliefs reflecting their views of the origin of the universe and man's place in it. They had four different narratives explaining the origin of man. Their cosmology described their kings coming down from the sky, and in the Gilgamesh myth they told of the great deluge punishing mankind for its sins.

The Amorites, who conquered the Sumerian-Akkadian civilization m about 2000 BCE made their capitol at Babylon and developed their own myth, Enmu Elish, and celebrated their annual spring New Year festival beginning in 1700 BCE. This myth began with the creation of the gods themselves, resulting in their Sun-God, Marduk, in whose honor they built a great ziggurat pyramid about 2100 B.C. at Ur.

Their myth then had Marduk, almost as an afterthought, creating humanity by mixing divine blood with dust. In this "pagan" view mankind shared in divinity, having derived its nature from the gods. (See Boccaccio's "Genealogy of the Gods")

At 15 years per generation since the beginning of Sumerian cuneiform writing in 3400 BCE, through succeeding civilizations, there have been about 460 generations.

Egyptian

In prehistoric Egyptian times the great goddess Nun was believed to have given birth to Atun, who created the universe. Subsequent gods were mostly male, beginning with the earliest dynasties. Their pyramids at Saggara were built about 2600 BC and the Great Pyramids at Giza built about 2500 BC. They developed hieroglyphic writing about 3000 BC. There were progressions from Horus as Falcon, through Seth, Atun (Ra), the god-king Osiris (and his sister-wife Isis), then to the high god Amun, then briefly to the monotheistic god Akhnaton, and then back to Amun, under Tutankamun. Genealogically the god Geb (earth) and the goddess Nut (sky) were believed to have been the parents of Osiris and Isis, Seth and Horus. Osiris and Isis then became the parents of the boy Horus. So, from Geb and Nut came all the children of Egypt. As is well known, Egyptians, throughout their long history, have had a strong belief in life after death, as told in: their "The Book Of The Dead." The entire culture of ancient Egypt, from 3000 BCE through 300 CE, was dedicated to a quest for immortality. The belief in life after death was so palpable, not only for the Pharaohs and their nobles, but for all the common people (and their pets) that pyramids and monuments and burial sites were dedicated to preparation for and actual life after they died. The Egyptian myths of resurrection and judgment day after death have carried over directly into Judaism, Christianity and Islam.

Archeologists have developed accurate records of the many dynasties and generations of Egyptian Pharaohs, from 3950 BCE to 332 BCE, equivalent to 190 generations. The actual number of generations per generation is 15 years. At 20 years per generation from Alexander to the present time, add another 100 generations. Thus a total of 290 generations nom 3950 BCE to the present.

Chinese

Prehistoric, Taoism and Confucianism

The Chinese creation myths include several elements: creation from a primal "cosmic egg" containing Chaos, a mixture of Yin-Yang, female-male, passive-aggressive, cold-heat, dark-light, and wet-dry. From the egg came Phan-Ku, the giant who separated Chaos into its many components. Phan-Ku is said to have labored for 18,000 years during which he created the mountains, valleys, rivers and oceans and the sun, moon and stars. This myth says further that it was fleas in Phan-Ku's hair that became human beings!

Other Chinese myths: The original Chaos was divided into sky and darkness, and Yang and Yin. When Yang became one and the five elements were separated, humankind was born. The "Gold-One" came from the sky and stood before man, "The Yellow One", and taught man "How to stay alive and read the sky".

Taoism's origins can be traced to prehistoric religions in China, to the composition of the "Tao Te Ching" (3rd or 4th century BCE) or to the activity of Zhang Daoling (2nd century AD). Or, it may only have arisen later by way of contrast to the newly arrived religion of Buddhism.

Lao-Tsu is said to be the founder of Taoism, who taught that "Creation is the Way, the Tao itself, and "Being for the Taoist comes from Non-Being". Obviously, at least to me, Taoism is a mysterious system of thought, which cannot be fully expressed, in this very short summary. Another interpretation is "the map is not the territory", in other words, no matter; how complicated the description, it always lacks the entirety of what is.

Taoism has never been a unified religion and has always consisted of different teachings based on many different original revelations. Beyond the Chinese folk religion, various rituals, exercises, or substances are said to positively affect one's physical health.

For a more complete discussion of Taoism and the world's many other creation myths, see "A Dictionary of Creation Myths", by David and Margaret Leeming, (Oxford U. Press, 1994), and "In the Beginning", by Virginia Hamilton and illustrated by Barry Moser (Harcourt, Inc. 1988). Both these books have extensive bibliographies.

Confucianism, founded by Kung Fu-Tzu in the 6th century BCE during what we now call "The Axial Age", is not, strictly speaking, a religion. It is however still a very strong influence in Chinese culture as a code of behavior and ethics, written originally for members of the court.

Chinese dynasties are well recorded and extend backwards in time to at least 3000 BCE, roughly 300 generations to the present day.

Other Pre-Judeo - Christian Beliefs
Zoroastrianism

Zoroastrianism was the ancient religion of Persia. It was founded about 3500 years ago by the prophet Zarathustra. Arising out of the polytheistic traditions of ancient India and Iran, he was one of the first monotheists in human history. The basic scripture of Zoroastrianism is a set of five poetic songs called the "Gathas", which were composed by Zarathustra himself and have been preserved through the millennia by Zoroastrian priests. The most important thing about Zoroastrianism is the dedication to ethical and moral excellence. The motto of the faith is: "Good thoughts, Good works, Good deeds." This threefold path is the center of the faith. Unfortunately, Zoroastrianism reached its zenith of power in Persia by 600 CE, with over 50 million adherents, and was then supplanted by Islam during its military expansion. There are now only about 200,000 adherents, mostly in America and India. They are quite tolerant of intermarriage and do not proselytize so they are continuing to diminish from their once glorious past as a great world religion.

Dharmic Religions

Dharmic religions are a family of religions that have originated from the Indian subcontinent. They encompass Hinduism and three other religions that have spawned from it – namely, Buddhism, Jainism, and Sikhism. The theology and philosophy of Dharmic religions center on the concept of Dhanna, a Sanskrit term for "fixed decree, law, duty", especially in the spiritual sense of " natural law, reality".

Hinduism is considered to be the oldest living religion in the world. Having its foundation in the Vedic civilization that dates back to at least 2500 BCE, Hinduism has no single founder and is based upon a number of religious texts developed over many centuries that contain spiritual insights and practical guidance for religious life. Among such texts, the four Vedas, namely Rig Veda, Sama Veda, Yajur Veda, and Atharva Veda are the most ancient. Other scriptures include the eighteen Puranas and the epic poems Mahabharata and Ramayana. The Bhagavad-Gita, which is contained within the Mahabharata, is a widely studied scripture that summarizes the spiritual teachings of the Vedas.

Hinduism is the third largest religion in the world, with approximately one billion adherents.

Buddhism ("the teachings of the awakened one" is a dharmic, non-theistic religion, a way of life, a practical philosophy, and arguably a form of psychology. Buddhism focuses on the teachings of Gautama Buddha who was born at Lumbini Garden in ancient India (now modern day Nepal) around the fifth century BCE. Buddhism spread throughout the Indian subcontinent in the five centuries following the Buddha's passing, and propagated into Central, Southeast, and East Asia over the next two thousand years.

Today Buddhism is divided primarily into three traditions: Theravada, Mayhayana, and Vajrayana. Buddhism continues to attract followers worldwide, and is considered a major world religion. World estimates for Buddhists vary between 230 and 500 million, with most around 350 million. It is the fifth largest religion in the world, behind Christianity, Islam, Hinduism and traditional Chinese religion. Buddhism is the fourth largest organized religion in the world, and the monk's order "Sangha" is among the oldest organizations on earth.

The original Buddha was concerned primarily with the practical alleviation of suffering by reducing desire, "becoming enlightened". He did not concern himself with theology, metaphysics or genealogy. For instance, Buddha is said to have asked, "If you are shot in the leg with a poisoned arrow, does it make any difference what wood the arrow is made of ? "Reincarnation" was introduced in Buddhism in later years by followers of Buddhism.

Jainism is a religion and philosophy originating in ancient India. It stresses; spiritual independence and equality of all life with particular emphasis on non-violence. Self-control is vital for attaining realization of the souls' true nature. It does not recognize a God-head, rejects the Vedas, but strongly adheres to "dharma, moksha and nirvana".

Sikhism is a religion that began in the sixteenth century CE with the teachings of Nanak and nine successive gurus. The word Sikh comes nom the Sanskrit word for "disciple", or "learner". The principle belief in Sikhism is faith in one God and the pursuit of salvation through disciplined, personal meditation on the name and message of God. There are over 23 million Sikhs in the world which make it the sixth largest religion in the world. Most Sikhs live in the Punjab region of India.

Shinto

Shinto is the indigenous religion of Japan. It began in prehistory and is the background for all Japanese culture. For a discussion of its history and practice see page 157 of this book under "Shinto Shrines". Buddhism was imported to Japan from China in approximately 600 CE.

All other religions have their own beliefs about the creation of the universe and mankind. Many are quite colorful and imaginative, telling of man's creation from animals, or the earth, or nom various gods. A recently published "Encyclopedia of Gods and Goddesses", by Michael Jordan (Facts on File, 2004) lists and describes over 2500 gods known throughout human history. The history of mankind is "saturated with gods".

Abrahamic Monotheism,
The Bible: Old and New Testaments –
Biblical Genealogies

The Judeo-Christian Bible, both Old and New Testaments, contains some remarkable genealogies. First, in the Old Testament, in Genesis: Chapters 1 and 2, after God creates "heaven and earth" in six days, He then creates man and woman in two versions), and mankind begins with Adam and Eve. Then, Chapters 4 and 5, "The book of the generations of Adam", Adam and Eve beget Cain and Abel, who, in turn, beget children (with whom?) who, in turn, beget a series of ten generations culminating in Noah. Then, "After Noah was five hundred years old, Noah becomes the father of Shem, Ham and Japheth."

To keep these biblical generations in perspective, the average life span of the biblical descendants from Adam to Noah was about 900 years, with an average age between generations of about 100 years. Noah, for instance, is said in the Bible to have lived 500 years before having his three sons; then lived 100 years more before the Flood, and then lived on for 350 years more, dying at the age of 950!

In Genesis: Chapter 10, the generations of the sons of Noah; Shem, Ham, and Japheth, are described thus: "These are the families of the sons of Noah, according to their genealogies, in their nations: and from these the nations spread abroad on the earth after the Flood."

Shem's descendants are then described in Chapter 11, and after ten more generations we get to Abram, who later, on the instructions of God, leaves Ur of the Chaldeans to go to the land of Canaan where he assumes the name "Abraham". Some modern historians date Abram's departure from Ur at 2800 BCE. Other historians can find no archeological or non-Biblical evidence that Abram ever actually existed except as a strongly persistent myth. One of Abraham's later descendants was Moses who is said to have led the Hebrew Exodus from Egypt at about 1250 BCE. . Subsequent descendants; Kings Saul, David and Solomon reigned from 1030 to 931 BCE.

Other biblical genealogies occur throughout the Old Testament; particularly in Chronicles.

The New Testament Genealogies
The New Testament genealogies are found in Matthew and Luke. The first chapter of Matthew begins with; "The book of the genealogy of Jesus Christ, the son of David" the son of Abraham." Matthew then traces 14 generations from Abraham to King David, and 28 more generations from David to Jesus, totaling 42 generations.

64   THE MEANINGS OF GENEALOGY FOR SCIENCE AND RELIGION

In Luke, Chapter 3, verse 23, traces Jesus' genealogy backwards in time to David in 41 generations, then on to Abraham in 15 more generations, totaling 56 generations from Abraham to Jesus. A difference of 14 generations between the Luke and Matthew versions of Jesus' genealogy.

Luke then proceeds to list 20 more generations from Abraham to Adam, a grand total of 76 generations from Jesus to Adam. A comparison of the Luke and Matthew genealogies also shows many differences between the names as well as the number of the descendants. No explanation is made in either Gospel for the differences, or for the apparent break in lineage from Joseph because of an immaculate conception. It is clear, however, that both the Apostles Luke and Matthew thought it was of great importance to link Jesus to Isaiah's Old Testament prophesy of the birth of "Immanuel" from the house of David.

The two versions of the mankind's creation are also reflected in the two versions of Abraham's Covenant with God, and the two stories of Noah's Ark. Also, as is now well known, the Gospels in the Canon, and the Gnostic and 35 other Gospels excluded from the Canon, contain many different and some contradictory versions of the life of Jesus.

The chronological dates from the time of Abraham to the birth of Jesus are estimated to be from 1950 BCE to 4 CE. Using 20 years per generation this approximately 200 year time period computes to 100 generations, plus 100 more generations from Jesus to the present, totaling 200 generations.

Greek, Roman and European Royal Families

Greek and Roman histories begin later; from 500 BCE to the present is approximately 150 generations. European royal family histories generally begin between 400 CE and 600 CE, roughly 60 - 75 generations.

The Qur'an - Islam

Islam, founded by Muhammad in 600 CE is based on the belief that Muhammad is The Messenger of God, speaking the revealed Word of God, as a prophet in the line of Adam, Abraham, Moses and Jesus, perhaps implying a kind of descent from the Biblical genealogies.

In the original Qur'an only Chapter 1 of Genesis was recited describing God's creation of man and woman equally together at the same time. Later commentaries on the Qur'an imported the Chapter 2 version, describing women as created from Adam's rib and the story of temptation by the apple and woman's sin as the cause of mankind's fall from Grace, from the Judeo-Christian Bible.

THE SCIENTIFIC VIEW
OF THE UNIVERSE

a. The Big Picture - the Big Bang

It is now generally agreed among scientists that the Universe we can observe and measure is approximately 14 billion years old, starting with the "Big Bang". It is also generally agreed that there are about 100 billion galaxies in the Universe, and that our "Milky Way" galaxy contains more than 100 billion stars. Our Sun is one minor star on the periphery of our galaxy.

The theory of the Big Bang, now confirmed by modern astronomy, is that the Universe began with an unimaginable expansion of matter and energy, from an also unimaginably small beginning, creating what is now seen to be the entire universe, which is still expanding at an accelerating rate. For an excellent, easily readable book about this subject see "Big Bang. The Origin of the Universe" by Simon Singh (Harper Collins, 2004). And see also Steven Weinberg's "The First Three Minutes". There are, of course, still a great many unknowns related to this theory, such as "string theory", and "dark matter", completely beyond the scope of this book, as well as this author.

b. Evolution

Our Earth, one of the nine planets revolving around our Sun, is generally agreed to have been formed about 4.5 billion years ago, and life first appeared in its primordial single-cell form about 3.5 billion years ago. Multi-cellular life developed about 1.8 billion years ago. Plants moved to dry land and, during the "Cambrian explosion", between and 500 million years ago, all the animal species diversified dramatically. Then, 250 million years later, there was a mass extinction called the "Permian-Triassic extinction", killing off 90% of the then existing animal species.

At 225 million years ago dinosaurs and small mammals began to evolve. The dinosaurs dominated until 65 million years ago when they were made extinct, probably by the collision of a huge asteroid with the Earth. From then on mammals evolved into larger animals and ultimately became dominant, with mankind's precursor emerging in Africa about 6 million years ago.

Scientific evidence of facts in support of Darwin's theory of evolution and natural selection, as amended over time, is overwhelming. There are, of course, gaps in the evidence considering the vast scale of time and geography, but if new scientific discoveries require amendments to the theory they will be made, as it is with all scientific knowledge.

However, as I have previously quoted the renowned biologist Theodorus Dobzhansky (1900-1975) saying; "Nothing in biology makes sense, except in the light of evolution".

Ever since Charles Darwin published "The Origin of Species" in 1859, and Descent of Man in 1871, laying the foundation for the theory of Evolution, and the subsequent accumulation of veritable mountains of confirming factual scientific evidence from all the physical sciences, the prevailing scientific view of the origin and variety of life on earth, including mankind, is evolutionary.

Geology

Influential to Darwin's thinking was Charles Lyell who, in 1830, wrote "Principles of Geology". This work summarized and carried further the 17th century work of the Dane, Nicolaus Steno, and the 18th century Scot, James Hutton ("the fathers of geology") and Georges Cuvier, the French fossil scholar. Altogether these men created the science of geology, answering the age-old question of "why are there sea-shells on the tops of mountains?" From the time of the Greeks the naturalists said it was because the earth was formed by the upheaval of the sea bottoms. But the Abrahamic religions taught that the earth was formed by God as told in Genesis and the seashells were on mountains because they were left there after the great flood as told in the biblical story of Noah's Ark. The Rev. James Ussher, the Archbishop of Armagh, Ireland, had, for instance, declared in 1658 that "God had created the earth on October 23, 2004 B.C.".

Nicolaus Steno (1638-1686) was a brilliant student who was a friend to Spinoza in Holland and became most famous as a highly skilled dissector of biological specimens, including human cadavers. Later in life, he became a part of the "Cimento", a Medici supported group of scientists in Florence, Italy, some of whom had been students of Galileo. There Steno became interested in the structure of the earth and the question of "seashells on mountains". His observations of the landscape in Tuscany led him to conclude that most of the earth's surface was made up of sediment laid down over thousands of years at the bottom of seas which had receded and then been upended and moved into new shapes and forms such as mountains. He perceived and wrote about many principles of geology in his book "De Solido", much of which is still valid today. But the last years of his life he spent as a devout convert from Lutheranism to Roman Catholicism, leading to his ultimately becoming a titular Bishop in Hannover, Germany where he became friends with Gottfried Liebniz, the great mathematician. Steno conformed his geology to Genesis by asserting that the floods of the Creation and Noah would have been enough to create the earth landscapes he had observed. Steno subsequently moved from Hannover to Munster and then to Hamburg where he died in poverty. Steno's connection with the church contributed to his being forgotten as a scientist.

However, in the late 18th century, James Hutton, a retired gentleman farmer who was also part of the Scottish Enlightenment in Edinburgh, observed the same phenomena in the landscape of Scotland as Steno had in Tuscany. He had, essentially, "rediscovered" what Steno had found. However, Hutton carried the thinking a few steps further by speculating about the amount of time necessary for such geologic changes. He estimated it as "indefinite", which was of course contrary to the teachings of Genesis. And Hutton was not a Roman Catholic so he didn't carry any religious baggage. And Cuvier, the French paleontologist, confirmed that fossils illustrated clearly that the earth had undergone many, many catastrophic geologic revolutions. This growing body of scientific work had already begun to change the Biblical view of the past, which held that the earth was just a few thousand years old.

By the beginning of the 19th century most geologists had agreed that the earth was millions of years old. However, during Darwin's time there was still a dispute whether there were enough millions of years to support the theory of Evolution. Lord Kelvin, then a famous physicist and mathematician asserted that based upon the laws of physics, as they were then understood that the earth could not have been old enough to sustain the theory of Evolution. It was not until the early 20th century, with the discovery of radioactive elements, uncovering a previously unknown source of heat energy in the solar system, that the age of the earth could be determined at billions of years. Thus the scientific basis for the millions of years required for Evolution had been laid by 18th century geology and confirmed by 20th century physics.

John McPhee, the author of excellent books on geology, (among many other subjects) put the answer to the "seashell question" best when he said in "Annals of the Former World", if by some fiat I had to restrict all this writing to one sentence, this the one I would choose; The summit of Mount Everest is marine limestone."

Taxonomy:
Linneaus, Buffon, Humboldt.
The Chicago Botanic Garden
Preceding these men were of course the great classifiers of all living things, The Dutchman Carl Linnaeus, the Frenchman, George Buffon in the mid 1700's, and the inspirational naturalist and world traveling German, Alexander Humboldt in the early 1800's. It was they who laid the foundation for the modern science of taxonomy. For an excellent review of all these men's work see "Finding Order in Nature, the Naturalist Tradition from Linnaeus to E.O. Wilson", by Paul Lawrence Farber (Johns Hopkins Press, 2000)

Gregor Johann Mendel (1822-1884)
Mendel's Laws of Inheritance
The basic principles of heredity, the science of "genetics", was discovered by Gregor Johann Mendel (1822-1884). Mendel was an Augustinian monk who enjoyed gardening and was a natural scientist, a careful observer and a creative thinker. He observed that plants with different traits standing next to each other retained the essential traits of their parent plants and were not affected by the neighboring plants' traits. This simple observation gave birth to the idea of heredity. Mendel's extensive experimentation - he cultivated and tested some 28,000 pea plants - generated Mendel's Laws of Inheritance, which apply to all living plants and animals.

When Mendel published his findings in 1866, virtually no one in the scientific community took notice, and they were temporarily lost in obscurity. Mendel then became the Abbott of his monastery, ceased doing further research, and died in 1884. His Laws of Inheritance remained "unknown" until 1900 when they were "rediscovered", and subsequently merged with Darwin's theory of evolution into the modern evolutionary synthesis beginning in 1920. Although Mendel was aware of Darwin it does not appear that Darwin knew of Mendel's Laws.

It is however now agreed that, "Mendel's name marks not only the beginning of genetics as a scientific discipline in its own right, but also the beginning of the systematic use of mathematics, quantified measurements and applied statistics in biology." (Biography of Mendel, by Eisenhaber and Schleiffer, Vienna, 1997 - 1999)

For an excellent beautifully illustrated, narrative of the history and facts of evolution please see "Evolution, The Triumph of an Idea", by Carl Zimmer. (Harper Collins, 2001) It describes the history of the idea of evolution the gathering of confirming evidence, humanity's place in evolution, and evolution's place in humanity. In other words, that humans are not "descended from apes", but that both humans and apes share an ancient common ancestor millions of years ago. It further illustrates that the basic mechanism of evolution is Natural Selection; that individual organisms don't evolve, but populations do, and that evolution is not synonymous with progress.

In November, 2005 Norton published a single volume collection of Charles Darwin's four greatest works; "The Voyage of the Beagle" (1845), "On the Origin of Species" (1859), "The Descent of Man" (1871), and "The Expressions of the Emotions in Man and Animals"(1872), The collection,

"From So Simple a Beginning" is edited by Dr. Edward O. Wilson, Harvard Professor of Biology, Emeritus and author of twenty other seminal books on biology. Professor Wilson also written an introductory essay to each of Darwin's books and an introduction and epilogue to the collection. Wilson's essays are worth the price of the collection by themselves.

Norton is also the publisher of the Norton Critical Edition of "Darwin" (2001), authored by Dr. Philip Appleman, including his own poem "Creation" reprinted in this book at page 57.

c. Creationism and Intelligent Design
Fundamentalist Religion
The teaching of evolution in America has had a difficult past because of resistance by American Protestant Fundamentalists. The first legal challenge to teaching evolution came in the trial of John Scopes in 1925 in Tennessee when Clarence Darrow, represented the evolutionists, against William Jennings Bryan who was representing the Fundamentalists. Bryan's literal interpretation of the Bible was exposed as absurd, but the Tennessee jury still found for the Fundamentalists. The public embarrassment of the Fundamentalists was so great that they mounted a long

campaign to discredit evolution in the American educational system. As a result, most high-school boards of education, wanting to avoid controversy, simply stopped buying science textbooks that presented evolution.

Just as Darwin had the Rev. William Paley as a religious critic of evolution in the 19th Century, there are still a small number of primarily American Protestant Fundamentalists critics of evolution. They are "Creationists" and "Intelligent Design" theorists, but they have not yet been able to present credible scientific to back up their criticism.

In the 1980's two famous cases, McLean v. State of Arkansas in 1981, and Edwards v. Aguillard in 1986 decided that "Creation Science" is not science and could therefore not be required to be taught in public schools, as a violation of the Federal Constitution's First Amendment separation of church and state.

The Fundamentalists changed tactics and raised the theory of "Intelligent Design" claiming that - Nature is too complicated not to have been created by a supernatural "intelligent designer". This theory was promulgated for many years through various writers and public relations activities organized by the Discovery Institute of Seattle, Washington, and financed by some other fundamentalists, finally coming to litigation in the case of

Kitzmiller v. Dover School District in Dover, Pennsylvania in 2004. The case was decided in December 2004 and, once again, the federal court decided that "Intelligent Design" is not science and should not be taught as science in a public school. In this case the judge, a Republican appointee of President George W. Bush, went so far as to characterize the School Board's decision to adopt "Intelligent Design" as an alternative to evolution in a public school science course as "breathtakingly inane". The judge went on to state: "The students, parents, and teachers of the Dover Area School District deserved better than to be dragged into this legal maelstrom, with its resulting utter waste of monetary and personal resources."

The same battle has continued among the members of the Board of Education of Ohio, which has previously permitted the anti-evolution "Critical Analysis", another euphemism for "Intelligent Design" in its science curriculum. On February 14, 2006 the Board decided to reverse its previous decision and eliminate the "Critical Analysis" language from its curriculum, thus taking "Intelligent Design" and "Creationism" out of the science curriculum. Curiously, the Board member leading the group arguing for this reversal, Martha Wise, is a self-declared "Creationist". She has been criticized by fellow Creationists, but says, "How could

I dare do something like this if I say believe in God? I can do that because I believe there are two separate issues here. One is the teaching of good science. The other is the teaching of creationism, and I think that is important too, but I think that should be taught in any other class or at church or at home...not in a science class."

Even President George W. Bush, a self-described "born-again Christian", has publicly urged that "Intelligent Design" be taught as an alternative to evolution. At the same time, the president's own science adviser, Dr. John Marburger III, has publicly stated: "Evolution is the cornerstone of modern biology and Intelligent Design is not a scientific concept." Strange world!

The Roman Catholic Church Position
Perhaps the Dover case will counter the unusual New York Times op-ed article written in July, 2005 by Austrian Cardinal Schonborn which contradicted Pope Paul II's 1996 encyclical recognizing that evolution is "more than a hypothesis". It was later learned that the Cardinal's article was usually submitted to the Times by the public relations firm which represents the Discovery Institute, the intellectual home of "Intelligent Design". So, the Discovery Institute has even reached a Roman Catholic Cardinal to help their cause, encouraging him to contradict the late Pope John Paul II! Since the Dover case was decided in December, 2005, the official Vatican newspaper, "L'Osservatore" has, however, labeled the Dover decision as "correct".

In 1996 it was widely reported that Pope John Paul II's encyclical recognized that "the theory of evolution is more than just a hypothesis". In his message the Pope indicated further that he regarded "the human soul is of immediate divine creation, but that scientific evidence seemed to validate the theory of evolution through natural selection."

In short, the Roman Catholic view is that religious faith and evolution can coexist. The teaching of evolution in Roman Catholic schools continues as a standard part of the curriculum. (New York Times, October 25, 1996) "In 1992, in a similar statement to The Academy, a group that advises the Papacy on scientific matters, the Pope rectified the Church's famous perception of Galileo for asserting that the earth moved around the sun." Ibid.

Thus, the Roman Catholic Church has concluded that religious faith and evolution and science can coexist and that "naively literalist" interpretation of the Bible is dangerous and can lead to a "false certitude".

The Traditional Protestant Church Position

Many traditional Protestant Churches, which are not fundamentalist, also subscribe to the teaching of evolution as valid science and embrace the historical-critical method of Biblical interpretation. Recently a group of Methodist, Lutheran, Episcopalian, Presbyterian; Unitarian, Congregationalist, United Church of Christ, Baptist, and a host of community churches, have organized "The Clergy Letter Project" in support of the teaching of evolution. Over ten thousand Christian clerics have signed the letter, which concludes:

"We urge school board members to prescribe the integrity of the science curriculum by affirming the teaching of the theory of evolution as a core component of human knowledge. We ask that science remain science, and that religion remain religion, two very different, but complimentary forms of truth."

Hopefully, the Dover case decision, the decision by the Ohio Board of Education, the recent statements by the Vatican, and the Clergy Letter Project will persuade most other school boards to separate science from the religious teachings of Intelligent Design and Creationism and put a stop to this wasteful conflict. However, this hope may be in vain because, as Patricia Princehouse, a biologist and director of the Ohio Citizens for Science, said; "The one thing we have learned about creationists is that they never give up".

For the record, there are really five different evolutionary hypothesis: (1) the scientific, Darwinian explanation, (2) the "Creationist" religious explanation - a literal reading of the Biblical book of Genesis, holding that "God" created the Universe and all life in six days abut 6,000 years ago, man did not descend from hominids, but was created personally by "God" and is the only creature to have a "soul", and there is no evolution, the whole cosmos is static, (3) the "liberal" religious explanation, which includes the Roman Catholic and the Traditional Protestant positions, holding that science and religion are complimentary, man has descended from hominids, but his "soul" comes from "God", (4) the Goethian position - brings Johann Wolfgang Goethe's "science" up to date - generally accepting Darwin, but adding a hierarchy, with man as "the highest form of organization", adopted by Anthroposophy and Theosophists, and (5) the Teilhardian position, according to the teachings of the Jesuit Paleontologist, Pierre Teilhard Chardin, where consciousness and matter are aspects of the same reality, man is not, distinguished by his "soul", but by his "mind", all humans are "united in a single Divine Christ consciousness" (credit: http://www.kheper.net/evolution/alternatives.htm).

Thus, Darwinian evolution is the only completely scientific explanation, with each of the other having a religious or philosophical aspect.

d. The Epic of Creation

For an excellent overview comparing the theological and scientific treatments of the creation and history of the universe, the formation of the earth, and the origin and evolution of life to modern mankind please refer to: The Epic of Creation, presented annually in a weekly Monday evening course during February and March at the Lutheran School of Theology at 55th Street and Ellis Avenue in Hyde Park, Chicago, Illinois. The course outline is available from the school. The class is offered as part of the seminary curriculum and is also open to the public free of charge.

The Big Bang and Theology
"The Epic" begins for scientists with the "Big Bang", the beginning of the Universe. Most scientists I know do not presume to even speculate on what the state of the Universe was before the Big Bang. I once asked this question of Professor Jim Cronin, a University of Chicago Nobel Laureate and Big Bang physicist, at a small Sunday evening gathering in our Methodist church parlor. His answer was, quickly and simply, "Nothing". He went on to say that scientists can only deal with natural phenomena that they can measure.

Professor Cronin went on to tell the following anecdote to illustrate his point; a physicist was once climbing up the "Ladder of Knowledge" and when he got near the top he looked up and saw that there was already another man sitting on the top rung of the ladder, with his chin resting in his hand, looking contemplative. The physicist asked the man, "Who are you and what are you doing up there?" The man looked down, smiled, and said; "I'm a theologian, and I've been waiting for you." The obvious point is that what came before the Big Bang is a theological question and not a scientific one.

So, the Big Bang physicists are not presuming to tell us what happened before the Big Bang. Most good scientists I know are quite humble people who are awed by the infinite enormity and complexity of the Universe. One of them said to me, "Since we don't know the essence of being, "Why is there something, rather than nothing?" It is as if we are living inside an enormous mystery."

Ever Changing Science -
From Steady State to Big Bang
As an example of how science changes is the fact that while I was a science student in the 1940's and 50's the prevailing theory of cosmology was called "steady state", advanced" by Sir Herman Bondi and his colleagues Fred Hoyle and Thomas Gold. "In

1965 Dr. Robert Wilson and Dr. Arno Perizias, microwave scientists working for Bell Laboratories inadvertently, and serendipitously, discovered the actual cosmic microwave background (CBR) which was the key to proving the "Big Bang" theory of the origin of the universe. Ironically the existence of CBR was predicted by Herman, the proponent of the steady-state theory. The Big Bang theory "had actually been suggested in 1927 by Georges Edmund LeMaitre, a Belgian astronomer and Jesuit priest such are the circuitous ways of scientific discovery. And, the name "Big Bang" was created derisively by Fred Hoyle who could never accept the idea because it contradicted his steady-state theory.

DNA

And, until 1952, Drs. Watson and Crick had not yet discovered the process and form by which DNA replicates itself and is thereby the key to reproduction by all living things. When I was studying embryology the processes of reproduction and differentiation were said to be caused by "precursors" which, simply said, meant they were unknown.

Tectonic Plates

And, it was not until the 1960's that the data was proved to confirm the theory of Tectonic Plates being moved around on the surface of the earth forming continents, by huge undersea volcanic action caused by the molten magma underneath the sea floor. The picture of the evolving and changing shape of the earth's continents also provides the answers to many questions about the similarities and dissimilarities among species now and previously existing on neighboring, but now separated continents.

Computer technology

Technology has also, in many more ways, changed dramatically during my lifetime. The advent of the modern computer; first with vacuum tubes and then with microchips, has revolutionized communication, transportation and even science itself with its astonishing computational and information storage and retrieval power.

e. Deep Time - Geologic Time Scale

The geologic, "deep time" scale is so vast it is very difficult for us to grasp its significance. The Field Museum of Natural History in Chicago does an excellent job of graphically showing deep time with a standing chart located at each station in its new exhibit "The Evolving Planet". Another succinct description is by Carl Zimmer, the author of an excellent, beautifully illustrated book, "Evolution" (2001).

"While these few pages can't do full justice to the majestic depths of life's history, one thing is clear: our own time in this universe is inconceivably brief. No longer can human history match the scale of natural history.

If the 3.5 billion years that life has been on earth were a summer day, the past 200,000 years, which saw the rise of anatomically modern humans, the origin of complex language, or art, religion, and trade, the dawn of agriculture, of cities, and all of written history - would fit into the flash of firefly just before sundown."

Or, from the MacMillan Visual Desk Reference, "If the history of the earth were represented as a one revolution of a clock, human evolution would represent the last 19 seconds of the hour."

And, for yet another metaphor of the relationship of the recent brief time of mankind's existence to the geologic time scale of the universe, I find the story told by John McPhee, the author of "Basin and Range" (1980), very helpful:

"David Brower, for example, the founder of Friends of the Earth and emeritus hero of the Sierra Club, has tirelessly traveled the United States for thirty years delivering what he himself refers to as "the sermon", and sooner or later in every talk be invites his listeners to consider the six days of Genesis as a figure of speech for what has in fact been four billion years. In this adjustment, a day equals something like seven hundred and fifty million years, and thus, "all day Monday until Tuesday noon creation was busy getting the earth going". Life began on Tuesday noon, and

"the beautiful, organic wholeness of it developed over the next four days." "At four PM Saturday, the big reptiles came on. Five hours later, when the redwoods appeared, there were no more big reptiles."

"At three minutes before midnight, man appeared. At one-fourth of a second before, Christ arrived. At, one-fortieth of a second before midnight the Industrial Revolution began." "We are surrounded with people who think that what we have been doing for that one-fortieth of a second can go on indefinitely. They are considered normal, but they are stark raving mad". Brower then holds up a photograph of the world - blue, green, and swirling white. "This is the sudden insight from the space ship Apollo," he says. "There it is. That's all. We see through the "eyes of the astronauts how fragile our life really is."

"McPhee continues: "human consciousness may have begun to leap and boil some sunny day in the Pleistocene (2,000,000 years BCE), but the human race by and large has retained the essence of its animal sense of time. People think in terms of five generations "two ahead, two behind and heavy concentration on the one in the middle - themselves. Possibly that is tragic, and possibly there is no choice. The human mind may not have evolved enough to be able to comprehend deep time. It may only able to measure it.

f. The Origin and Development of Humans

The current scientific view of the evolution of mankind is that the earliest proto-human ("hominids") emerged in Africa as a separate species from their mammalian ancestor between 5,000,000 and 6,000,000 years ago.

It now appears that a great many pre-hominid varieties of Miocene (22- 6 million years ago) apes ranged throughout Europe and Eurasia, having originally migrated from Africa and then returning to Africa before evolving into hominids.

Then, through subsequent mutations into a variety of intermediary hominids; Ardipithecus ramidus, Australopithecus anamnesis, A. Aferensis ("Lucy"), (3.5 million years ago"), A. Africanus, Homo habilis (the toolmaker), and Homo erectus, the first truly human-like, but still very primitive human being (2 million years ago). Homo erectus migrated from Africa into Asia about 1.8 million years ago, and Europe more recently, from 500,000 to 1 million years ago, but subsequently became extinct, as did all the other intermediary hominids. The recent discoveries of other hominid species, such as Kenyanthropus rudolfensis, Peranthropous bosei, and Homo ergaster, illustrates the ever-changing nature of science, requiring reconsideration of the previously known archeology.

There were periods of ancient time during which three or more species of hominids co-existed.

Since prehistoric people had a much shorter life span than modern man, we can safely estimate 15 years per generation for their lives, thus estimating 120,000 generations for the span of the earliest Homo erectus species. At 10 years per generation we get 180,000 generations. And, going all the way back to 6 million BCE, the very first bi-pedal hominid, the Hom Orrorin in Africa, we get between 400,000 and 600,000 generations, at 10 or 15 years per generation.

In Europe Homo erectus evolved into or was displaced by Homo Antessor in Gran Dolina, Spain, based on reliably dated fossil records dated about 800,000 years ago. Antessor, in turn, evolved into or was displaced by the subspecies Sima de la Los Huesos, at Atapuerca, Spain, which subsequently evolved into the Homo Neanderthalis whose 300,000 year old fossils have been found in Germany near Dusseldorf. Our direct ancestors, Homo Sapiens, probably emerged in Africa about 200,000 years ago, and then emigrated from Africa to the Middle East about 90,000 years ago and from or through there to Europe and Central Asia about 60,000 years ago.

Homo Neanderthalis became extinct about 30,000 years ago and Homo Sapiens (people like us) emerged in

Africa about 200,000 years ago. Homo Sapiens is the only pre-historic hominid to have developed a body of art and complex stone and bone tools, beginning about 60,000 years ago. Archeological evidence of their remarkable skills and artistic creativity can be found today in many sites in southern France and Spain. Modern mankind has remained essentially the same species for the last 60,000 years.

At 15 years per generation the Neanderthals had 18,000 generations for their 270,000 years of existence. At the same rate we Homo Sapiens would then have had 4,000 generations to get from our post-African origins 60,000 years ago to the present time. And it would have taken 14,444 generations to get to the present from our African origins 200,000 years ago. We are not only very recent arrivals on earth in terms of geologic time, but also in evolutionary time.

Surveying the history of mankind's generations one can quickly see that one's own genealogy, even if it can be researched back 10 generations is only going back a very small percentage of the time of human history. And, remember what we said earlier, that going back ten generations we each have about 1,000 ancestors. Thus it should now be very clear that we are all part of an enormous, well mixed pool of genes. We are, in short, all members of the same human family.

It is also important to remember that most of what we know about pre-historic man has been discovered very recently. Neanderthal man was first discovered by a German miner in the 1856, and was not properly identified as pre-historic until the late 19th century. Cro-Magnon man was not discovered until 1868 in Les Eyzies De Tayac in the Dordogne in France. The cave art at Lascaux, France was not discovered until 1940, and the cave art at the Chauvet Cave in the Ardeche, France was not discovered until 1995. Most of the over 250 sites of prehistoric man in Southern France and Northern Spain have been discovered during the last fifty years. And DNA genetic analysis of pre-historic man is even more recent, since DNA was not discovered until 1953 and not applied to this research until the 1970's.

**g. Population Genetics,
Human Migration, Spencer Wells,
Geographic Project**
It is however now quite easy to search your DNA "roots". Oxford Ancestors, located in Oxford, England, will search both your "Y" male line and/or your matrilineal DNA history back into ancient history, for a fee. For an interesting exposition of the history and work of Oxford, Ancestors, read "The Seven Daughters of Eve", by Dr. Bryan Sykes. They can be reached on the Internet at http://www.oxfordancestors.com.

Another of the Oxford geneticists, Dr. Spencer Wells, who is now supported by the National Geographic Magazine, has written some recent books describing his DNA studies confirming the archeological evidence that prehistoric man came out of Africa, in successive waves of migration. "The Journey of Man, A Genetic Odyssey" (2003) and "Deep Ancestry, Inside the Geographic Project", National Geographic (2006) also supports a personal genetic search program: http://www.genebase.com.

According to Wells, the first wave of Homo erectus hominids came to Central Asia and then to present-day China and Indonesia about 1,800,000 years ago. Subsequent waves came out about 900,000 years ago and "turned left" as it were, settling in northern Spain as Sima de los Huesos, at Atapuerca.

Next, the Neanderthals either descended from the Sima or were a subsequent wave of emigration from Africa, settling in present-day Israel and sites in Europe, such as present-day, Germany, France and Czechoslovakia. Lastly, our direct ancestors, Homo Sapiens left Africa about 90,000 to 60,000 and followed the old emigration routes to Central Asia, Eastern Asia and Europe.

Some brave Homo Sapiens souls trekked and perhaps sailed along the coastlines all the way to present-day

Australia about 50,000 years ago. Others crossed present-day Siberia and crossed the Bering Sea land bridge that existed 15,000 to 20,000 years ago into present-day Alaska, then migrating all the way down to Chile, leaving settlements along the way in present-day North, Central, and South America.

For a while, between 30,000 and 40,000 years ago Homo Sapiens coexisted alongside Neanderthal and Homo erectus man until they became extinct about 30,000 years ago.

The wide diversity of appearance of Homo Sapiens is just that; appearance. We humans are quick to notice differences in appearance, and typically react negatively, to people who are "different" than our own family or clan or tribe. For centuries we have believed and acted fiercely on the belief that mankind is made up of many "races", with some, usually one's own "race" being superior to the others; Our human skills of discrimination have probably helped us survive and compete successfully as prehistoric men, but the same skills have also caused great havoc and suffering.

Migration to What Is Now England and Ireland
Recently, Dr. Stephen Oppenheimer, a medical geneticist at Oxford, announced that the results of his genetic research indicate that the conventional wisdom about the ancestry

of most English and Irish people is probably wrong. The conventional wisdom has been that the Irish are descended from Celts and the English from the Anglo-Saxons who invaded from north Europe and drove the Celts to the countries western and northern fringes. (Reported in the Science Section of the New York Times on March 6, 2007)

Oppenheimer's research, which is not agreed to by all genetic scholars, is that the principal ancestors of today's English and Irish populations arrived from Spain about 16,000 years ago, speaking a language related to Basque.

The "Spanish" migrants would have come to what is now England and Ireland by simply walking north along the Atlantic coastline, since there was then no English Channel or Irish Sea, or even a North Sea. The glacier melt had not yet filled the valleys that were subsequently flooded by these seas.

This new migrant, hunter-gatherer population would have settled an empty land and then later survived a cold spell that we call the "Younger Dryas" that lasted from 12,000 to 11,000 years ago. Much later, 6,000 years ago, agriculture finally came to the "British Isles" from its birthplace in the Near East with a Celtic migration. These Celtic immigrants were few in number but spread their farming techniques and language throughout Ireland and the western coast of

England. Later immigrants arrived from northern Europe and had more influence on the eastern and southern coasts. They too spread their language, a branch of German, but these invaders numbers were also small compared to the local population.

Ireland received the fewest of the subsequent invaders: their DNA makes up about 12 percent of the Irish gene pool. DNA accounts for 20 percent of the gene pool in Wales, 30 percent in Scotland, and about 33 percent in eastern and southern England.

Dr. Oppenheimer's book, "The Origins of the British, a Genetic Detective Story" was published in 2006 by Carroll and Graf. And, Bryan Sykes, the Oxford geneticist referred to above, agrees with Oppenheimer, saying, "by far the majority of people were present in the British Isles before the Roman Conquest of AD 43. The Saxons, Vikings and Normans had a minor effect, and much less than some of the medieval historical texts would indicate." Sykes own book, "Saxons, Vikings and Celts; the Genetic Roots of Britain and Ireland", tells the rest of his interpretation.

So, once again, scientifically based DNA research and analysis has altered the conventional view of history. However, it must also be said that genetic similarity does not necessarily generate cultural similarity. For example, the Irish and the English have been in constant conflict for centuries, as have the genetically similar Serbians, Croatians, and Muslims in the former Yugoslavia, and many of the people of the constantly warring near and middle east.

h. A Brief History of Human Population Growth

The history of human population is another vast subject but for the purpose of this summary view of genealogy, suffice it to say that for the first few millions of years of mankind proto-hominid and prehistoric existence the total human population was in the tens and hundreds of thousands, at most. DNA studies, for instance, produce an estimate that the first Homo Sapiens group of humans to leave Africa about 60,000 years ago were less than one hundred people. This condition of small family related groups of hunter-gatherer prehistoric people prevailed until the beginnings of our historical time, approximately 8-10,000 BCE, when agricultural and urban development began. From then until the beginnings of the Roman Empire the growth was modest, but significant, resulting in Roman censuses of males from age seventeen to sixty of between 4,000,000 and 6,000,000. It is therefore estimated that the total world population at the time of the Roman Empire was approximately three hundred million.

From then until 1750 CE the total world population increased to approximately one billion. The period since 1750 CE is characterized by very rapid and rapidly accelerating growth. This period represents only about .02 percent of mankind's history, but over 90% of the increase has occurred during this time. In 1962 the total world population was estimated to be three billion. We are now (2007) estimated to have doubled to six billion human beings on earth, with the growth rate still accelerating. Some say we will peak at ten billion, but the United Nations recently revised its long-range forecast of population growth to 9.5 billion people by 2050.

Among the 6 billion people now on the earth approximately 2 billion are Christians; 1.5 billion are Muslims; 1.5 billion are Chinese of unknown religious choice; 900 million are Hindus, 360 million are Buddhists; 14 million are Jews; and the rest made up of small sects such as Shinto, Jainists, Sikhs, Confucians, Taoists and aboriginal native religions.

In America our official population census has been counted every ten years since 1790. Our first census counted a total of 3.17 million "white" people and 760,000 "Negro" people, totaling 3.93 million people. The total population increased dramatically year by year, fueled mainly by immigration at about 35% to 38% per year until 1860 when it reached a total of 31,440,000, including 4,440,000

Negroes, mostly slaves. Slave importation was outlawed in 1808. The total American population reached 300,000,000 in 2006.

So much for the gene pool and total human population. DNA research has determined that mankind is literally all related to itself, coming out of Africa thousands of years ago and dispersing itself all over the world. In this remote sense all Americans, and everyone else, are "African-Americans". We are all out of the same genetic root. It is clear however that it is very difficult to verify one's genealogical roots specifically back very far in the total human existence, except for the tracing of some "X" and "Y" genetic markers that can identify one's remote ancestral migration path.

i. Primatology, Behavioral Evolution, Biological and Cultural
Biological Evolution - Who we were - Who we are now
As the primatologists Jane Goodall and Franz De Waal illustrate in their work our closest primate relatives pre-figure our own aggressive, war-like propensities in the male-dominated, competitive, chimpanzee ape societies, and our peace-loving, erotic propensities in the female-dominated, cooperative societies of the bonobo ape. Chimpanzees, like young male humans, are fully capable of forming marauding gangs that hunt monkeys for food, and also engage in preemptive killing wars with chimpanzees from neighboring troops. And, when young Chimp males win the competition for dominance among the males of their own troop, they will frequently kill off the newborn offspring of other males to gain sexual access to their "widows".

The predatory sexual practices of young chimp males is chillingly similar to sexual predation by young human males. Testosterone seems to work its will among all primates. It is not "original sin", but the testosterone of primate male puberty that seems to be the cause of much of the dark side of primate societies. Both males and females seek reciprocally pleasurable sexual relations, but it is the aggressive male who initiates and takes sexual possession of the female. The female should clearly not be blamed for the temptation of males as told in the Genesis tale of the Garden of Eden. It is the females who nurture and teach their offspring. Males don't need temptation; they can get into trouble all by themselves. The instinctive male desire to have sex and propagate its own genes drives his aggressive behavior. The 10% -15% greater size of males, and their greater kinetic muscle strength, compared to females, plus the biological fact that it is females who conceive, bear, nurse and nurture the children, sets the stage for the traditional subordination of females by males.

The male consignment of females to lives as sexual objects and partners, and "domestic labor" has only recently begun to change toward equal rights and opportunities in some Western cultures. Many middle-eastern, African, Asian and many Latin American cultures continue to subordinate women in the worst ways through polygamy, slavery, prostitution, genital mutilation, "honor killing" and the denial of most basic human and property rights.

The 20th century advent of Western culture's Women's Suffrage and the development of birth-control pharmaceuticals and technology, plus more democratic and open communication systems have only recently begun to free women from subordination. However, the behavior of our primate "cousins" shows all too clearly the source of the self-propagating behavior patterns of our own human societies. We are still primarily concerned with survival and reproduction.

One of the best summaries of the science of primatology is "Sociobiology, The New Synthesis", by E.O. Wilson, (Harvard Belknap Press, 2000) See also Fraanz De Waal's, "Tree of Origin" and "Our Inner Ape", and Jane Goodall's "The Chimpanzees of Gombe: Patterns of Behavior" (Harvard U. Press, 1986)

Dr. de Waal has also done considerable research on the subject of primate "morality". Although he concludes that non-human primates do not possess human morality, they have many distinct behavior traits that are the "emotional building blocks" for the evolution of human morality. Dr. de Waal has documented clear evidence of four kinds of primate behavior; (1) empathy, (2) the ability to learn and follow social rules, (3) reciprocity and (4) peacemaking, as the basis of their sociality. "Social living requires empathy, which is especially evident in chimpanzees, as well as ways of bringing internal hostilities to an end. Dr. de Waal has found that every species of ape and monkey has its own protocol for reconciliation after fights. If two males fail to make up, female chimpanzees will often bring the rivals together, as if sensing that discord makes their community worse off and more vulnerable to attack by neighbors. Or, they will head off a fight by taking stones out of the males' hands." Dr. de Waal believes that these actions are undertaken for the greater good of the community, as distinct from person-to-person relationships, and are a significant precursor of morality in human societies.

They also have hierarchical social structures and rules of behavior, practice mutual grooming, care for their young, share food, and a have a level of self-awareness that only apes and humans seem to possess.

Dr. de Waal sees human morality as having grown out of primate sociality, but with two extra levels of sophistication. People enforce their society's moral codes much more rigorously with rewards, punishments and reputation building. They also apply a degree of judgment and reason for which there are no parallels in animals.

Religion can be seen as another special ingredient of human societies, though one that emerged thousands of years after morality. There are clear precursors of morality in non-human primates, but no precursors of religion. So it seems reasonable to assume that as humans evolved away from chimps, morality emerged first, followed by religion. Dr. de Waal says, "I look at religions as recent additions. Their function may have to do with social life, and enforcement of rules and giving narrative to them, which is what religions really do."

As Dr. de Waal sees it, human morality may be severely limited by having evolved as a way of banding together against adversaries, with moral restraints being observed only toward the "in group", and not toward outsiders. "The profound irony is that our noblest achievement - morality - has evolutionary ties to our basest behavior - warfare. The sense of community required by the former was provided by the former."

For a more complete discussion of Dr. de Waals' work please see his books, "Good Natured" (1996) and "Primates and Philosophers" (2006). See also Marc Hauser's book, "Moral Minds" in which he argues that the human brain has a genetically shaped mechanism for acquiring moral rules, a universal moral grammar similar to the neural machinery for learning language. See also the New York Times Science Section, March 20, 2007.

j Biological Evolution – who we were – who we are now
A frightening look at the violent capabilities of chimpanzees is "Deep Jungle", by Fred Pearce, a book companion to the PBS series of the same title. Close-up videos of chimpanzees hunting, catching, killing and eating monkeys illustrates the roots of our "hunter" propensities. Other close-up videos of a troop of Chimpanzees tracking, capturing and killing another chimpanzee from a neighboring troop also illustrates dearly the roots of our capacity for gang and war-like killing. The pictures of members of the marauding chimpanzees returning to the killed chimpanzee and beating it once again are particularly tragic. They are awful reminders of the recent videos taken of continued police beatings of arrested and handcuffed people they have arrested and subdued. Our primate and other mammalian "cousins" are certainly capable of "wild-dog-pack" or

"hyena-pack" killing behavior. And you need only read the daily newspapers or watch the evening TV news to see that mankind is still capable of the same behavior.

Another excellent book about "Who we were" and "Who we are now" is "The Origin of Mind, Evolution of Brain, Cognition, and General Intelligence", by David Geary (American Psychological Assn., 2005). This book could just as well be cited under "Brain Science", but since it covers both Homo erectus and Homo Sapiens, it is just as appropriate to include it here. Geary's general thesis is that the real story of the biological arms race that fed human brain development actually has only two acts. In the first act, humans achieve "super-predator" status, probably around 800,000 years ago at the latest, with Homo Erector's mastery of fire. That, along with the ever-developing making and using of tools, allowed humans to become masters of their ecological domain. This had enormous survival and reproductive consequences. Once ecological mastery was achieved, "an evolutionary Rubicon was crossed." After that point the effects of extrinsic forces of natural selection diminished, and within species competition became the principal hostile force of nature, guiding the long-term evolution of behavior capacities, traits and tendencies."

"In the second act, the natural, cyclical contractions of ecological resources force social competition among small bands for diminishing resources. In such a situation where social competition intensifies, the stage is set for a form of runaway selection, whereby the more cognitively, socially and behaviorally sophisticated individuals are able to outmaneuver and manipulate other individuals to gain control of resources in the local ecology and to dominate the behavior of other people."

k. Cultural Evolution
Mankind's cultural evolution has propelled Homo Sapiens far beyond what his earliest origin indicated in Africa over 200,000 years ago. The evolutionary development of our remarkable brains, principally our cerebral cortex, provides the biological basis for our cultural evolution. The acquisition and development of spoken language from earliest times, and its subsequent development into written language beginning about 5,000 BCE, enabled mankind to pass on learned experience from parents to children, and then, as libraries of written knowledge accumulated, to build a data base of experience available for use by all subsequent generations. From the libraries and the institutions of learning, and the unleashed creative capacity of the human mind, came the technical, legal, religious,

business and artistic innovations that have covered the globe in a burgeoning variety of cultures.

The cultural evolution of mankind is of course a monumental subject, which fills countless museums and libraries. Suffice it to say here that the evolution of human culture from the earliest stone tools and weapons to more sophisticated tools, weapons and art, musical instruments such as 100,000 year old flutes (which must have occasioned or accompanied dancing) and ceremonial burials of the dead; then to the development of written language, the bronze age and the iron age, and through the origins of agriculture and the building of towns and cities, with codes of behavior and laws (the Ten Commandments and the Laws of Hammurabi),and formalized and institutionalized religions. Then the development of modern science and technology all the way to the present. Thus our cultural evolution has propelled mankind forward in time to our present state of affairs where we dominate the physical world, but we are still caught up in seemingly perpetual strife. As Darwin said, we are still limited by our animal self, "the indelible stamp of our lowly origin." We are basically primates, but with a remarkable brain. However, if we don't properly use our brains, we will simply be the same primitive animals as our primate cousins. Hopefully our cultural evolution will someday overcome our baser instincts.

Chicago Culture

On the bright side however, in some parts of the world, such as Chicago, Illinois, we do enjoy an incredible culture of freedom and affluence, unimaginable to most humans throughout human history. Most of us are relatively safe, have good housing and transportation and access to a virtually unlimited array of products and services. We have hundreds of beautiful parks, a magnificent lake front system of parks and athletic facilities and world famous amateur and professional sports teams. We have over 100 legitimate theaters, hundreds of television channels of electronic entertainment, restaurants, the Chicago Symphony Orchestra and all kinds of other music, Ravinia, the Lyric and other grand opera companies, many dance companies, the great Universities of Chicago and Northwestern and Illinois (and others) with their outstanding faculties and libraries, the Newberry and Chicago Public and other independent libraries, The Pritzker Military Library, the Arts Club of Chicago, the Art Institute of Chicago, the Field Museum, the Museum of Science and Industry Shedd Aquarium, the Planetarium, the Chicago History Museum, the Oriental Institute, many, many other cultural institutions; such as the Chicago Literary Club, the Cliff dwellers, the Fortnightly Club of Chicago, the Antiquarian Society, the

Cultural Center, The Chicago Humanities Festival and many others. Chicago is also a city of many great hospitals and rehabilitation centers and hundreds of Christian churches, Jewish synagogues and Muslim mosques. In Chicago our cultural cup does "runneth over".

American Culture – The American Dream of Equal Rights for All People

As Americans we all share in the unique experimental culture that is America. I say experimental because our founders set forth the audacious principle of "All men are created equal" even though there were great inequalities at the time of our founding. Most of the founders owned slaves, who were certainly not seen or treated as equal, and women were very much second-class citizens without the right to vote or equal employment or legal status.

The Fundamental Right of Habeas Corpus

The fundamental right of Habeas Corpus ("Produce the Body") had its origins in ancient Anglo-Saxon common law, predating even the Magna Carta of 1215 when the English Nobles challenged King John's assertion of arbitrary power. In legal terms it is a prerogative writ - a procedure to which you have an undeniable right. It is an extraordinary remedy at law. "Upon proper application, or even on naked knowledge alone, a

court is empowered, and is duty bound, to issue the Extraordinary Writ of Habeas Corpus commanding one who is restraining liberty to forthwith produce before the court the person who is in custody and to show cause why the liberty of that person is being restrained. Absent a sufficient showing for a proper restraint of liberty, the court is duty bound to order the restraint eliminated and the person discharged. Habeas Corpus is fundamental to American and all other English common law derivative systems of jurisprudence. It is the ultimate lawful and peaceable remedy for adjudicating the providence of liberty's restraint."

As with other features of English common law and practice, by the time of the American Revolutionary War, the Writ of Habeas Corpus was clearly established in all of the British Colonies in New England and was generally regarded as part of the fundamental protections guaranteed by law to each citizen. The American Constitution at Article 1, Section 9 states that: "The Privilege of the Writ of Habeas Corpus shall not be suspended, unless when Case of Rebellion or Invasion the public Safety may require it."

The most controversial Habeas Corpus case in pre Civil War American history was the Dred Scott Case, when it was perniciously decided that since Scott was a slave and was therefore not a "person" as constituted by the Constitution, he did not have a right to petition for a Writ of Habeas Corpus. This case was subsequently overturned many years later.

The American Bill of Rights
The foundation for American's equal rights was also laid, first in the Declaration of Independence of 1775, then codified more specifically in the first ten amendments to the Constitution, "The Bill of Rights", adopted by the States and declared in force December 15, 1791. Its predecessor was the Virginia Declaration of Rights, written by George Mason. (I have recited The Bill of Rights as follows here because very few American have actually read them.)

1. Religious establishment prohibited. Freedom of speech, of the press, and the right to peaceably assemble and petition the government for redress of grievances guaranteed.

2. "A well-regulated militia being necessary to the security of free State, the right of the people to keep and bear arms shall not be infringed." The "Right to bear arms" is conditional, as a part of a well-regulated militia. This right has been repeatedly decided by many Federal courts to grant the "collective right" to bear arms as a part of a well-regulated militia, and not the individual right to bear arms. The National Rifle Association has for many years publicly asserted that the amendment grants the individual right to bear arms, but the courts have never agreed, until June, 2008 when the U.S. Supreme Court, in a controversial, 5 to 4 decision, struck down a Washington, DC gun control law. The case was DC vs. Heller, deciding that there is a common law right to bear arms which pre-exists the 2nd Amendment, providing the basis for an individual right to bear arms. The Courts's decision allowed for the regulation of arms in many circumstances, but asserted the individual right to bear arms for hunting and "self defense". As a practical matter the individual right already exists in the minds of many citizens. The Court's decision and its dissents will surely spawn many subsequent cases trying to define its limits and its application.

3. "No soldier shall, in time of peace, be quartered in any house without the consent of the owner, nor in time of war but in a manner prescribed by law."

4. "The right of the people to be secure in their persons, houses, papers, and effects, against unreasonable searches and seizures, shall not be violated, and no warrants shall issue but upon probable cause, supported by oath or affirmation, and particularly describing the place to be searched, and the persons or things to be seized."

5. "No person shall be held to answer for a capital or otherwise infamous crime unless on a presentment or indictment of a grand jury, except in cases arising in the land or naval forces, or in the militia, when in actual service, in time of war or public danger; nor shall any person be subject for the same offense to be twice put in jeopardy of life or limb; nor shall be compelled in any criminal case to be a witness against himself, nor be deprived of life, liberty or property, without due process or law; nor shall private property be taken for public use without just compensation."

6. "In all criminal prosecutions, the accused shall enjoy the right to a speedy and public trial, by an impartial jury of the State and district wherein the crime shall have been committed, which districts shall have been previously ascertained by law, and to be informed of the nature and cause of the accusation; to be confronted with the witnesses against him; to have compulsory process for obtaining witnesses in his favor, and to have the assistance of counsel for his defense."

7. "In suits at common law, where the value in controversy shall exceed twenty dollars, the right of trial by jury shall be preserved, and no fact tried by a jury shall be otherwise re-examined in any court of the United States than according to the rules of the common law."

8. "Excessive bail shall not be required, nor excessive fines be imposed, nor cruel and unusual punishments inflicted."

9. "The enumeration in the Constitution of certain rights shall not be construed to deny or disparage others retained by the people.

10. "The powers not delegated to the United States by the Constitution, nor prohibited by it to the States, are reserved to the States respectively, or to the people."

As clearly stated, and as important as the Bill of Rights is, they were not effectively enforced until beginning after World War I when the ACLU was organized, as the first of many similar organizations, to resist the abuses by the United States attorney general during the "Palmer Raids". The development of civil liberties law under the Bill of Rights and subsequent laws establishing citizen's rights continues until the present. It is for these reasons that I have always called the ACLU "The most conservative organization in America", because it is dedicated to conserving the most important legacy we have as Americans, freedom from government abuse.

No real democracy is possible without civil liberties. The right to vote is meaningless without freedom of speech and peaceable assembly. There are many examples of military dictatorships, which have false democracies. Majority rule must also protect the rights of minorities and individuals.

It took a bloody Civil War to at least prohibit slavery by the Thirteenth Amendment to the Constitution, abolishing slavery, and the Fourteenth Amendment, the "Equal Protection" amendment, but it took another century for even nominal equality to be achieved by the sons and daughters of slavery. Reconstruction was defeated when President Grant withdrew Federal Troops from the south in 1871 and thus set the stage for the nightmare of Jim Crow and the Ku Klux Klan which returned the south to virtual slavery replete with lynching and rank racial and social segregation. Ironically the Fifteenth Amendment, the "Equal Rights To Vote" Amendment, prohibiting the denial of the right to vote by any State on account of race, color or previous condition of servitude was also ratified in 1871. But from then on Black Americans suffered separate and miserable schools, separate and miserable housing, "back of the bus" transportation, separate restaurants, drinking fountains, virtually no voting rights, no rights to organize labor, segregated professional - medical and legal - organizations, segregated entertainment facilities, and humiliation everywhere, even to stepping off the sidewalk to let whites pass.

And many white, segregationist Southerners became more and more and more mean spirited as virtual rulers in a continued virtual slave society. Both the masters and the slaves are badly damaged in a slave society.

The 19th and the 20th centuries saw the legal abolition of slavery in Portugal, France, England, and North and South America. There is however still slavery and "virtual slavery" still being practiced in many Asian, middle-eastern and African countries. Next to war itself, slavery has been a continuous scourge in the cultural evolution of humanity.

The American Civil Rights Movement
It wasn't until just before World War II and the courage and tenacity of A. Philip Randolph (1889-1979), the president of the Brotherhood of Sleeping Car Porters, that black Americans were able to begin to assert their rights as citizens. The National Labor Relations Act, passed under President Roosevelt's first term, gave all working people the right to elect their bargaining representatives. After twelve years of frustrating failure to get the Pullman Company to bargain with the Sleeping Car Porters, Randolph was able to force Pullman's management to recognize their union and bargain with them in 1937. Next he forced President Roosevelt to recognize the rights of minorities to have

equal employment opportunity in World War II defense contract work. It was Randolph's basic insight, now obvious, that you couldn't be free unless you had a job. Freedom is based upon economic independence. Then, after World War II, during which the American armed services were rigidly segregated, Randolph threatened a black draftee's boycott and another march on Washington to protest for integration of the armed services, President Truman resisted, but once again Randolph's tenacity and the justice of his cause prevailed, and Truman reluctantly ordered the integration of the armed forces in 1948. Many years later, in 1963, Randolph, at age 74, once again organized a massive March on Washington for Jobs and Freedom, passing the Civil Rights leadership torch to Rev. Martin Luther King. One of the direct results of this march was the enactment of the 1965 Voting Rights Act. Randolph achieved these rights by threatening to organize peaceful, but massive protest marches on Washington, D.C.

One of Randolph's biographers, Karen Chenoweth, says; "For the first time, (during World War II) because of federal jobs, a substantial Black middle class could begin to develop." "It would be hard to overstate the importance of A. Philip Randolph to the last century of American history. It would also be hard to overstate the

deep shadow into which his memory has faded."

Randolph's views were best stated by him: "Freedom is never given, it is won". "At the banquet table of life, there are no reserved seats. You get what you can take and keep what you can hold. If you can't take anything, you won't get anything. And you can't hold anything without organization." (This quote is inscribed on the bust of Randolph located in the passenger concourse of the Union railway station in Washington, D.C.)

""Let the nation and the world know the meaning of our numbers. We are not a pressure group. We are not an organization or a group of organizations. We are not a mob. We are the advance guard of a massive moral revolution for jobs and freedom..."
A. Philip Randolph

As John Lewis said in 1963, then a young leader of the Student Nonviolent Coordinating Committee and now a Democratic congressman from Georgia, "If Randolph had been born in another period maybe of another color, he probably would have been President. In another land he probably would have been, maybe, Prime Minister... But in a real sense, he was head of the building of a new nation, a better America."

A great many other Americans, both black and white, followed Randolph's leadership during the post World War

II Civil Rights Movement and joined together to help make America's promise of equality come more true. People such as John Hope Franklin, Thurgood Marshall, Roger Wilkins and Presidents Eisenhower, Kennedy and Johnson are prominent examples, among many others. We are still a very imperfect democracy, but we moved considerably forward during the 20th century.

Women's Rights

One area, coincidentally led first in America by Frederick Douglass, the escaped slave who became an influential Abolitionist and influenced President Abraham Lincoln to make the Emancipation Proclamation, has been Women's Rights. Douglass was one of the first public figures to see and speak out about the subordination of women's rights as similar to slavery. The cause was moved forward further by many brave women advocates for women's suffrage rights to vote, first in England and then in America before and after World War I, culminating in the 19th Amendment to the U.S. Constitution, ratified in 1920, granting the right to vote to Women. The increasing recognition of women's rights and their participation in business, politics, the professions and the arts has made America a much more credible land of opportunity for all.

Slavery and Apartheid

It is important to consider civil liberties when we talk about who we are as people. For without freedom for everyone our society will continue to be flawed by many who are subordinated and by others who are their masters. One of the great lessons of slavery is that it negatively affected both the slaves and the masters. The slaves were abused and the masters were the abusers, and the system depended upon actual or threatened violence for its enforcement. It killed freedom for both the slaves and the masters. And we need freedom to flourish and be a creative, productive people. Science, business and religion certainly need freedom to flourish.

Outside of America there have also been some remarkable examples of 20th century heroism on behalf of freedom. Nelson Mandela, who suffered decades of imprisonment in South Africa and then emerged to become its Prime Minister during the relatively peaceful overthrow of Apartheid. Bishop Tutu shares the same honor with Nelson Mandela, both Nobel Laureates.

One of the bravest and great South African authors, Alan Paton, in his "Cry The Beloved Country", spoke poetically and prophetically about the end of Apartheid and the possibility of peace when he wrote:

"For it is the dawn that has come, as it has come for a thousand centuries, never failing. But when that dawn will come on our emancipation, from the fear of bondage, and the bondage of fear, why, that is a secret."

An interesting historical fact connecting slavery in Haiti and America is the successful slave rebellion in Haiti led by Toussaint L'Ouverture against both the French and the British who wanted possession of Haiti for its sugar, timber and slaves. L'Ouverture led the revolution in the 1790's, but was captured and sent to prison in France where he ultimately died. But his deputy, Jacques Dessalines, was victorious over the French, who also succumbed to tropical disease. The French loss made Napoleon I decide against further pursuit of territorial gains in North America. President Thomas Jefferson was therefore able to negotiate the purchase of the Louisiana Territory, consisting of 530 million acres of land stretching from New Orleans to the Canadian border, from the French at a price of $15 million U.S. dollars. The purchase doubled the land area of America! Thus, the successful slave revolution in Haiti turned into the Louisiana Purchase for America.

The Culture of War
The history of humanity is in one sense the history of its wars. From the time of Homer's Iliad (500 BCE?), the history of the Trojan War, through the 5,000 plus wars of recorded history, to the present, when some of the same wars of 2,000 years ago are still being fought by the same cultures in the middle-east.

Mankind is clearly a war-like animal. And, most of mankind's wars have been fought with some kind of religious justification, on both sides, many times with both sides praying to the same god! One-way to measure the quality of a culture is to examine the history of its wars: their causes and their conduct.

Prior to World War I America projected its power in Asia to protect its commercial interests in both China and Japan. In 1853 an armed American Fleet commanded by Admiral Perry "opened communication" with the Emperor of Japan, which had been self-isolated for over 200 years, in order to obtain trading rights and coaling stations for its military and commercial ships. (see Robert Tomes's "'The Americans in Japan", Appleton, 1857). American forces were also stationed in Tientsin, China to protect its diplomatic and commercial interests, and participated with British, German, Japanese and French forces in putting down the Boxer Rebellion in 1900.

World War I
World War I, the precursor of all modern warfare with the machine-gun, airplanes, radio, telegraphy, telephones, tanks and massive, wholesale

slaughter, was fought among the world's most "civilized" cultures: England, France, Germany, Austria, Italy and Russia. Over 9,000,000 soldiers killed. And each of the combatants on all sides was praying to the same God for support. "Gott Mit Uns" was even emblazoned on German soldiers' belt buckles.

America came into combat in World War I in 1918, late in the game, but made a significant contribution on behalf of England and France. All the combatants were exhausted by 1918 so the infusion of fresh American troops tipped the scale against Germany. America's professed reason for entering World War One was to help "Win the war to end all wars", an honorable, if illusory goal.

World War II
In World War II the Allied forces of England, America, Russia and France risked extraordinary treasure and blood to overcome the attacks by German Naziism, Italian Fascism, and Japanese Militarism. The formation of the United Nations in 1945 following WorLd War II has at least established a forum for debate and resolution of some international disputes. The subsequent facing down of Soviet Communism, the Korean and Chinese Communists during the Korean Conflict, and the continued attempts by the United Nations, however flawed, to resolve international disputes and conflicts illustrates

mankind's attempts to make the world a better, more just, and more democratic place to live.

American Wars
I think it is worth telling the story of America's wars in some detail because the story serves to tell "who we are" in ways that are both complimentary to our culture and also devastatingly critical of our culture. It is "Who We Are", good, bad and indifferent, "warts and all."

America was of course born by the conquest of the North American continent, beginning in the 16th to 17th centuries. The Spaniards were first, coming in through Central America and what is now Mexico and Florida. Next were the Dutch and English, coming in through what we now call New York and New England. And then the French coming in through what we now call Canada. Each of the European conquerors came in search of lands to colonize, and wealth, and also as missionaries for the Christian religion. Each colonial power also regarded the native Indian populations as "heathens" to be exploited, converted to Christianity, or killed as the circumstances warranted. When the Indians died of the smallpox or other European diseases carried by the colonials their deaths were seen to be caused by "God" on behalf of the colonials! So much for benevolent Christianity.

The Europeans succeeded by conquering the land and committing what we now see was genocide on the American Indians. The full story is long and complicated, but in the end, it was a relentless decimation of probably 4 - 6,000,000 Native American Indians by 1900. The few survivors were herded into "reservations" of otherwise unwanted land after repeated betrayals by the Europeans and Americans of treaties made and broken. Please see your local library for the complete well-documented history. One of the most eloquent and sad books on the subject is, "Touch The Earth", by T.C. McLuhan (Promontory Press, 1971), which tells the story of the 19th century American Indian in his own words. "Everywhere the white man touches the earth, it is sore."

The American Revolution of 1776 to 1783 resulted in the Treaty of Paris granting America the sovereignty of the original 13 colonies from the Maine boundary with Canada to the Florida boundary with Spain. The long, disorganized and in many ways unpopular war against the British could not have been won without the courage of many brave revolutionary Americans and the help of France, which supplied many officers, money and its navy, making the critical difference at the final battle of Yorktown. The American Constitution, and its first ten amendments, known now as the Bill of Rights was created by the American Founding Fathers after much wrangling in Philadelphia and still stands as the world's template for our uniquely free and democratic government. So, the American Revolution was certainly a "good war" in result. America subsequently added to its landmass in huge steps, some by peaceful acquisition and some by acquisitions forced by acts of war.

First, Thomas Jefferson negotiated the Louisiana Purchase from Napoleon I in 1803. By paying France $15,000,000 U.S. Dollars. Jefferson doubled the size of America in one peaceful transaction, obtaining title to all the 530,000,000 acres of land between New Orleans and the Canadian border. Second, Thomas Jefferson sent the Lewis and Clark Expedition to Oregon and claimed the northwestern part of the American continent for America. This claim was later certified by the Oregon Treaty with England in 1846.

In 1819 Florida was purchased from Spain for $5,000,000 under the Adams-Onis Treaty. The Independent Republic of Texas was annexed peacefully by America in 1845.

America then invaded Mexico in 1845 and after winning the war, acquired California, Arizona, Nevada and New Mexico by paying $15,000,000 to Mexico. In 1819 the present border with Mexico was completed by the Gadsden purchase in 1853 for another $10,000,000.

Unfortunately, America's subsequent behavior as a military power has left a lot to be desired. Beginning with the American overthrow of the legitimate monarchy of Hawaii in 1893, followed by the American invasion of Cuba, beating Spain and taking over its government from the Cuban revolutionaries in 1898, then similarly invading and taking over Puerto Rico. Then after Commodore Dewey destroyed the Spanish fleet in Manila Bay in 1898, America paid Spain $20 million for all of Cuba, Puerto Rico and the Philippines. The problem was that the Philippine revolutionaries did not agree and expected to have their sovereignty, which America denied. The ensuing war between American Marines and Philippine guerrillas was won by America in 1902, after 3 1/2 years of jungle fighting that left 4,374 Americans dead and 16,000 guerrillas and at least 20,000 civilians killed. Another "regime change" was accomplished by America in Nicaragua in 1912. In each of these "regime changes" America justified its involvement on the basis of protecting its commercial interests and extending "Christian democracy."

Next in this sorry chain of "regime changes" was Iran in 1953, at the instigation of Britain whose British Petroleum had been nationalized by the Iranian Prime Minister, Mohammad Mossadegh. America, with the willing cooperation of Secretary of State John Foster Dulles and his brother Allen Dulles, head of the CIA, engineered the physical overthrow of Mossadegh and the installation of the Shah. The reason given was "to roll back Communism", but there was never any evidence that Mossadegh was either a Communist or a Communist sympathizer. He was, in fact, a dedicated Iranian nationalist. This "regime change", of course, came back to bite America many years later, with the overthrow of the Shah and the installation of the Islamic Iranian government that bedevils America to the present.

Guatemala was next on the list for "regime change" which was accomplished by our military and CIA backed coup, in 1954, once again at the behest of John Foster Dulles on behalf of the United Fruit Company which had huge banana growing interests in Guatemala. And, once again, "anti-Communism" was the professed reason for the coup.

Perhaps the worst "regime change" that produced enormous unintended consequences for America was the nullification of the Vietnamese election scheduled for 1956. We nullified the election because it appeared certain that the northern nationalist leader, Ho Chi Minh, would win. Ho had made serious overtures to America for help, but was rebuffed as too independent and probably "leftist". But the Chinese Communists were also leery of his independence. In the event we picked a South Vietnamese Catholic, Ngo Dinh Diem as our man and we installed him as prime minister with the approval of Emperor Bao Dai, then living in Cannes. Dulles died in 1958, Eisenhower lost interest in Vietnam and John Kennedy was elected president. He offered and sent American soldiers and fighter planes and other military hardware, but the South Vietnam government was too corrupt and too ineffective to lead the country. Vietnam was only 10% Catholic and Diem's only credentials were that he was Catholic and "anti-Communist".

The upshot of all this trouble was that when Diem offered to negotiate with North Vietnam Kennedy gave up on him and decided to replace him. The "replacement" turned into a bloody assassination managed by the CIA, to the horror of president Kennedy. The result was that America then took over the day-to-day management of the Vietnam war which was eventually, under presidents Johnson, Nixon and Ford, lost to the North Vietnamese in 1975 after a loss of over 55,000 American soldiers and millions of Vietnamese. The war also radically changed American politics for the worse from then on.

Next, in 1973, was the overthrow of Salvador Allende, the duly elected president of Chile. His election made

the American government and many American businessmen panic. "He was a life-long anti-imperialist and admirer of Fidel Castro who had vowed to nationalize the American owned companies that dominated his country's economy." ("Overthrow", by Stephen Kinzer, Holt, 2006) This sad story ended in 1973 with the killing, or suicide, of Allende while he was under the military coup's attack, followed by the installation of General Augusto Pinochet as president. The subsequent government of Pinochet was turned out in disgrace many years later after it was proved that they had deprived many Chileans of their lives and civil liberties during what amounted to a corrupt military dictatorship.

In October of 1983 President Reagan, on the fervent advice of his zealous staff, ordered the invasion of the tiny Caribbean island of Grenada, on the pretense that its newly installed "leftist" government posed a risk to some American medical students living and studying there. The students didn't request protection and could have been rescued if that was the true reason for intervention. But Reagan and his advisers saw an opportunity to accomplish a public relations coup by diverting the news and asserting American power. During the Grenada "crisis" word had come that terrorists had blown up a marine barracks in Lebanon killing over 200 U.S. Marines. The result of the American invasion of

Grenada, an island the size of Nantucket, was a Gilbert & Sullivan operetta war with much confusion and unnecessary killing, including a number of patients in a local mental hospital. The American force was overkill, with airborne troops, fighter-bombers, over 6,000 assault troops and heavy weapons. After the Grenada, "Urgent Fury" operation, Reagan announced to Congress that, "Our days of weakness are over!", "Our military forces are back on their feet, and standing tall." America then pulled the rest of its troops out of Lebanon.

And next was Panama in December of 1989. General Manuel Antonio Noriega, the commander of the Panama Defense Forces, was an incredibly corrupt, vicious, enormously wealthy, CIA informant, drug dealer and politically powerful man who thought he was above the law. He thought, erroneously, that President George H. W. Bush who was inaugurated in January, 1989, would be his friend, particularly since he had known him from Bush's CIA days. But Bush was looking for a way to get rid of his "wimp factor" image and was very sensitive to appearing indecisive. The then president of Panama, Hugo Spadafora, was brutally assassinated in 1989 and the president Noriega installed to replace him was not as obedient as Noriega expected. When Noriega then installed another president

against the wishes of the Panamanian people, Bush sent American troops to warn Noriega. The warning wasn't effective and Bush then ordered a full-scale invasion of Panama. The invasion was a massive show of force including 3,000 airborne troops and heavy air power.

There was, predictably; much devastation, and many civilian casualties and the Panamanian defense forces, mostly police men, quickly surrendered. After a few days of dramatic posturing Noriega was captured and whisked away to jail under indictment. He was subsequently convicted and he is still sitting in jail, in Miami, probably forever.

America became involved in Afghanistan during the 1980's under the presidencies of Carter and Reagan, in a successful attempt to support the Afghan's guerrilla war against Soviet Russia which had occupied Afghanistan and which had lost 15,000 soldiers fighting the Afghanistan insurgency. In 1986 Mikhail Gorbachev, the new Soviet leader, told the Politburo that the Afghan war had become a "bleeding wound" and had to be ended, which he did by withdrawing the remaining 8,000 Soviet troops in 1989. The CIA and the American government celebrated and promptly forgot about Afghanistan. But the local Islamic force, which called itself Taliban, didn't forget and they took over the country, ruling it according to strict Islamic Fundamentalism.

The rest is well-known recent history. Osama Bin Laden, a wealthy Saudi Arabian "Wahabi Muslim" revolutionary, used the country as his base for training terrorists and ultimately struck the Trade Towers, using Taliban trained Saudi Arabians, in New York City on September 11, 2001. The obvious American response was to attack Afghanistan to overthrow the Taliban and hopefully capture Osama Bin Laden. But America only occupied some of the main cities in Afghanistan and contracted the apprehension of Bin Laden to Afghans. It is now June of 2008 and neither the Afghans or the American forces have been able to capture or kill Bin Laden. And, the Afghan warlords are back in power and the opium crop has reached an all time high level.

America then turned its military attention to Iraq, and invaded the country in March, 2003. It was claimed before the invasion that the Iraqi government, under the command of its brutal dictator, Saddam Hussein, possessed Weapons of Mass Destruction, which posed an "imminent threat" to America and other countries. The United Nations had been unable to find any evidence of such weapons and was continuing its inspections when the American government,

under George W. Bush's presidency, launched its "pre-emptive" strike against Iraq. This strike was made against the specific public advice of General Brent Scowcroft, George Bush Senior's National Security Adviser during the previous war with Iraq to free Kuwait. Many others also strongly advised against the war, namely all the mainline Protestant churches and the Roman Catholic Church, as being contrary to the religious Canons of a Just War. All other European countries, except Britain, Italy and Spain, also voted against this war.

As is now also well known, no weapons of mass destruction have ever been found in Iraq and the war has continued now into its fifth year, with the American and British forces and the Iraqi people suffering from a continued insurrection, and now sectarian violence between the Shiite and Sunni factions. This latter violence is one of specific reasons cautioned against by Brent Scowcroft when he advised against starting the war.

And, it now also appears that one of the major unintended consequences of the Iraq war is that Iran has gained increased influence in the Middle East through its close association with the Shiite majority in Iraq, also a problem noted by Scowcroft. The newly elected government of Iraq has publicly made friendly diplomatic contact with Iran, which has pledged its aid to help rebuild Iraq. It also appears that the often stated justification for deposing Hussein by helping Iraq become a democratic country is in serious jeopardy because of the religious fundamentalism of its Shiite majority. And, beyond Iraq, America's unhappy involvement there as an occupying force, now openly identified with torturing prisoners and committing some inevitable atrocities of war, has made Iraq a hotbed of terrorism, and has made America a pariah among most middle-eastern countries. Our close alliance with Israel has also aligned America with the Arab Middle East's traditional enemy. The most recent war between the Hezbollah in Lebanon and Israel has only exacerbated the escalation of military violence in the Middle East.

Thus the American invasion of Iraq, professed to protect against Hussein's aggressive threat and also to create a democratic ally for America in the middle-east, has already backfired into a "royal-mess", now threatening to spiral out of control into a greater confrontation between America and England and many middle-eastern countries.

So, it appears to me at least, that America has strayed a long way from its founding principles of democracy and civil liberties, much of which it enlarged by peaceful acquisition, into a recent course of military adventur-

ism and "regime changes" of countries which it perceived as threats to America's security or commercial interests. The real irony of many of these changes is that they have actually turned out to be contrary to our stated interests, actually harming our security and commercial interests.

The end of World War II put America into a global contest with Soviet Russia, known as the "Cold War" which shaped American foreign policy from 1945 to 1989 when Soviet Russia collapsed during "Perestroika" under premier Gorbachev. President Ronald Reagan's willingness to deal with Gorbachev and proceed forward with nuclear disarmament was also a significant factor in helping end the Cold War. It is frequently said that America "won the Cold War" by its resolute anti-Communism. My own view is that Soviet Russia collapsed under the weight of its own incompetence and ruthless oppression of its conquered people. Soviet Russia failed as a concept and style of government and as an economy.

America survived and still has a relatively vibrant economy, although the gap between its very rich and the middle class and the very poor has grown significantly in recent years. And we have gone from a country with a substantial financial surplus to one with a serious substantial deficit, also in recent years.

And America has been left with the huge, expensive "military-industrial complex" that president Eisenhower warned us about when he left office in 1960. America now spends over 550 billion dollars per year on its military operations, more than all other countries put together! This is certainly one important definition of "Who We Are".

James Carroll's recent book, "House of War" (Houghton Mifflin, 2006) a history of the rise of America's military history during the past sixty years since the end of World War II. It is a frightening chronicle concluding that the "Pentagon has, since its founding, operated beyond the control of any force in government or society. It is the biggest, loosest cannon in American history, and no institution has changed the country more." He quotes Eisenhower again when he described the Pentagon as "a disastrous rise of misplaced power." Carroll knows whereof he speaks. He literally "grew up" in the Pentagon where his father, Lt. General John Carroll, was the first Director of the Defense Intelligence Agency. James Carroll later became an ordained Roman Catholic priest, but resigned the order and has become a scholar and the author of many excellent books. He has been an astute student of the Defense Department for many years.

The problem for us now is that the Cold War has been replaced by the "War on Terrorism", another perpetual war, which lays claim to endless additional financial outlays for "Defense". Some political figures seem to welcome the War on Terrorism as a replacement for the Cold War. It gives them and the nation a war-like sense of mission. And it also provides the basis for further erosions of our civil liberties in the name of national security.

The reason for reciting this long litany of American "regime changes" is simply to show that our beloved America is not always a benign force for good in the world, as much as we would like to believe. The facts are otherwise. We certainly have the capacity and we have done many good deeds as a nation, but we have also behaved very badly against the interest of many other countries who have done us no harm, and, ironically and unintentionally, against our own interest. We are still, unfortunately, capable of acting like the worst of our primate cousins.

I have long been convinced that America should never have changed the name of the "War" Department to the "Defense" Department. My logic is that while we can all get enough of "War" we seem to never get enough of "Defense". What we call things can have a profound effect on how we behave toward them. Let's go back to calling it the "War Department" to see if we can decide we have enough war and reassert control of our peace-time lives.

There are some minority political voices calling for cutting the "Defense Department" expenses in half and investing the difference in our schools and medical care. Good idea, but it would mean overturning generations of political habits and dismantling our military-industrial complex. However, by the way we spend our national resources, we must now be defined as a war-like state. So, for the present this is "Who We Are".

Our Unique "Time Bubble" of Freedom, Affluence and Relative Safety
The Age of Non-Renewable Fossil Fuels

Western" civilization has lived for the past fifty years, during what must be described as a unique "time bub-ble" of freedom, affluence, and rela-tive safety. Unique in all of human history. Ever since the invention of the steam and internal combustion engines over one hundred years ago we have lived in the age of coal, gas and oil "fossil" fuels, which we are rapidly consuming and which will someday, perhaps one hundred years from now, be effectively consumed. The age of fossil fuels has enabled the industrial revolution to create this "time bubble" which has bene-

fited a substantial number, (but still less than one half) of the human population with an extraordinarily high standard of economic life. But coal, gas and oil are simply not going to be readily available forever and, as they become scarce, the western way of economic life will be severely impacted. Automobile and airplane travel will become prohibitively expensive unless practical substitutes for coal and oil can be developed and massive programs for energy conser-vation can be implemented. America will be most severely affected since we are the country most dependent upon automobile and air travel, petro-chemical products, and food produc-tion and distribution.

This impending crisis has been known for some time since 1957 when a Shell Oil Co., scientist named Marion Hubbert analyzed world oil production and consumption and concluded that the world's discovery and production of oil would "peak" in the 1970's. He was ridiculed at the time, but it is now broadly agreed that he was right, and the world is now on the down slope of oil discov-ery and production, at the same time that world consumption is growing rapidly - with China and India, and most of the developing economies of the world, just at the beginning of their industrialization.

The problem is further compounded by the fact that most of the world's reserve oil supply is in the Middle East under the political control of notoriously unstable governments. And, even though their reserves are vast, all fossil fuels are finite and non-renewable, and are being consumed at a rapidly increasing rate. Once they are used up they are gone forever and there will be no more being created.

It is also true that the alternative energy sources most discussed in the public forum; nuclear, solar, hydrogen, bio-fuels, coal-conversion fuels, wind and wave energy sources, are simply not likely to be available within the next fifty years to do more than produce a small amount of alternative energy compared to the likely greater loss of oil based energy. It is likely that the world's economies will begin to feel the effects of the beginning of this oil shortage within the next ten years. Oil prices will continue to increase and the world of "cheap oil" will come to an end, with serious economic consequences.

A number of books and DVD's have been recently published by responsible authors, notably the DVD, "A Crude Awakening", available for rental on Netflix.com or for purchase on Amazon.com. These publication sources will lead you to the library of other publications telling the same story.

However, even though this huge impending crisis has been known by many scientists for fifty years, the self-interest of the oil producers and the automobile and airplane industry, and our corruptible Congress, have denied its existence and procrastinated taking any serious action to deal with it. The politically unspoken, but obvious reason for America's recent military intervention in the Middle East - Kuwait and Iraq - is for control of oil production and supply. And control of oil supplies was one of the significant reasons for World War II. Religion and political ideology are many times only a "cover story" for the real economic power reason for war.

"Global warming" will also cause significant changes in our way of life during the remainder of the twenty-first century. The negative impact of these changes will probably occur at the same time as the world's population reaches its forecast maximum of 9.5 billion people. The economic gap between the developed country rich and the "third world" poor is already great and increasing. The impending oil shortage will only make the gap greater. The increasing stress on humanity will be extreme, and we already know how aggressively and combatively humans can act under extreme stress. So, there really isn't much time left for humanity to sort out and control its penchant for violent expression of its religious, ethnic and nationalistic beliefs. Hopefully our children and grandchildren and other descendants will be able to differentiate between their emotionally, "poetic", believing selves, and their rational, "prose", thinking selves and, through tolerance and cooperation, find peaceful resolutions to such looming problems.

BRAIN SCIENCE, THE BIOLOGY OF BELIEF AND EVOLUTIONARY BEHAVIOR PATTERNS

Neuroscience and Neurotheology

"From the old Dualism of "Mind and Brain" to the "New Dualism" of the emotional and rational brain."

The founder of neuroscience in America was Dr. Paul D. MacLean who just recently died at age 94. In the 1940's Dr. MacLean began his research at Yale University. He developed the theory of what he called the "triune brain" to explain the brain's evolution and attempt to reconcile rational human behavior with its more primal and violent side. As part of his theory he described the brain's center of emotions as the "limbic system", including the hippocampus and the amygdale. He proposed that the limbic system had evolved in early mammals to control their "fight-or-flight" responses and react to both emotionally pleasurable and painful sensations. To Dr. MacLean the presence of the limbic system also "represents the history of the evolution of mammals and their distinctive family way of life". These concepts are now broadly accepted in neuroscience.

The "triune brain" consists of (1) the limbic system, (2) the more primitive reptilian system which he called the "R-Complex" (the sympathetic system which controls muscle movement and breathing), and (3) The neocortex which controls speech and reasoning and was the last to arrive in evolution. Each of these systems compete in the human and their conflicts help explain the extremes of human behavior. As Dr. MacLean observed, surveying worldwide violence and intolerance, "language barriers among nations present great obstacles" He also observed, "But the greatest language barrier lies between man and his animal brains; the neural machinery does not exist for intercommunication in verbal terms."

After an academic career at Yale Dr. MacLean moved to the National Institute of Mental Health in 1957 where he was chief of the laboratory of Brain Evolution and Behavior. He retired in the early 1990's. His principal work was "The Triune Brain in Evolution; Its Role in Paleocerebral Functions".

"Brain Science" has become during the last 50 years one of the most important disciplines in the biological sciences. It employs many thousands of scientists in research centers around the world. One of the most prominent is the Center for Neural Science at New York University, once headed by Dr. Eric Kandel a Nobel Laureate in Medicine and Physiology in the year 2000. It is now headed by Dr. Joseph LeDoux who is also the founder of the LeDoux Laboratory at the Center.

Also prominent in brain science research is Dr. V.S. Ramachandran, prolific author and research scientist and professor and director of the Center for Brain and Cognition at the University of California, San Diego, and adjunct professor at the Salk Institute for Biological Studies in La Jolla, where the late Francis Crick, Nobel Laureate and co-discoverer of DNA also worked.

And at the University of Chicago, another prominent researcher and prolific author is Dr. Martha McClintock who is Professor of Psychology at the University of Chicago and Director of the Institute for Mind and Body where she designed and oversaw the construction of the Biopsychological Sciences Building. The Institute for Mind and Body's mission is to promote research on the reciprocal interactions between social behavior and psychological states, at the behavioral level of analysis, and, at the biological level of analysis, neuroscience, endocrinology, immunology and genetics. The actual integration of the biological and psychological sciences is now occurring.

The application of molecular biology techniques to the study of the brain has developed an extraordinary new understanding of the complex workings of the brain, as a critical part of the human organism as well as general cell growth development and effective drug therapies for brain malfunctions. Combined with genetic engineering the prospects are for even greater human benefits for the future.

All of this research begins with a detailed understanding of the complex inner workings of the over one billion neurons and their trillions of interconnections in the average human brain. What makes them connect, what turns them on and off and how they relate to the rest of the human body from which they get sensory input and to which they transmit information. The study requires knowledge of biochemistry, physics, anatomy and modern biology.

For anyone interested in these subjects I highly recommend reading some of the excellent books referred to here.

In recent years a number of neurophysiologists, neuropsychologists, medical doctors and biochemists have also undertaken research into the workings of the brain using non-invasive technology: Such work began many years ago using electroencephalographs (EEG) and computer assisted topography (CAT). The recent development of magnetic resonance imaging (MRI) systems has greatly enhanced the effectiveness of such research to measure the brain's responses during programmed mental and emotional states, including religious experiences. This latter research is sometimes referred to as "Neurotheology".

I mention neurobiology here because it is the science of the neuro-biological basis for behavior, thought and belief. The modern scientific concept of the brain is that it is "the mind" and is not distinct or separate from its functions, as advocated by Descartes and other "Dualists", beginning with Plato. It is not "I think, therefore I am.", as the great French philosopher Rene Descartes famously proclaimed 1637. It should be, rather, "I am, therefore I think.", or "I have a brain, therefore I think." And beyond these simple aphorisms, it is most important to understand that we are who we are because we can remember what we have thought about. "Memory, From Mind to Molecules", (Scientific American Library, 2000)

Neuroscientists trace the evolution of the brain, and its various functional parts as part of our emotional and rational thinking. Neuroscientists and primatologists also describe the extraordinary processes by which human, as well as many animal species, have evolved physical ritual practices that bind them together as mates and communities, and, in the case of humans, are part of religious rituals and myths. We are biological organisms and our religions are expressions of our biology. The human mind is an incredibly powerful instrument, but it is not just a computer - it is a vital dynamic part of a complex biological organism. Understanding the connection between our biology and our religious practices is an important part of understanding the differences and connections between religion and science.

Neuroscience research and literature has grown rapidly and is too diverse and complex to summarize in this essay. For the serious reader who would like to explore the subject in more detail I highly recommend the following authors: J.B. Ashbrook, "Mind..." "Zygon, September, 1997.Vol 32; Michael Shermer, "How We Believe"; Francis Crick, "The Astonishing Hypothesis";

Antonio Damasio, "Descartes' Error" and "The Feeling of What Happens", LeDoux, "The Emotional Brain"; Gazzaniga, "The New Cognitive Neurosciences" and his new book, "The Science Behind What Makes Us Unique"; and Drs. Andrew Newberg and Eugene D'Aquili, "Why God Won't Go Away" (Ballantine, 2001), Daniel Dennett, "Breaking the Spell, Religion as a Natural Phenomenon" (Viking, 2006). See also Jean Pierre Changeux's "The Physiology of Truth: Neuroscience and Human Knowledge,", "Conversations on Mind, Matter, and Mathematics", and "What Makes Us Think? A Neuroscientist and a Philosopher Argue about Ethics, Human Nature, and the Brain"; and, lastly, Edelman and Tononi's "A Universe of Consciousness: How Matter Becomes Imagination". And each of these author's books has extensive bibliographies for further reference.

Two recently published books also require special mention, because they present the history of neuro-science in very compelling ways. The first is Carl Zimmer's "Soul Made Flesh" (Simon & Schuster, 2004), and Dr. Eric Kandel's "In Search of Memory" (WW Norton, 2006).

Zimmer's book is the story of a remarkable group of men who were gathered at Oxford University in England in 1662 by Thomas Willis to study the brain as a biological organ, then held to be the seat of the "Soul". Among those he gathered were two men later known mostly for their work as architects; Christopher Wren, and Robert Hooke, plus Robert Boyle, later known for his discovery of Boyle's Law. Together they created a new science of "Neurology" ("the doctrine of the nerves") and began what we still call and live in, "The Neurocentric Age". "It is a fascinating book that reads like a mystery novel."

Kandel's book is also a very well written story of his life as a neuroscientist, ultimately leading to his being awarded the Nobel Prize for Medicine and Physiology in 2000 for his work on the cellular and molecular process of memory. Kandel's book is a marvelous textbook for understanding neuro-science and the history of biology during the past 50 years. It is written for non-scientists so it is wonderful window into what is otherwise an arcane world. Interleaved with the science is Kandel's autobiography beginning in Vienna from which he and his family were forcibly expelled by the Nazis in 1938. It is thereby an exciting adventure, which culminates in his organizing a seminar in Vienna in 2004 discussing the failure of Austria to redress its World War II participation in the Holocaust. The seminar was successful to the extent that he was welcomed by the then president of Austria, Heinz Fischer, whose own wife's father had been imprisoned by the Nazis.

Embryology - From Magic To Molecular Biology – "Evo-Devo"

Research in molecular biology has discovered the detailed inter-cellular and intra-cellular Processes that create organized growth, reproduction and communication between cells. When I was studying biology in college over 50 years ago these details were not known. The answer to the question of how this growth occurred was only "by the action of unknown precursors." This cellular biology was most compelling to observe, particularly in embryology. To see under a microscope the fertilization of the egg of a tadpole, its automatic division into a "blastula" of geometrically multiplied cells, which then, some nine hours later, again automatically, begins to "gastrulate". Gastrulation is the process of forming into three layers of differentiated cells, the innermost layer "endoderm", the middle layer "mesoderm", and the outer layer "ectoderm". Then further remarkable changes occur, creating the neural tube for the future brain and spinal cord the digestive system, the vascular system, the fins and eyes and the internal organs. The whole process is quite magical and exciting to witness.

But, until molecular biology matured as a science it was simply "magical". Now much of the process is understood in terms of biochemistry, wherein the chemicals serotonin, acetylcholine, dopamine and various proteins and enzymes, under the guidance of various genes, trigger and shape the growing embryo. The process of becoming a tadpole is a wonderful complex, but now mostly understood biological process. And it is the same kind of process that forms each of us human beings as embryos! We are, in short, biological phenomena.

And, while it has long been believed that the connection between embryology and evolution is fundamental, it has only recently been demonstrated through breakthroughs in the science of genetics how these phenomena are actually related. It has recently been discovered that; "most of the genes first identified as governing major aspects of fruit fly body organization were found to have exact counterparts that did the same thing for most animals, including ourselves. This discovery was followed by the revelation that the development of various body parts such as eyes, limbs, and hearts, vastly different in structure among animals and long thought to have evolved in entirely different ways, was also governed by the same genes in different animals. The comparison of developmental genes between species became a new discipline at the interface of embryology and evolutionary biology - evolutionary development biology, "Evo-Devo" for short. (From "Endless Forms Most Beautiful - The New Science of Evo

Devo and the Making of the Animal Kingdom", by Sean B. Carroll, W.W. Norton, 2005) If you are going to read any book about biology, "Ev-Devo" by Sean Carroll should be the first on your list. Carroll is a leading research biologist at the University of Wisconsin – Madison, and an excellent and enthusiastic story-telling writer.

The Human Biological Life Cycle
Human beings emerge from the embryo to birth, about 50/50 males and females, and then, from infancy into consciousness, instinctively acquire language, grow up into puberty, and males and females become sexually mature men and women. During these early years the human brain grows explosively into a remarkably complex biological organ, making humans truly unique among all living species. At puberty women begin to ovulate, producing ovum (eggs), which can become embryos if fertilized by male sperm. Women's pelvic structure widens to accommodate prospective births and they develop breasts for nursing children. Men develop sperm and the capacity and desire to have sexual intercourse. Young men and women "fall in love", biologically, psychologically and romantically. Thus the stage is set for reproduction. Men and women become attracted to each other, mate sexually, and have and nurture children, forming family groups. Males are 10% - 25% larger than females, kinetically stronger, and more aggressive, which unhappily explains why females have been subordinated by males for most of primate and human history. A small minority of both male and female humans, probably less than 5%, are biologically homosexual. All human males have residual nipples, resulting from the early development of secondary sex characteristics before the later development of sexual identity. Sexual identity is not simply"all male", or "all female", but rather that each human being possesses a spectrum of male-female characteristics.

During adult human lives we continue primate behavior patterns in our tribalism, aggression, violence, territoriality, social hierarchies, and even our capacity for sharing, cooperation, reciprocal grooming, generosity, kindness, love and altruism. Our biology drives our behavior. We also express our cultures by what we learn, from our parents, our peers, our religions, and our institutions of learning. Both men and women experience joy and suffering, die early or grow into old age, and ultimately die. Each of these phases of life and behaviors is governed partly by our biological selves, which have evolved over millions of years from our ancient primate, mammalian past, and partly by our cultural selves which have also evolved over the thousands of years of human culture.

Human biology programs the parts of our brains that control our ordinary emotions, behavior and expressions. Fear, anger, phobias, love, anxiety, pleasure, disgust, and many more subtle feelings, as well as facial expressions and "body language", are all shared by all humans among many different cultures. The evolutionarily "primitive" parts of our brains, the amygdala (the "fight or flee" brain center) the insular and rest of the limbic system, combined with the hippocampus, plus the "rational", thalamocortical system make up the major regions of the brain, all of which provide us a certain number of "hard-wired", instinctive reactions and the capacity to learn all the other things we learn.

Our primitive survival as a species resulted primarily from our capacity to compete successfully against other species because our behavior is "hard-wired" for survival and for procreation, and the protection and the nurturing of our offspring. Our subsequent survival has resulted from our ability to incorporate what we have learned from our cultural evolution into our behavior.

Unfortunately, without the influence of some civilizing experience, young males in particular can behave in ways that our culture now defines as criminal. Fighting between males for physical supremacy, seducing and having sex with women, and marauding and even killing neighboring groups of the same species, are each part of the biologically evolved behavior of primates.

Civilizing experience is best learned from one's parents in the context of a loving and caring family life. Civilized, ethical, behavior is not readily taught as a subject, like arithmetic, it is, rather, learned as a way of life, participating daily as a member of a family, with ethical parents. Absent such a family context, some institutional forms of care, such as sports teams, religious institutions, or schools, or even military service, can provide a substitute civilizing influence. Other, uncivilized forms of group organization, such as criminal gangs, will of course teach uncivilized behavior.

CREATING SUPERNATURAL
GODS AND GODDESSES

Transactional Gods

Most religious systems are based on belief in a supernatural God, or Gods, who created the universe and mankind; that such a Creator God is human-like and is concerned with and cares about the lives and behavior of mankind; and that such Gods express their concern through intervention in human affairs via benevolence or punishment. In other words, most religions are founded on a belief in what I call, "transactional gods" who care about mankind and can be communicated with and dealt with as if they actually existed. Gods with whom you can "do business".

Most religions also include belief in a spiritual life, supernatural "souls", "demons", or "spirits" that are separate from the physical body and continue to exist beyond the end of earthly life. Other supernatural beings are "angels" and "saints" and "ghosts" and "devils", etc., etc. There is of course no scientifically valid physical evidence for such supernatural beings, but they are widely believed to exist and are spoken of and spoken to as if they do actually exist. The concept of "soul" is of critical importance in Christian theology - providing, as one example, the religious basis for being against any abortion because the "soul" is deemed to "come into being at conception". Both Plato and Socrates taught elaborate theories of the existence of the Soul, and Demons, and the Christian religion adopted most of their ideas as part of its theology.

"Misplaced Concreteness"

There are obviously risks inherent in the mental process of imagining supernatural gods, souls and spirits. One of the risks is similar to what the great philosopher, Alfred North Whitehead, called "the fallacy of misplaced concreteness". Let me give an example: If an attempt is made to explain a natural event (rain, or lightning, or a flood, or an earthquake) by ascribing its cause to the supernatural, such as a "god" or other supernatural "being", and the supernatural being is described in concrete terms, such as an all powerful, human-like giant, we have "misplaced concreteness". The abstract "god" is turned into a concrete being, with whom people will attempt to communicate, or placate by prayer or sacrifice, to prevent the recurrence of a flood or earthquake, or obtain the recurrence of the rain. It appears throughout human history that people are readily prone to such misplaced concreteness.

In my view the same misplaced concreteness has been applied to the concepts of "soul", "spirit", "life-after-death" and even "consciousness", just as Dualism created the concept of "mind". In each of these cases there does not appear to be any physical evidence of their concrete existence, but because we have named the abstract experience of remembered events, as if the memory is itself concrete, we treat them as if they have a concrete existence. It seems to me they are each Chimeras, like the smile on the face of the Cheshire cat. But they are very powerful Chimera. For many people they might as well be real.

The Soul, for instance, does not actually have a concrete, scientifically demonstrable, existence, but it is included in theology as if it did, and serious decisions are based upon this misplaced concreteness; such as the absolute prohibition against abortion because of the belief that the Soul "comes into existence at conception". We all surely remember the essence of another person's life, and we can refer to that essence as their soul, but its existence is purely in our minds, as a memory.

The "existence" in our brains of these "Chimerical" illusions can however profoundly shape our behavior, and our views of the world. Their "existence" in our brains is sometimes more powerful than if they actually existed in the external world. They can be the memories of our knowledge of another person, or of ourselves (our self-consciousness), or of events that may or may not have actually occurred. The world is necessarily only our perception of the world - as it exists in our brains.

To lose an illusion, is generally regarded as a loss of innocence, like losing our belief in Santa Claus. So there is a sense of loss and regret if we lose an illusion about the existence of a soul. But, if the illusion really didn't exist in the first place, all we have "lost" is the illusion that they existed. As a friend from the Wilmette Trinity United Methodist Church, Dr. Parker Palmer, once said to a patient he was counseling when she complained of "being so disillusioned"; Palmer said, "Congratulations!, you have rid yourself of an illusion, you are now closer in touch with reality! Rejoice!"

"Trans-substantiation", the Roman Catholic dogma that proclaims priest blessed Eucharist wine and bread is "trans-substantiated" into the actual blood and flesh of Jesus, is still adhered to as an important part of Catholic ritual, even to the point that Eucharist communion is not offered to Protestants because they are not Roman Catholic. The adherence to this dogma actually impairs the authority of the church in these modern times when it is obvious to nearly every-one, Protestant and Catholic alike, that there is no actual trans-substantiation. This is another one of those persistent illusions that have been promulgated for so many centuries that it has taken on the attributes of incontrovertible fact. Alfred North Whitehead's "Misplaced Concreteness" at its utmost.

But, as logically absurd as trans-substantiation may be, it does provide many people with a feeling of transcendence and unity with the "body and spirit" of Jesus. The "feeling of transcendence" has been demonstrated to be a neurological event which is "very real" to the person having the experience. I can only say that such an experience is an emotional, or "poetic" experience, and not a rational one.

The same can be said of "The Apostle's Creed" which recites in part that Jesus was born of the Virgin Mary and was raised from the dead three days after his crucifixion. A good friend of mine at Trinity United Methodist Church in Wilmette many years ago spoke up in our book group and said "I've been saying The Apostles Creed for forty years in this church and I never have believed it to be actually true." (This man is a highly educated retired vice president of strategic planning for a major energy company.) We discussed his statement and concluded that what he really meant was that he could not accept that the Creed was scientifically true; that is to say that no one, including Jesus, could be physically raised from the dead, and that no one could be physically born from a virgin. But we also concluded that the recital of the Creed was an important part of Christian ritual and, as such, generated feelings of unity with other believers and a profound sense of belonging to the Christian church. Thus, although it may not be scientifically true, it has become emotionally, or "poetically" true for many people. (It certainly was emotionally true for my own mother who read and recited it during the many times of stress in her life.)

Another man in the same book group, Bob Piros, who is also a highly educated retired chemical engineer and CEO (and fraternity brother and fellow veteran of the WW II 82nd Airborne Division), could not accept our division of belief into "poetic" and "scientific". For him you must either believe something or not. He is still a good friend whose judgment, integrity and sincerity I greatly respect, even though we disagree on this subject.

For an interesting exploration of the supernatural and the natural see Alan Lightman's newest book "Ghost", (Random House 2007) Ghost is a fiction novel, but is grounded in Lightman's unique life experience as, first, a theoretical physicist and, second, as a dual professor of physics and the humanities at Massachusetts Institute of Technology in Boston. Lightman has written eleven other books. Some novels and some non-fiction, such as "Einstein's Dreams" and Great Ideas in Physics.

a. Naming the Gods - Misplaced Concreteness

Once an abstraction, like a god, is given a name, becomes a noun, it is very easy for people to give it the attributes of a concrete being and ascribe to it behavioral characteristics that give it a personality with whom believers in the god can deal. And, although most religions have prohibitions against "graven images", most religions also accept and even promote the display of iconic images of their gods, in paintings or sculpture.

In the 8th century the Eastern Christian Church in Constantinople reacted against these displays in a revolt of the "Iconoclasts", those who wanted to "break the images." The destructive violence of this 8th century revolt within Christianity decisively widened the schism between the Papacy and the Eastern Church. Thus the "fallacy of misplaced concreteness" had very real consequences.

Under some facilitating circumstances the images of gods can come into being via "altered" or "anomalous" forms of consciousness; "dreams", "visions" or "voices" or other mental "experiences". Such "experiences" can be profoundly more real to the person having the experience than ordinary experience. This "super-reality" of such an experience can then lead to a belief in the actual, concrete existence of such a "divine" god and provide the basis for a belief system - yea, a whole theology that provides answers to other questions that can also be answered by the same supernatural god.

It seems obvious to me (but also obviously not to many other people) that the "supernatural", or divinity, or any "other-worldly" states of being beyond the three Spatial dimensions, plus time, that we can sense and measure, are purely the result of our creative imaginations. Our minds are incredibly creative and are not bound by any rules of evidence. If we can think of something we can also believe it "exists", even though there is no tangible, concrete evidence for its actual existence. Thus we are capable of a "new dualism", whereby we can "think" or "believe" both emotionally and rationally, even though such beliefs and thoughts may be self-contradictory. Our brains do not always edit our thoughts and beliefs for consistency.

And, since our sensory input systems; ears, eyes, touch, taste or smell, can create images and memories in our brains, these same images and memories can be recalled and cause us to believe that they have actually reoccurred. Once we have "recorded" an image or experience it can be recalled and recombined with other such experiences in dreams, or simply in our faulty memories. Our brains can process information both ways; first, as it comes in from the external world, and, second, as it is recalled from our brains and is re-expressed in our memories.

Dr. Andrew Newberg records that many people have such very vivid "dreams" and "visions" and hear very vivid "voices" which some times "tell them what to do", and in some cases are "more real than ordinary experience", particularly during religious meditation or other religious experiences. And the literature of religious experience is filled with the voices and visions of people in trances induced by meditation, or fasting, or hallucinogens, or alcohol or certain kinds of very repetitive, rhythmic dancing. In short, human beings are capable of hearing voices or seeing visions as a matter of internal mental experiences, not caused by external visual or auditory stimuli. We confuse the images and sounds generated inside our brains with the images and sounds generated outside our bodies and sensed by the receptors connected to our brains.

Most very young children instinctively create imaginary "friends" with whom they talk and play for hours, and, they insist, are "real". And yet these same children also seem aware that these imaginary "friends" are "make believe". "Let's pretend" is a normal process of children's play. Children therefore seem to be able to function quite well with the simultaneous appreciation of make believe and ordinary, "literal" reality. They seem naturally capable of shifting back and forth between "poetry" and "prose".

And yet the gods are dealt with in adult human conversation as if they really do exist and can be communicated with. It never ceases to amaze me that this basic confusion is allowed to continue and is participated in by otherwise very rational and highly educated people. There are frequent attempts to ascertain "what God wants us to do", or "what is God's purpose", etc. Theology abounds with speculation about what the gods meant and what they would have us do. So much strife and so much confusion could be resolved if only people would go back to the beginning and realize that "misplaced concreteness" of the abstract is at the root of the problem.

The human mind is certainly "a many splendored thing", capable of extraordinary feats of memory and imagination. But it is also capable of "many splendored confusions". In particular, confusion between the Concrete and the Abstract. For example, the most elementary aspect of language is the naming of concrete things, such as "a lion. "The next step up the ladder from the concrete toward the abstract, is to identify more than one lion, as "lions" - the plural of "a lion." And then, the next step toward abstraction would be to identify lions as "animals", a large category of living things, still concrete things, but a "category", an abstraction. In other words, the word animal stands for some concrete living things, but now as an abstract category. And farther up the ladder towards greater abstraction one gets to all living things, both animals and plants. And then to all "matter", both living and inanimate. And then, ultimately to the "supernatural", beyond "matter"- the ultimate abstraction - to the gods.

It is by naming an abstract category that the potential for confusion arises. For by naming anything, whether concrete or abstract, the implication is that the named abstract category exists in the same way that the concrete things exist. The problem is that anything that can be named is presumed to "exist". Thus, if someone names a "god" it can be presumed to "exist" in the same way a lion exists.

Thus, the almost countless gods named by human beings over the course of human history, and prehistory, have been presumed to "exist" and have therefore been given the attributes of existence. However, since they do not have any actual concrete existence, and are therefore the products of human imagination, they are free from any of the constraints of actual existence. They "exist" beyond the laws of physical phenomena and can therefore do all kinds of things not possible for mere mortal beings.

"Misplaced Concreteness" is similar to Immanuel Kant's "transcendental illusion" which he described as mankind's attempt to exceed the fixed bounds of possible experience. In his "Critique of Pure Reason", Kant says, "We are not satisfied with the exposition merely of that which is true, but likewise demand that account be taken of that which we desire to know....and what we desire to know above all is how it all fits together." As Mark Lilla says in his "The Stillborn God", "Neither "nature" nor "world" is an object of possible experience, in Kant's terminology. They are what he calls "regulative ideas" that we develop to make sense of how specific things fit into the order of all other things and ideas. One of reason's functions is to develop fictions like these and employ them to regulate the employment of our understanding, which is limited to what can be experienced in space and time." Lillas goes on to say, "Hobbes saw our interest in science as arising mainly from our desire to master the environment, and through it our fears. Kant saw it arising from something noble within reason itself, something much closer to what Aristotle called our desire to understand". Lilla also says, "The need for ideas is subjective, in the sense that it arises from our own limitations, not from some feature in the world. We need ideas to order our own thinking, so we posit them. Yet we also have a tendency then to take such ideas as if they were real objects, entities that might be experienced. This is precisely what happens with metaphysical ideas and in particular, given our perceived need for him, with the idea of God. Those who have spoken confi-

dently of God's nature or their experiences with Him -- from church fathers debating the Trinity to modern mystics like Swedesboro -- have all fallen victim to transcendental illusion, taking an idea for a real presence."

Lilla goes on to say that "Kant saw very little use for the idea of God in modern science...,but he did think that a highly developed, and highly disciplined, conception of God was absolutely crucial for ordering reason in what he call its "practical" employment, that is , in our active, moral lives." .... "Our noble ideas of God could have arisen only from our highest faculty, our reason. That is why there is no shame in saying that God is something that man needs. Religion has roots in needs that are rational and moral, even noble. Once we see that, we can then start learning how to satisfy those needs rationally, morally, and nobly."

One of the more interesting discussions of these phenomena is the book, "The Mind In The Cave, Consciousness and the Origins of Art", by David Lewis-Williams (Thames & Hudson, 2002). In this book the author reviews the story of pre-historic art and compares it to what is now known about evolutionary psychology and neurophysiology. His major conclusion is that the emergence of a "higher order consciousness" in Homo Sapiens enabled the creation of their magnificent cave art and the many other artistic artifacts of their culture. He attributes this capacity to a neurological change, compared to the "primitive consciousness" of the Neanderthals. The author also considers at some length the capacity for Homo Sapiens, and for modern man, to have "altered", or "anomalous", or "transcendent", or "out-of-body" mental experiences, which provide the basis for religious experience.

As for dreams, something we all experience - almost every night during sleep - a therefore very "normal" mental experience, David Lewis-Williams has this to say: "Sleep, dreaming and the activity of the brain in altered states of consciousness are part and parcel of the electro-chemical functioning of the neurons." ... It seems therefore probable that dreaming is something that came about when, during evolution, the early limbic system became fully articulated with the evolving thalamocortical system. Some researchers believe that dreaming is what happens when sensory input to the brain is greatly diminished: the brain tries to make sense of the resultant stream of images. Be that as it may, we still need to ask if sleep is of any value to people and certain animals; if it is not, why did it evolve? After all, chances of survival in a hostile environment are reduced by sleep. The answer is

that, in deep sleep, the brain manufactures proteins at a faster rate than during waking. Proteins are essential for maintaining the functioning of cells, including neurons, and in sleep, the human body builds up a reserve of proteins. Sleep (together with the dreaming that takes place in REM sleep, the prelude and postlude to deep sleep) is therefore biologically, rather than psychologically, important, and the brain evolved in such a way as to facilitate sleep for good biological reasons. There was no evolutionary selection for dreaming as such - only for the manufacture of proteins."

"Dreaming is a non-adaptive, but not maladaptive, by-product. The content of dreams themselves is not significant. Yet people have always felt it necessary to "explain" dreams, be it as voices of the gods or invasions by devils. More modern dream analysis by Freudians and Jungians is simply a contemporary way of giving meaning to dreams. It is, in the strict sense of the word, a modern myth that tries to make sense of a human experience that does not require that sort of explanation."

On the other hand, there are some traumatic real-life experiences that become the subject of recurring nightmares, occasioning the same fears and physical reactions as the original traumatic real-life experience. War combat, or other life threatening experiences are in this category.

Lewis-Williams also refers to Julian Jayne's "The Origins of Consciousness in the Breakdown on the Bicameral Mind", which says that in Homer's Iliad" the characters have no concept of free will. They have no conscious minds; they do not sit down and think things out. It is the gods who act who tell men what to do... "These gods were inner voices that were heard as distinctly present-day schizophrenics hear voices speaking to them, or Joan of Arc heard her voices. The gods, Jayne's concludes, were "organizations of the central nervous system... The god is part of the man ... The gods are what we now call hallucinations."

Yet in the Odyssey (also ascribed to Homer), which follows the Iliad historically by as much as a century, we are in a world of plotting and subterfuge. The gods have receded, and men take the initiative. This change, Jayne's argues, resulted from the breakdown of what he calls the bicameral mind.

But Lewis-William's "prefers to think in terms of primary and higher-order consciousness, the development of the second having taken place much earlier than the Iliad - at the emergence of Homo Sapiens in Africa. Thereafter, it was culturally specific definitions of altered consciousness that determined whether people heeded their inner voices or not. Emancipation of the mind from the imperative of voices and visions has in fact been a slow, stop-go-retreat process, one that is still incomplete. When and how did it become possible for people to stand back and contemplate their own thought processes, recognize that the voices they heard and visions they saw came from within and not from external sources?"

Homo Sapiens's mental capacity, even compulsion, to perceive the world and analyze the cause and effect connection between events has provided us with an enormous evolutionary advantage. The fact that the human species can understand the world better and quicker than competing species can mean the difference between life and death. The capacity to articulate our cause and effect understanding of the world through speech with fellow human beings, and therefore cooperate to achieve a common objective gives us an even greater advantage. This combination of mental skills has given us the ability to win out over all other living species and to virtually tame the natural world in many ways.

But these same mental skills can also lead us into false conclusions, with unintended consequences. If we "create" a god as a result of having an anomalous mental "experience", and we subsequently believe in such a god, which in actual fact exists only in our mind, we risk making important decisions or taking significant action based purely upon an illusion. "Supernatural" gods are unfortunately as unreliable as a child's "Santa Claus". They are imaginary beings who may provide short-term feelings of comfort and hope, but no actual, tangible results.

Or, if, for instance, we misidentify a supposed enemy and attack someone who turns out to be a friend, or an enemy who turns out to be much stronger than our "intelligence" told us. Or, when rituals celebrating the recurrence of natural events become confused with the actual cause of the natural events; such as when Sun worshippers, fearing that the Sun will not rise again unless they perform their morning rituals, or that the longer days of Summer won't return unless they perform the Winter Solstice celebration on the shortest day of the year in December. Or, when Witch Doctors, or some modern day charlatan "faith healers", make incantations that fail to cure actual illness. Our mental skills, in short, are not mistake proof, or confusion proof, and can lead us into trouble by causing us to act before we are properly informed, or causing confusion between a religious ritual and the actual cause of a natural event.

b. Mythology - Omnipotent Gods
All of which brings us to the world of mythology, mankind's continual attempts to explain the unexplainable

through stories of the supernatural. Some of the best known popular histories of mythology are Joseph Campbell's "Hero with the Thousand Faces" and "The Mythic Image", and "The World of Myth", by David Adams Leeming, and "A Short History of Myths", by Karen Armstrong. See also Mercia Eliade's "Shamanism", Princeton U. Press (1962) for a comprehensive review of the role of the Shaman in the history of religion. And, for an excellent review of the "homemade varieties of American Christianity", see American Originals", by Paul K. Conkin. This book tells the fascinating story of the unique brands of American Christianity, including: (1) the Humanists, Unitarians and Universalists, (2) the Apocalyptic, Adventists and Jehovah's Witnesses, (3) the Mormons, (4) Spirituals, Christian Science and Unity, and (5) the Estatics: the Holiness and Pentecostal movements.

My own personal view is that we human beings have created and struggled with the confusions between what is in the real world and what we have imagined in our mythologies for many thousands of years. We "name" an abstract idea or image, such as a "god" to explain the cause of otherwise inexplicable events and we define the idea, or god, as "supernatural", thus avoiding the embarrassment of not having any scientific evidence. But having the benevolent and omnipotent "god" provides its believers with answers to otherwise unanswerable questions. Thus, anxiety is relieved even though the "god" is illogical and invisible.

One of the great public conundrums illustrating the problem of the imaginary omnipotent and invisible "god" is the debate that ensued following the earthquake that devastated Lisbon, Portugal in 1755. The earthquake occurred on a Sunday morning and killed tens of thousands of people worshiping in the many churches and cathedrals of Lisbon. Many Christian believers claimed that the earthquakes was evidence of God's displeasure with the bad behavior of the people of Lisbon. Voltaire (1694-1778) publicly took up the opposing argument, that the earthquake was a natural event without any supernatural basis. Voltaire cited as part of his argument the "Epicurean Paradox", described by the Greek philosopher Epicurus (341- 270 BCE). The Paradox is:

"God either wants to eliminate bad things and cannot, or can but does not want to, or neither wishes to nor can, or both wants to and can. If he wants to and cannot, he is weak - and this does not apply to God. If he can but does not want to, then he is spiteful - which is equally foreign to God's nature. If he neither wants to nor can, he is both weak and spiteful and so is not a God. If he wants to

and can, which is the only thing fitting for a God, where then do bad things come from? Or, why does he not eliminate them?"

This paradox remains unresolved for many people in the present day world. For instance, immediately after the September 11, 2001 attack on the World Trade Towers in New York City, the American Tel-Evangelists, Pat Robertson and Jerry Falwell made a similarly absurd, and I would say, blasphemous, claim that the attack was "God's punishment" for what they saw as the "liberal evils" of American "secular humanists". Just as absurd is the hopelessly foolish comment that, "God works in mysterious ways".

Many people still seem to prefer having an illogical, invisible God to whom they look for justice, even though the evidence for such a God is nil. There are of course other examples selected to prove that "God rewards the righteous" since there are many examples of events turning out well for "righteous" people. But there are also countless, unselected, examples of the reverse being true. The best Biblical answer to the paradox that I know is the book of Job in the Old Testament. When Job, after being stripped of all his possessions, and his health, and his family, even though he has lived a completely righteous life, asks God, "Why have you done this to me?" gets God's reply. God says, in short, "Who are you to ask me for justice? Where were you when I created the Universe?" In a later addition to the original story of Job, God restores Job's goods, health and family, but in the first verses of Job we are still left with the profound, and unanswerable questions; "Who are you to ask me for justice?" and "Where were you when I created the Universe?"

Where was God in the Concentration Camps?

And, the most horrific modern-day example of the confusion caused by the idea of a just and omnipotent God is the Nazi Holocaust, which killed 6,000,000 Jews and also 6,000,000 other non-Jews. It is illustrated dramatically by Elie Wiesel's story in his book, "Night", when a fellow prisoner in the Auschwitz-Buna concentration camp asks aloud while their group was forced to watch the hanging of a young boy, "Where is the merciful God, where is He?". The same man repeats his plea when they are forced to march past the hanged boy, "For God's sake, where is God?". Elie Wiesel writes, "And from within me, I heard a voice answer: "Where is He?" This is where, hanging here from this gallows ..."

Also, when Pope Benedict VI recently visited Auschwitz, to appropriately pay his and his church's respects to the people who suffered there, he was moved to ask the rhetorical question out loud; "Why was God silent?" To even ask such a question shows such a profound misunderstanding of the history of the church and the Holocaust that I am stunned. The Pope is an otherwise intelligent, even brilliant, man, but the idea of an omnipotent and just God is so embedded in his psyche that he can't let it go. Shouldn't he have asked; "Why was humanity, and the church, silent?"

The answer to the problem seems to me obvious: there simply is no god or gods to whom humanity can look or depend upon for justice. We are on our own. It is up to us to provide justice to our fellow human beings. We can't get justice from God, nor blame injustice on God.

It is also high time we stopped calling natural disasters "Acts of God", and do our best to prepare for their prevention, or at least for the amelioration of their effects. And it is long overdue for humanity to stop trying to justify its war making as "god inspired", or "god's will".

The twenty million total dead from World War I, the millions of Armenians killed in 1905 by the Turkish government, the thirty million total dead from World War II the thirty million Russians killed by

Soviet Russia, the additional thirty million killed by Mao-Tse-Tung in China, and all the other recent and ongoing genocides can't be blamed on god or "god's will". They are all our fault as human beings.

So, the confusion caused by the "misplaced concreteness" of an abstract "god" can and has created monumental confusion and pain and suffering, which should be avoided if at all possible.

On the other hand, since most people will continue to find comfort and hope in the belief in a "transactional god" and "life-after-death", perhaps the only practical solution to the problem of "misplaced concreteness" is to remember that such beliefs are "poetic expressions", "parables", or "metaphors", meant to express feelings, but not scientifically verifiable facts.

Sanity requires that we constantly make the distinction between what is happening only inside our brains from what is actually happening in the external world. Sanity requires that we be as free of illusions as possible so we can deal effectively with reality. The idea of a "just god" may be a poetic one, but not a poetic one on which we can depend.

c. The Myths of Eden, the "Paradise before the Fall"

One of the most persistent myths presented by the book of Genesis in the Old Testament is that of the Garden of Eden, the paradise that presumably existed before the fall of man after the temptation of Eve by the Satanic serpent. The fundamental problem with this myth is the idea that Nature is a paradise. Nature is NOT a paradise. Nature can, of course, be magnificent in its awesome beauty, but it is also brutal, cruel and pitiless. Most biological organisms sustain their lives by acting as predators on other biological organisms. Wild animals are, in fact, wild. They either kill and eat other animals or simply harvest and eat plants. And primates, including humans, kill other animals for "sport", that is for purposes other than food. Such as war. And, as much as our poetic selves would like to believe it, the lions do not lie down peacefully with the lambs, or any other animals.

And Nature is not inexhaustible - another myth. We are depleting and polluting it. And not just recently, causing global warming, but for all of mankind's existence - denuding the land of forests, killing off animal species for food, drying up lakes and rivers by wasting and diverting water resources, and polluting streams, rivers and the air with our technology. Nature was not only never a paradise, but we have been making it less paradisal by our reckless and careless behavior.

The Paradise myth is, I suppose, necessary as a precursor to the myth that there is a caring, omnipotent god who will take care of humans if they will obey his commands. This second myth is as absurd as the first. There certainly does not seem to be any credible evidence that there is a caring, omnipotent god or other supernatural power concerned about god-given justice here on earth. The evidence is, in fact, to the contrary. All of which is to say that, at least as far as I am concerned, humanity needs to rid itself of these two fundamentally erroneous myths and focus more energetically on creating our own systems of justice and conserving the earth's resources.

These myths are of course very useful to any religious institution wanting to control its believers with the idea of Original Sin, which requires constant confessionals and the payment of penances to obtain religious salvation.

d. The Myths of Life-After Death and Life-Before-Birth

The confusion and potential disillusionment caused by belief in some kind of "life-after-death" is well known, but is also included in most systems of religious belief. While the usual rationale for supporting such a belief is the comforting belief that we will be re-united somehow with loved ones who have died, it also undercuts the belief when no evidence can be shown for its truth. And the belief continually sets the stage for abuse by those who promise it and thereby profit from the grieving survivors. The promise of life-after-death and re-uniting with deceased loved ones in "Heaven" is, in my view, the basis of a vast funeral industry that too often preys upon and profits from the hopes and fears of innocent, grieving people. Grief is a real, natural, and very difficult experience. We all need to express our profound sense of loss when we lose a loved one. It is important to memorialize the virtues of departed friends and loved ones. But it need not be a grandiose enterprise.

The use of the myth of "Life After Death", by the Christian and Islamic religions in particular, as the basis for punishment in "Hell" or rewards in "Heaven" after death is fundamental to their theologies. Every Tympanum (sculptured frieze) over the front entrance to every Cathedral in Europe shows a graphic portrayal of Judgement Day and the punishments or rewards that await the dead.

Isn't it much better to simply say "we don't know what happens to us after we die", in the same way that "we don't know where we were before we were born." Both of these answers beg the existential question of "Being" which I personally have not been able to find adequately answered by anyone throughout history. I am therefore perfectly comfortable with the thought that our "Being" is purely a function of our being alive as a biological organism, and that we did not"exist" before we were born anymore than we can continue to "exist" after we die. It seems to me the only "immortality" available to any of us is the living memory of whatever good (or bad) deeds and descendants we leave behind.

Curiously, at Genesis iii, Verses 17-19 of the Old Testament, God admonishes Adam for eating the forbidden fruit, by saying, "Cursed is the ground for thy sake" Then, God continues, "In the sweat of thy face shalt thou eat bread, till thou return unto the ground; for out of it wast thou taken: for dust thou art, and unto dust shalt thou return". This idea is later expanded upon in the Protestant Book of Common Prayer's funeral service, "In the sure and certain hope of the resurrection to eternal life through our Lord Jesus Christ, we commend to Almighty God our brother; and we commit his body to the ground: earth to earth; ashes to ashes, dust to dust". (In Christian theology it is of course the "soul" that goes to Heaven.) For

those who insist on having comfort from a belief in life-after-death I can only suggest that it be regarded as a "poetic expression" and not as a statement of verifiable fact.

e.Without a God in a purposeless universe, what purpose can we have? Perhaps the most succinct answer I have found for this question is the one stated by Phillip Pullman, the author of a recent book, "The Golden Compass", which was also made into a motion picture of the same title.

Pullman's answer is: "We are creatures of the Universe -- we haven't come from anywhere else -- and we have plenty of purpose. Looking after this planet -- there's a purpose. Discovery, curiosity, the preservation and increase of consciousness – through science and through art as well as through love – those are great purposes, and the Universe itself brought them into being." (From his speech before the World Humanist Congress in June, 2008)

My own answer is that mankind has many biological purposes. Each of us has a primary purpose to survive as individuals and as groups of affiliated individuals; families, tribes, or nations. We defend ourselves against threats, we obtain food for nourishment, we select mates, procreate and nourish and protect our offspring. We compete with each other and with other groups of humans and other species for control of resources and the environment. We express our concern for others, loved ones, friends and people in need, by stating and acting upon altruistic purposes. All of these purposes, and many similar ones, are of course earthly, natural, purposes. Some of us also seek supernatural, cosmic, spiritual, purposes which are often expressed in religious language.

f. Religion as Man's First "Science"
Early religions were man's first attempts to explain the universe and the world they lived in. Astronomy was man's first "science" and it was also part of man's first religions. Astronomy was also tied closely to what we now call Astrology, the belief that the Stars and Planets could foretell and control earthly and human events. The daily reappearance of the Sun and the monthly rotations of the Moon were seen as causing events here on earth. The warming rays of the Sun and the resurgence of plants in the spring, and the coincidence of the Moon cycles with female menstruation cycles were profound evidence of cause and effect to prehistoric man.

And the stars, which were very bright and profusely evident every clear night in the clean and unpolluted prehistoric skies, showed recurring patterns that compelled early man to explain in human terms. Stonehenge, in England, over 5,000 years old, and Sumerian astronomy in Mesopotamia, also over 5,000 years old, evolved into Western and Islamic astronomy, which was until recently a fundamental part of religious belief and observance.

So, mankind's extraordinary capacity to perceive and analyze the universe and the world, and his propensity to "concretize" the abstract notions of gods led him easily into constructing mental images of "real" gods who controlled events here on earth. Our compulsion to understand the universe and world has led us into both religion and science.

g. How and When Does Knowledge Become Belief?
This problem of understanding how and when knowledge turns into belief and action is a fundamental one. When and how does knowledge become belief? When do we stop considering and begin acting? Drs. Newman and D' Aquili's neurophysiology tells us that the process of the left-brain and the right brain joining circuits neurologically is the moment when knowledge becomes belief. It may not be that simple in our complicated brains, but it surely does happen inside our brains. At some point we stop considering and start acting. And once we commit to action there is very little time left to change course and adjust our actions.

In fact, it appears from common sense observation that once a course of action is committed it is very difficult to pull back. "The trains are loaded" syndrome which pushed the Germans forward with their plan to start World War I in August, 1914, even though last minute intelligence and second thoughts suggested delay, is all too common in human history.

Neurophysiology also shows us that there is no automatic filter, or editing function in our brains that "audits" whether emotional evidence presented to us is in fact rationally or objectively true. In other words emotionally based evidence, "dreams" of "'visions" or "voices" presented to our brains, is not audited for its objectivity. Or, in more other words, emotional or religious evidence presented to our brains is not required to pass a scientific or legal evidence test inside our brains. In fact, since much religious or emotional evidence is more powerful and memorable, it many times trumps whatever rational or scientific, or even ethical, test may challenge it.

Nazi officers in charge of concentration camps could and did return home at the end of a "hard day's work at the camp", beating, starving and killing prisoners, and listen to classical music, drink fine wine, and play with their beloved children. No ethical fuses blew.

Or, less melodramatically, we persist in admittedly stupid behavior even when "we know better" and we over-react to threats of physical danger. The brain is not primarily organized to be "rational" or to find "objective truth", or act ethically, but, more importantly for the human organism, to help us survive in the short term. In other words, survival and avoiding the possibility of trouble in a dangerous world is more important than the reality of trouble, or ethics. "Better be safe than sorry" and "Power trumps truth". Fear doesn't generate truth, but it does generate protection and power. Our biology protects our survival first.

h. Superstition: Belief Defies Reality

Superstition, a kind of low intensity belief, operates in the same way. For instance, Astrology, a superstitious belief system which has been around since Babylonian times, still persuades 30-40 percent of the American public. Surely, even before the Babylonians recorded their belief in astrology, humans were looking toward the heavens and perceiving what they believed to be meaningful patterns among the stars. No matter how often astrology has been debunked, it still exists. This human compulsion to find patterns in patternless data is called "apophenia" in statistics.

Televangelists also understand this process. They require an emotional setting, enhanced by crowds of people, fiery preaching with cadenced, trance inducing rhythms, calling on the supernatural gods, music, guilt, insecurity, references to sacred scripture, "faith healing" experiences, making people close their eyes and fervently pray, communicating with their gods, and so forth. It can and does work for some people who are now and have always been ripe for "psychosomatic" or "faith" healing. Many more people just desperately want to believe in something larger than themselves, particularly if it is said to be supernatural and is believed in by many other people in a large, singing, emotional crowd.

Many of us know that some people hold religious beliefs which defy rational understanding, and yet they are firmly held, and their believers staunchly defend their "truth" in spite of serious rational challenges. Why is this so? My own personal observation is that it is almost as if the more rationally absurd the professed belief may be, the more tightly it is held by the believer. Such a belief must be so important to the well being of the believer that he will defend it to the death. It is not subject to rational challenge. The value of the belief is in its certainty and subjectivity - it is "owned" by the believer and he will not give it up. And it becomes more valuable the more it is challenged and maintained.

As Luigi Pirandello (1867-1936), the great Italian author and playwright, puts it in the words of L'Ignata, the protagonist who is believed to be someone she is not in the play "As You Desire Me": Other characters say: "She's mine, she's mine - no, she's mine", not because she looked like their own flesh and blood - but because they wanted to believe. L'Ignata exclaims: "Doesn't matter about proof. Doesn't even matter about common sense. If you need to believe in something enough, then you believe it. Look at me, you believed in me without a shred of evidence."

An early 19th century American prophet, William Miller, a farmer from New England, prophesied the end of the world, based on the Biblical Book of Daniel, to occur by March 21, 1844. When that date passed without event he set a new date, October 22, 1844, and when that date also passed, his followers stayed together, but called the following day, "The Great Disappointment." One of his followers picked up the cause, predicted that the world would end "someday" and founded the "Seventh Day Adventists."

As one commentator said, "Being wrong does little harm to a good apocalyptic movement". "The apocalyptic worldview, in fact, is like that awful beast in the old science fiction movies - blasts from the ray guns of history only make it stronger."

A University of Minnesota sociologist, Leon Festinger, in his book "When Prophecy Fails", addressed this very paradox in a 1956 study he and two colleagues did of a failed apocalyptic prophecy.

The results of their study led Festinger to conclude that, "a committed believer, faced with irrefutable evidence contradicting his belief - with what Festinger called a "disconfirmation"- would redouble rather than diminish his efforts to defend his view. Stranger yet, the more harshly reality dealt with a belief, the more feverishly the believer would work to convert others."

Festinger wrote on, "A man with a conviction is a hard man to change. Tell him you disagree and he turns away. Show him facts or figures and he questions your sources. Appeal to logic and he fails to see your point." (Bryan Urstadt, Harper's Magazine, August, 2006)

i. "The True Believer" (Harper & Row, 1951)" by Eric Hoffer

One of the most original thinkers and writers about belief as it applies to mass movements was Eric Hoffer (1902-1983). He was almost entirely self-taught, having lost his sight when he was a boy and recovering it only as a young man. He was occupied during the rest of his life mainly as a longshoreman in San Francisco, which gave him the means and the time to spend his free time in libraries where he became an apt pupil of Michel de Montaigne's "Essays", whose style of thought and writing he emulated. Hoffer's first, and best, of his ten books is "The True Believer". I recommend it for everyone's library as a way to decode the mind of the "true believing" fanatic and the psychology of mass movements, in history and the modern world. The following excerpt will give a brief example:

"The most decisive qualities for the effectiveness of a mass movement leader seem to be audacity, fanatical faith in a holy cause, an awareness of the importance of a close-knit collectivity, and, above all, the ability to evoke fervent devotion in a group of able lieutenants."

"Exceptional intelligence" noble character and originality seem neither indispensable nor even perhaps desirable. The main requirements seem to be: audacity, and a joy in defiance; an iron will; a fanatical conviction that he is in possession of the one and only truth; faith in his destiny and luck; a capacity for passionate hatred; contempt for the present; a cunning estimate of human nature; a delight in symbols (spectacles and ceremonials); unbounded brazenness which finds expression in a disregard of consistency and fairness; a recognition that the innermost craving of a following is for communion and that there can never be too much of it; a capacity for winning and holding the utmost loyalty of a group of able lieutenants. This last faculty is one of the most essential and elusive. The uncanny powers of a leader manifest themselves not so much in the hold he has on the masses as in his ability to dominate and almost bewitch a small group of able men. These men must be fearless, proud, intelligent and capable of organizing and running large-scale undertakings, and yet they must submit wholly to the will of the leader, draw their inspiration and driving force from him, and glory in this submission."

Josie and I heard Eric Hoffer speak and met and talked with him in Chicago in 1980. He was a most engaging, thoughtful and modest mannered man. He was also a modern day, and all too prescient, reincarnation of Machiavelli, but he addressed his thoughts to the public and not just to "The Prince.", but to the public of ordinary men and women.

Thus, we have seen that although there are very different kinds of evidence, the objective, scientific/legal kind, and the subjective, emotional/religious kind; there is no necessary connection in the brain between the two, and it is entirely possible that one form of evidence can trump the other. The examples of this are as common as the eyewitness's misidentification of a suspect in a police line-up, and the mistaken religious zealot's belief that he or she has witnessed a "miraculous" depiction of a religious icon. In both cases the witness believes that what he or she saw is "true", and their brains tolerate the contradiction between their subjective belief and the objective evidence. Beware the "true believer."

j. God Is Not Dead - In fact, new Gods are being born every day

So, God is not only not dead, but new gods are being reborn every day to the new people who are born every day. As young people grow up and emerge into adult consciousness they ask the same fundamental questions about birth, death and suffering, and many find that god-centered religions provide them with their best answers. We need gods, and we will accept them, or create them, with dreams, visions and voices, just as we need kings, tribes, churches, synagogues, mosques, love, hope, food and sex; Gods are one of the things that makes us all too human. In the absence of other resources Gods and other supernatural beliefs can give us hope and solace in times of trouble and loss. Given the vast number and variety of gods and goddesses accumulated over the thousands of years of human history it seems quite obvious, to me at least, that we human beings "created" the gods, either consciously or unconsciously. They are, in short, what we want as gods. This is not to demean the gods, but simply to explain how there could be so many of them. And, once created, we want to believe and do believe in them.

As refered to previously, John Dominic Crossan wrote in "Jesus, A Revolutionary Biography", (Harper, 1995), speaking of the story of Christ's reappearance on the road to Emmaus after his resurrection; "Emmaus never happened, but Emmaus will always happen.", meaning that although physical resurrection from the dead is not scientifically possible, people who want to believe in Jesus will never let him die in their hearts. If they want to believe that Jesus continues to live, they will believe it, and no scientific or rational argument will persuade them otherwise.

The powerfully tragic story of Jesus' life, coupled with stories of many supernatural events, has become one of the most compelling stories in the history of mankind. Jesus' courage, his preaching a gospel of love, his betrayal by his closest friends, his cruel and painful crucifixion, his righteousness speaking out for the poor, for women, the sick, the hungry, the dispossessed, and the despised; and speaking out against economic and governmental injustice, has made him an icon of hope for those in need. And, even though many institutional and other sins have been committed in the name of Jesus, many people simply will not let him die. Jesus is far too important to their hope for a better life, either here on earth or in the hereafter, to let him die.

And the same can be true for any other religious prophet, such as Moses or Muhammad. History is all too full of the extent to which mankind has, and continues to, express belief in the life and reality of religious icons and prophets. The religious strife, which has consumed Europe and the Middle East for thousands of years, stands as frightening testimony to the intensity of these beliefs. The resurgent Iconoclasm of the Taliban destroying images of Buddha, and Islamic militants violently protesting cartoons showing Muhammad are only recent examples of the violent replay of history. The extraordinary irony is that most of history's violent expressions of belief have been committed in the name of religious prophets who preached peace and tolerance. The Koran, for instance, opens with an invocation of God's mercy and compassion and repeatedly urges its believers to practice patience and kindness.

Although Islam is now often associated with authoritarian regimes, it was once known for its cosmopolitan humanism and pluralism, and a spirit of open-minded inquiry. Islamic scientists preserved and expanded the mathematical and scientific knowledge of the Greeks and other ancient civilizations all during Europe's "dark ages", transmitting such knowledge to Europe when it emerged from the dark ages into the middle ages. The Bishop of Chartres, for instance, sent his engineering emissaries from France to the Islamic libraries and school in Toledo, Spain in the 1100's to learn their advanced technical skills to help him build Chartres Cathedral.

k. The Variety of Gods and Goddesses – Historical Pluralism

For a recently published compendium of supernatural gods, see the "Dictionary of Gods and Goddesses", by Michael Jordan, 2nd Edition (Facts on File, Inc. 2004). This dictionary provides a chronology and an alphabetical list and brief description of the 2,500 major Gods who have been recorded throughout human history.

It has an extensive bibliography. Another shorter, beautifully illustrated "Book of Gods and Goddesses", tells the story of the many polytheistic gods, the Near East, Europe, the Americas, Asia, Africa and Caribbean and Oceania, by Eric Chaline, (Harper 2004). A companion book to these books is: "In the Beginning, Creation Stories From Around the World", by Virginia Hamilton and illustrated by Barry Moser (Harcourt Inc. 1988), the story of mankind by various cultures throughout human history. Required reading for anyone interested in these subjects is: William James's "The Varieties of Religious Experience, A Study in Human Nature" (Penguin Classics, 1985, originally published in 1902). These books, together with James's "A Pluralistic Universe", plus all of Mercia Eliade's books provide what seems to me irrefutable evidence for accepting religious pluralism. There have simply been too many different gods and religions throughout human history for anyone to be exclusively true, and all the others false. The only rational explanation for the multiplicity of gods, and their continual ineffectiveness, is that they are all the products of our fertile, and eternally hopeful, imaginations.

l. Emile Durkheim, "The Elementary Forms of Religious Life"

In contrast to William James was Emile Durkheim (1858-1917), the French founder of Sociology as an academic discipline and profession. Durkheim's main inquiry and thesis was how individuals achieve social consensus. James's concerns were about the individual's variety of religious experience while Durkheim's was communal experience. He observed and postulated that social solidarity coherence could occur only if members of a society held certain beliefs and sentiments in common. "Without such collective beliefs, he argued, no contractual relationship based purely on self-interest could have any force." (Encyclopedia of World Biography)

Durkheim wrote many books and was appointed to a professorship of Sociology and Education at the Sorbonne in Paris in 1902 where he remained for the rest of his career. His final book, "The Elementary Forms of Religious Life" (1912), argued that the binding character of the social bond was to be found in religion, as communal participation endowed with "sacredness", "the transcendent image of the collective consciousness." He was seriously concerned about the European loss of faith, particularly in France where the Jacobins had destroyed Catholicism after the Revolution of 1796. The French had tried to fill the so-called "moral void" by inventing a synthetic Religion of Reason, or Saint-Simon's New Christianity and Comte's

Religion of Humanity, but were still struggling with the "loss of faith". They asked, as Dostoevsky did via his Ivan Karamasov, in "The Brothers Karamazov", "Once God is dead, does not everything become permissible?" "Would the end of traditional religion be a prelude to the dissolution of all moral community into a state of universal breakdown and anomie?"

m. "The Evolutionary Basis of Religious Ethics"

More recently, John Teehan, Associate Professor of Philosophy at Hofstra University, has examined "The Evolutionary Basis of Religious Ethics" in a remarkable article published in the September, 2006 quarterly issue of the Zygon Journal of Religion and Science. Its Abstract states his proposal most concisely:

"Abstract. I propose that religious ethical traditions can be understood as cultural expressions of underlying evolutionary processes. I begin with a discussion of evolutionary theories of morality, specifically kin selection and reciprocal altruism, and then discuss some recent work on the evolution of religion, setting out those features of religion that prepare it to take on a moral function in society. Having established the theoretical framework for the thesis, I turn to a close reading of early Jewish and Christian ethical teachings, as found in the Bible, in order to set out preliminary support for the proposal. My goal is to argue for the plausibility of the thesis and to indicate how, if correct, it provides new insight into Judeo-Christian moral traditions and into the phenomenon of religious violence. Such an approach to religious ethics has important meta-ethical implications. In the last section I consider issues such as the foundation of ethics and the possibilities and limitations of a secular ethics."

Teehan's article discusses the fundamental importance of supernatural gods to the evolution of religion. The survival advantage to people who "over interpret" threatening stimuli is obvious. "It is not the primitive mind "going wrong", but it is the human mind making a rationally justifiable attempt to bring coherence to experience." Teehan quotes Scott Atran, from his "In Gods We Trust, The Evolutionary Landscape of Religion" (Oxford, 2002) who says that: "Supernatural agency (gods) is the most culturally recurrent, cognitively relevant, and evolutionarily compelling concept in religion."

Furthermore, Teehan continues, "the counterintuitive nature of supernatural agents (gods), rather than being an obstacle to their acceptance as explanations actually seems to contribute to their resilience." In other words, the fact that gods are supernatural, and therefore not scientifically credible, actually enhances their credibility to believers, and makes them more likely to be recalled over time, and more fit for transmission from one generation to the next. Also, Gods that have "strategic information", that is, Gods who know what everyone is actually doing - from whom there are no secrets – "occupy a unique role that allows them to detect and punish cheaters and reward cooperators. In moral religions such gods are conceived of as "interested parties in moral choices." Communal belief in such gods therefore lowers the risk of cooperating and raises the cost of cheating by making detection more probable and punishment more certain."

Teehan continues, citing other research on the evolution of moral religions, to summarize their findings simply as; "Groups with effective moral bonds will have a survival advantage. And, "..belief systems that can internalize social control are more effective than those that rely on external controls. A fictional belief system, such as represented by religion, can function as a low-cost external control system and can be more readily internalized than a reality-based system." (David Sloan Wilson, "Darwin's Cathedral", 2002)

Kin selection is a critical factor in Judeo-Christian religion. "Jews are all children of Abraham. All Jews through their tribal lineage are members of one, extended family. Genealogy matters. This extended family is the basis of Judaism and Jewish morality .....” “A community cannot survive and prosper without a shared commitment to a moral system.” Teehan then explores further the very ethnic tribal nature of Judaism, compared to the more inclusive nature of the Christian community, and the greater difficulty of maintaining a moral code in a larger more ethnically diverse community.

Teehan explores the Biblical recitation of “Moses, after having received the Law and communicated it to his people, leading the Hebrews on what can be described as a blood-soaked trek to the Promised Land.” So, the Ten Commandment’s prohibition against killing applied to the members of the Jewish community, but not to dealing with those outside of the community.

“Morality develops as a tool to promote within-group cohesiveness and to better enable individuals to enhance their genetic fitness. This cohesiveness also functions as an adaptive advantage in competition with other Groups (Alexander 1987; Wilson 2002). Morality is a code of how to treat those in my group; it is not extended to those outside the group.” “Moses’ actions seem coldly calculating to modern readers and not what one would expect of a reli-

gious hero, but to the degree that morality serves evolutionary ends Moses ably fulfilled his role as moral leader of his community.”

Teehan’s conclusions, simply stated, are First; that while evolutionary moral theory may undermine the claims for transcendent, religion based, moral systems, this does not invalidate morality, or even religious morality. “Rather than being collections of divine commands, moral systems are records of the efforts of various human communities as they struggled to solve the problems of communal life and to create a better society. Their value is not that of conclusive truths but of moral experiments that need to be evaluated by their results.” Thus, evolution teaches us that both morality and belief in supernatural gods evolved as survival tools for mankind, but while morality can be enhanced by belief in gods, it is not dependent upon such belief.

And, second: that “despite this downgrading of the status of religious morality, an evolutionary approach suggests a crucial moral role for religion to play ... “One possible reading of this evolutionary story is that religion may play a necessary role in grounding moral obligation on a large scale. For a secular morality to function it may need to tap into the same emotional and cognitive resources accessed by religion. Whether or not such secular substitutes can be made effective, it is clear that religion is designed to play such a role. In fact, for better or worse, religion does play this role, and in all likelihood will continue to, for a vast portion of the global population. Because religion taps into such deeply ingrained psychological mechanisms it can serve to amplify and funnel human energies in any number of directions. Given this vast power to move people for good and for ill, and the central position of religion in so many of the challenges confronting us today, it is imperative to understand how religion functions."

n. The Evolutionary Basis for Belief in God or Gods

Beginning with Darwin in his "Descent of Man", published in 1871, evolutionists have observed man's pervasive and persistent propensity for religious thinking and behavior. Darwin said "A belief in all pervading spiritual agencies seems to be universal." Anthropologists observe that "Religions that share certain supernatural features - belief in a non-corporeal God, or gods, belief in the afterlife, belief in the ability of prayer or ritual to change the course of human events-are found in virtually every culture on earth". (Robin Marantz Henig, contributing writer for the New York Times)

Sixty per cent of Americans believe in the devil and hell, and seventy percent believe in angels, heaven and the existence of miracles and of life after death. Ninety-two percent believe in a personal God - a God with a distinct set of character traits ranging from "distant" to "benevolent".

Some recent books by anthropologists, psychologists, and biologists illustrate the discussion going on within evolutionary scientists about the evolution of religion. There appears to be agreement on the central theme; that religious belief is an outgrowth of brain architecture that evolved during early human history. What they disagree about is why a tendency to believe evolved, whether it was because belief itself was adaptive, or because it was just an evolutionary by-product, an alternative consequence of some other adaptation in the evolution of the human brain.

 Scott Atran, the anthropologist-psychologist author of "In God We Trust: The Evolutionary Landscape of Religion (2002) characterizes religious belief as that which takes, "what is materially false to be true" and what is materially true to be false". (i.e. life after death) Atran also wrote "Religions do not exist apart from the individual minds that constitute them and the environments that constrain them, any more than biological species and varieties exist independently of the individual organisms that compose them and the environments that conform them".

Some other scientists have also addressed Atran's questions; Pascal Boyer, now at Washington University, Justin Barrett, now at Oxford, and Paul Bloom at Yale. They have moved toward a theory that religious belief is a by-product of other evolutionary advantageous traits. The late Stephen Jay Gould, a well-known evolutionary biologist at Harvard had also proposed the idea of the "spandrel" in evolution to describe a trait that has no adaptive value of its own. A spandrel in architecture is the "V" formed at the intersection of two arches, having no value on its own.

Another theory that evolutionary psychologists apply to explain mankind's ability for causal reasoning is "agent detection", the capacity of humans to observe warning signs or patterns of shape and motion that serve to detect potential danger. Our senses are ever alert to the possibility of danger and, important for our survival, usually over-reacting in the interest of safety. We also have a capacity to perceive patterns and impose a narrative meaning to what we see. We are, in short, self-protective, story-telling organisms who want to make sense out of what we observe.

Atran and his colleagues describe a culture's agreed sense of what is, "Folk psychology" as essential to getting along in the contemporary world just as it has since prehistoric times. An important part of all Folk psychology appears to be religions which have supernatural gods, who can be dealt with through prayer or ritual, promise life after death, and provide a supernatural basis for moral codes. Also important in these religions, according to these "by-product" theorists, is that people are more likely to "pay attention to and remember things that are unfamiliar and strange, but not so strange as to be impossible to assimilate. Ideas about God, or other supernatural agents seem to fit these criteria. They are what Pascal Boyer, an anthropologist and psychologist, called "minimally counterintuitive": weird enough to get your attention and lodge in your memory but not so weird that you reject them altogether. Such as a God who has a human personality except that he knows everything, or a God who has a mind but has no body."

"But it is not enough for an agent to be minimally counterintuitive for it to earn a spot in people's belief systems. An emotional component is often needed if belief is to take hold. Religions stir up emotions through rituals - swaying, singing, bowing in unison during group prayer, sometimes working people up to a state of physical arousal that can border on frenzy. And religions gain strength during the natural heightening of emotions that occurs in times of personal crisis, when the faithful turn to shamans or priests. The most intense personal crisis, for which religion can offer powerfully comforting answers, is when someone comes face to face with mortality."

These researcher's conclusions certainly comport with my own observations. I would, in fact, take the conclusions one step further by stating that it seems to me that more absurd, or "counterintuitive" a belief is, the more tightly it is held by the believer. Mormonism, for instance is based on very "counterintuitive" beliefs, beginning with the "Book of Mormon", dictated by Joseph Smith in upstate New York in the 1820's during the "Second Great Awakening" of religious fervor in America. Smith's "revelation" recites the discovery of a number of buried "golden plates" said to be the works of an ancient prophet named "Moroni". The plates were said to be inscribed with a kind of hieroglyphics that resembled Egyptian writing, but were not decipherable by any scholars at the time. Smith said the story the plates told was that an ancient tribe of people

from the Mediterranean came to America and became the ancestors of the American Indians. (a popular belief at the time, for which there never has been any archeological or other evidence) Smith's belief also asserted that Jesus came to America "by subterranean vessel" during the three days between his crucifixion and his "being raised from the dead". Smith was able to persuade a few of his local friends of the truth of these beliefs and, by dint of energetic proselytizing, increased the number of believers substantially during his lifetime. For the full story of Joseph Smith and the Mormon Religion see "Mormon America" (1999).

The point of reciting this brief description of Mormon beliefs is simply to illustrate that very "counterintuitive" beliefs can be created and then believed by many followers. Mormons are among the world's most successful religious believers. They are in fact the fastest growing religious organization in the world. Members of the church are required to tithe 10% of their gross income to the church every year and mostly adhere to a very strict, and healthy, code of behavior which prohibits smoking, drinking alcoholic and carbonated beverages. The Mormon Church also requires each of its young people to enter a two-year period of missionary work in their late teens and early twenties.

One of the results of some of their missionary work is the creation of the world's largest database of birth and death records. Smith believed, based on his reading of some of St. Paul's letters, that the Bible requires the members of the families of those entering heaven to all be baptized. This belief has caused the church to organize a continuing effort to "baptized the un-baptized dead" so their kin can enter heaven. The church therefore continues to manage surrogate baptizing, using young Mormons to "stand in" for the "un-baptized dead" and actually go through the process of water immersion and baptism. This continuing effort has created a database of over two billion names with birth and death dates. It is of course a database of interest to genealogists and, as such, is made available on the Internet for genealogical use. When Jewish people objected to having some of their deceased relatives "baptized" the Mormon Church stopped doing so, but said no harm had been done since the baptism was "optional" to the deceased! This practice is, to me, one of the most "counterintuitive" of all beliefs.

But the other main point of referring to the Mormons is to note that they succeed in gaining believers and in creating a financially rich church, which gives comfort to its believers.

In other words, even though it may be very "counterintuitive" it can work, at least for Mormons.

Thus, religion, whether adaptive or a by-product, can be and probably has been a very important element of mankind's evolutionary "survival kit".

BIBLE INTERPRETATION - HUMANISM - FUNDAMENTALISM

a. Historical interpretation of the Bible

Biblical interpretation has been going on ever since the various books of the Old and New Testaments were written. Questions of which books are in and which books are not in the Old and New Testament Canons, and the meaning of their contents, have been debated for thousands of years. In the Christian church's early history, Gnosticism, Aryanism, Monatism and Marcionism were seen by the Orthodox Church to be heretical and were violently persecuted. Arianism, in particular, was a serious challenge to the Trinity and led to the Nicene Creeds of 325 C.E. and 381 C.E., which affirmed the Trinity and formally stated the orthodox interpretation of Christian faith, still adhered to today.

b. Modern Biblical interpretation

(It is important to note at the outset of this review that each of the following biblical scholars was, or is, a loyal Christian. Their biblical interpretations were not intended to damage the Christian church, but to make it more credible.)

(1.) Begins with **Herman Samuel Reimarus (1694-1768)**, a German philosopher of the Enlightenment who wrote an unpublished essay in 1755 asserting as a Deist that "human reason can arrive at knowledge of God and ethics from a study of nature and our own internal reality, so we do not need religions based on revelation. Reimarus denied the reality of miracles and is credited with initiating historian's investigations of the historical Jesus. Reimarus set himself the task of separating what the Apostles present in their writings from what Jesus himself actually said and taught during his lifetime." (Reimarus's essay was later published by his son-in-law Lessing in 1774 as "Fragments by an Anonymous Author") "Reimarus attacked the Bible as "abounding in error", but he also attacked atheism with equal effect and sincerity. He was said to be a man of high moral character, respected and esteemed by his contemporaries" - none of whom read his essay until after he died.

By separating the historical Jesus from the Gospel narratives modern biblical interpretation laid the academic foundation for modern Religious Humanism. In other words, for religious tradition without the supernatural.

(2.) Subsequently, other German philosophers like David Strauss (1808-1874) and Bruno Bauer (1809-1882) continued the work that Reimarus had started. Strauss's "Life of Jesus" (1835) scandalized Christian Europe with his portrayal of the "historical Jesus" whose divine nature he denied and his assertion that the miraculous elements of the Gospels were "mythical".

Albert Schweitzer (1875-1965) wrote in his "Quest For the Historic Jesus" (1906) that "there are two broad periods of academic research in the quest for the historical Jesus; namely the period before David Strauss and the period after David Strauss."

Marcus Borg, presently a founder of the Jesus Seminar and a widely published religious book author, says that Strauss's basic claims - that many of the Gospel narrations are mythical

in character and that "myth" is not simply to be equated with "falsehood" - have become part of mainstream scholarship.

(3.) Bruno Bauer was a controversial and very independent biblical scholar who disputed some of Strauss's theories but subscribed to his basic premise of Christian mythology. Bauer was also the first scholar to identify Mark as the first Gospel, probably based upon "Ur-Mark", an unknown author who predated Mark.

(4.) Albert Schweitzer (1875-1965) was the great theologian, musician and medical doctor who founded the medical missionary hospital in the French African colony of Gabon at Lamberene in 1913. His expressed intent was to "atone for the wrongs done to the Africans during French colonialism." Schweitzer was awarded the Nobel Peace Prize in 1952. He was, in my view, a "Religious Humanist Extraordinaire".

Schweitzer also made major contributions to the fields of theology and music, first a biblical scholar, and second as an organist and authority on the life and works of J.S. Bach. (Schweitzer's home can be visited as an historic site in his picturesque medieval hometown of Kaysersberg in Alsace, France)

Schweitzer's first academic achievements were in theology. His book, "The Quest For the Historical Jesus", published in 1906, reviewed the development of Life of Jesus research in German scholarship from the time of Reimarus in the 18th century to William Wrede in the 20th.

Schweitzer's essential contribution to historical Jesus research is his view that Jesus' life must be viewed in the context of the Messianic - Apocalyptic Jewish world of his time. Jesus advocated his belief that the world was soon coming to an end and that all people must be prepared to meet their God. In Schweitzer's view Jesus was simply wrong, but his followers fastened on to his beliefs and restated them in mythical terms in support of their own beliefs.

As Bauer had said, "Jesus of Nazareth was the creation of a religious community in search of an ideal savior and redeemer. Schweitzer also described the Gospels as "dogmatic history".

In Schweitzer's view Jesus was simply a product of his times - specifically the apocalyptic eschatology that was then so prevalent, and thus Jesus is therefore someone who is alien to modern humanity.

Schweitzer's Christianity is therefore not tied to a biblical understanding of Jesus, but is translation of Jesus' "spirit" into a reverence for life - what he called a "practical mysticism". "By devoting oneself to the beings with which one comes into contact one devotes oneself to "Infinite Being" - to God. The power behind this reverence for life is pity. The capacity to empathize, to sympathize, with another's suffering."

In 1965 Schweitzer wrote: The fundamental fact of human awareness is this: "I am life that wants to live in the midst of other life that wants to live." A thinking man feels compelled to approach all life with the same reverence he has for his own. Thus all life becomes part of his own experience. From such a point of view, "good" means to maintain life, to further life, to bring developing life to its highest value. "Evil" means to destroy life, to hurt life, to keep life from developing. This, then, is the rational, universal, and basic principle of ethics."

"Practically, reverence for Life dictates the same behaviors as the ethical principle of love. On another level, though Reverence for Life makes the ethical principle of love rational, and calls for a widening of the circle to include all life. " In the words of his friend, Albert Einstein, "Schweitzer did not preach and did not warn and not dream that his example would be an ideal and comfort to innumerable people. He simply acted out of inner necessity. "

(5) Rudolph Bultmann (1884-1976) was another German philosopher who spent most his academic life at the University of Marburg at Marburg

an der Lahn, in Germany. (A place where I was billeted for a few days as a replacement infantry soldier in 1945 - and which I visited later as a businessman in 1965.) Bultmann is known mostly for his New Testament studies, which resulted in his landmark "History of the Synoptic Tradition" (1921), his "Gospel of John" (1941), and his lecture "New Testament and Mythology" (1941). His work became known widely outside of Germany in 1948 with the publication in English of his "Kerygma and Mythos". In this book he asserted the need to demythologize the New Testament. "To Bultmann "demythologizing" did not mean the elimination of the miracle stories, rather it meant their reinterpretation "existentially" in terms of man's understanding his own situation and its fundamental possibilities.

To Bultmann the story of the Resurrection is not an account of the reanimation of a corpse; instead it expresses the possibility of man's entrance into a new dimension of existence, free from guilt and anxiety and open to all people in love." See Bultmann's "Theology of the New Testament" (1951 translation)

Scholars have for many years, beginning prominently in the 20th century, through Bultmann's work, that the Bible has been compiled and selected out of a number of different writings produced by different authors over many centuries. Although claimed by the Bible's authors, and by some modern believers, to be "the revealed word of God" these writings are usually based upon oral traditions developed and passed down from generation to generation during many centuries of virtually total public illiteracy. These stories were therefore oral parables and metaphors that could not have been originally intended or capable of being interpreted "literally" by an illiterate public. Ancient Biblical times were thousand of years before what we now call "science", a time of magic, shamans and astrology, and a common belief in eschatology - the near coming of the end of the earth - so fervent belief in Biblical stories was probably the norm, but it could not have been "literal" in our modern sense of meaning.

Modern attempts by mostly "neo-literalist", or "fundamentalist" believers to interpret ancient writings "literally" are applying modern standards of meaning to documents that were created in a completely different context thousands of years ago.

(6.) Baruch Spinoza (1632-1677), Thomas Paine (1737-1809) and Thomas Jefferson (1743-1826) and many others of the "Enlightenment" described themselves as "Deists" who believed in an immanent God, but not

Biblical, God and also professed their belief that Jesus was the world's greatest teacher of ethics, but was not "divine" in any supernatural sense. (See my comments on Deism at page 182 in this book)

(7.) **The Roman Catholic rule for Bible Interpretation:** When the present Pope Benedict VI was Cardinal Ratzinger, the head of the Vatican Congregation for the Doctrine of Faith, he wrote the preface to a 1994 report by the Pontifical Commission of the Roman Catholic Church, which states:

"The historical-critical method of Bible interpretation is indispensable. Proper understanding of the Bible not only admits the use of this method, but actually requires it. Holy scripture is the "word of God in human language"; in short, the Bible "has been composed by human authors in all its various parts".

The Pontifical Report continues, saying in part:

"The fundamentalist approach is dangerous, for it is attractive to people who look to the Bible for ready answers to the problems of life. It can deceive these people, offering them interpretations that are pious, but illusory, instead of telling them that the Bible does not necessarily contain an immediate answer to each and every problem. Without saying as much in so many words, funda-

mentalism actually invites people to a kind of intellectual suicide. It injects into life a false certitude, for it unwittingly confuses the divine substance of the biblical message with what are in fact its human limitations." Bible Review (October, 1994)

("Postmodernism" theories of the "relativity of truth" have also affected Biblical Interpretation. For an excellent analysis and critique of this problem please see:

Dr. Van A. Harvey's "A Handbook of Theological Terms' and "The Historian and the Believer" and "Feuerbach and the Interpretation of Religion". Van Harvey is an emeritus professor of religious studies at Stanford University.)

(8.) **The Jesus Seminar**
For another interesting analysis of the application of modern scholarship to the New Testament please read John Dominic Crossan's "The Historical Jesus" Harper Collins, 1992). Crossan is a faithful Roman Catholic theologian and historian who, with his colleagues in the Jesus Seminar, addresses these questions with great skill, integrity, scholarship and faith.

Crossan has written many other best selling books, such as " Who Killed Jesus?", "Jesus, a Revolutionary Biography", "In Parables", and most recently "A Long Way From Tipperary", his autobiography in both personal and religious terms. In his view "It was inevitable and understandable that against secular rationalism would arise counter-strains of religious rationalism. If science and reason claimed a monopoly on truth, Christianity trumped them with biblical inerrancy, traditional conformity and papal infallibility. These were of course, the supreme victories of rationalism, the ultimate submission of sanctity to certitude. Secularism and fundamentalism deserve one another, and each is about as capable of destroying our humanity." Crossan's view of the historical Jesus interprets the many miracles and other incredible events of the Bible as "parables", never intended to be taken literally, but intended to communicate theological messages about justice and community and belief in God to illiterate people.

Crossan's life began in Ireland and proceeded through Roman Catholic schools to an American Monastery, to the priesthood, and then to a PhD. After teaching for a while he reacted against what he perceived as the unwarranted authority of the church, resigned his offices as a priest and married. But he never abandoned the Roman Catholic community and never lost his faith. He spent the rest of his academic career as a professor of religion at De Paul University in Chicago, from which he eventually retired as Professor emeritus.

Crossan's writings are quite controversial within both the Roman Catholic Church and Christianity in general, so when I once found myself seated at a memorial service next to the late Father John Richardson, C.M., then Chancellor of De Paul, I asked him how it was that Crossan was still active at De Paul, given his work with the Jesus Seminar. Fr. Richardson quickly said, with a big smile on his face, "We love Dom here at De Paul." Fr. Richardson went on to say that he and De Paul had complete confidence in Crossan's faith and the integrity of his scholarship.

"By the end of their (Jesus Seminar's) most visible period in 2000, the members had pared the sayings of Jesus down to 18 percent of those attributed to him in the New Testament and pictured him as a wandering teacher of "wisdom" who preached in riddles and parables about a God of love who preferred sinners to the wealthy, comfortable, and wise of the world. Gone, by and large, was the utterly mistaken eschatological prophet who preached the end of the world and never expected to found a church - much less a seminar - in his name."

"What the Jesus Seminar had tacitly acknowledged is over 80 percent of "Jesus" had been fictionalized by the Gospel writers. That is to say that, if we are to judge a man's life by his sayings, the greater portion of the literary artifacts known as the Gospels is fictional. If we are to judge by actions, then what actions survived historical criticism? Not the virgin birth, the Transfiguration, the healing of the sick, the purely magical feats like converting water to wine in Caana, or the multiplication of loaves and fishes. The Resurrection had quietly been sent to the attic by theologians in the nineteenth century. The deeds - except, perhaps, the attack on the Temple (Mark 11:15-19) - had preceded the words to the dustbin years before, yet scholars insisted the historical figure was untouched. Only faith could explain this invulnerability to harm." R. Joseph Hoffmann, (Free Inquiry, March/April, 2007)

I find Crossan's thinking and writing very compelling as a bridge between religion and science. He makes Jesus a credible human figure without ever giving up any of his divinity, or any of Crossan's faith in the Christianity of Jesus. But he is criticized by many, most recently by Garry Wills, a former Roman Catholic seminarian and a noted historian and Professor of History emeritus at Northwestern University. Wills has written many acclaimed works on religion and general history. His "Papal Sin" and "Why I am a Catholic" were New York Times bestsellers. Will's most recent book, "What Jesus Meant", in which he writes forthrightly as

a believer and not as a scholar, is very critical of Crossan's Jesus Seminar, labeling it as "the new fundamentalism", the meaning of which escapes me. (It is, after all, Crossan who sees himself as caught between the extremes of fundamentalism and secularism.)

Wills is also very critical of Thomas Jefferson's "The Life and Morals of Jesus of Nazareth" because it seeks to turn Jesus into a "mere moralist," in spite of the fact that Jefferson identifies himself as a Deist and praises Jesus' system of morals as the "most perfect and sublime that has ever been taught by man." Wills is joined in these criticisms by Martin Marty, a renowned Lutheran pastor and Professor emeritus at the University of Chicago School of Divinity. Both these critics are quite distressed by Crossan's and Jefferson's attempts to translate Jesus' life into human terms.

Both Wills and Marty seem to me to be engaging in "ad hominem" attacks on the Jesus Seminar, calling it "liberal-radical Jesus Seminar scholars who vote for the few "authentic" sayings of Jesus". They also quote the four gospel texts as their literal authority for finding out "What Jesus Meant", but don't see their own literalism as fundamentalism. Wills says that: "Jesus is not just like us, he has higher rights and powers". "He was called a bastard and was rejected by his own brothers and the rest of his family. He was an outcast among outcasts, ...homeless... He especially depended upon women, who were "second class citizens" His very presence was subversive. He was in constant danger...called an agent of the devil, ...never respectable... scandalous".

I do however agree completely with Garry Wills when he states in the following last few paragraphs of his book that it is justice and love that are at the core of "What Jesus Meant".

"Jesus' followers have the obligation that rests on all men and women to seek justice based on the dignity of every human being. That is the goal of politics, of "the things that belong to Caesar." But heaven's reign makes deeper and broader demands, the demands not only of justice but of love. Saint Augustine came in time to renounce the classical ideals of Plato and Aristotle, which exalted the intellect as man's noblest faculty. Augustine knew that the highest human faculty is love, the self-emptying love of Jesus: "A new instruction I have given you: love one another. As I have loved you, you must love one another. All will know that you are my followers by this sign alone, that you have love for one another" (John 13.34-35).

"'None knew better what Jesus meant than Saint Paul when he wrote:

"Were I to speak the languages of all men and all angels, without having love, I were as a resonating gong or jangling cymbal. Were I to prophesy and know all secrets and every truth, were I to have faith strong enough to move mountains, without having love, I were as nothing. Were I to give away all my possessions, or give my body to be burned, without having love, it would avail me nothing.

"Love is patient, is kind. It does not envy others or brag of itself. It is not swollen with self. It is not wayward or grasping. It does not flare with anger, nor harbor a grudge. It takes no joy in evil, but delights in truth. It keeps all confidences, all trust, all hope, all endurance. Love will never go out of existence. Prophecy will fail in time, languages too, and knowledge as well. For we know things only partially, or prophesy partially, and when the totality is known, the parts will vanish. It is like what I spoke as a child, knew as a child, thought as a child - which, now that I am grown up, I put aside. In the same way we see things in a murky reflection now, but shall see them full face when what I have known in part I shall know fully, as I am known. For the present, then, three things matter - believing, hoping and loving. But supreme is loving." (Corinthians 13.1-13)

What better way to end this commentary than with such New Testament poetry?

Anyone interested in learning more about Crossan's and his critics' views should read their books first hand and make up their own minds...Their full debate is beyond the scope of this essay.

(9.) The Jesus Project, by the University of California Committee for the Scientific Examination of Religion (CSER)

In January, 2007 the CSER fellows, invited guests, present and former members of the Jesus Seminar announced the beginning of a planned five-year study effort on the subject of "Scripture and Skepticism". This "Jesus Project" is the first methodologically agnostic approach to the question of Jesus' historical existence. "Did Jesus exist?" Its objective is to assess the quality of the evidence available for looking at this question before seeing what the evidence has to tell us. The Project regards the question of the historical Jesus as a testable hypothesis, and is committed to no prior conclusions about the outcome of its inquiry. The Project members are limited to a maximum of fifty scholars with credentials in biblical studies as well as in the crucial cognate disciplines of ancient history, mythography, archeology, classical studies, anthropology, and social history.

At the end of its five-year study period the Project will publish its findings. The Project is aimed at a probable reconstruction of the events that explain the beginning of Christianity - a man named Jesus from the province of Galilee whose life served as the basis for the beginning of a movement, or a sequence of events that let to the Jesus story being propagated throughout the Mediterranean. They profess their aim, like Pilate's (John 18:38) is to find the truth.

One of the members of the Jesus Project is Dr. Paula Fredriksen, the Aurelia Professor of Scripture at Boston University. She is a graduate of Wellesley College (1973), Oxford University (1974) and Princeton University (1979). Dr Fredriksen has written extensively on the subject of early Christianity. Her book, "From Jesus to Christ, the Origins of New Testament Images of Jesus" (Yale, 2000) is an excellent summary of the biblical interpretations reviewed here.

(10.) Reverend John Macquarrie, Scottish Theologian (1919-2007) Another modern biblical interpreter has been the recently deceased Scottish theologian, Rev. John Macquarrie. He was raised a Presbyterian and ordained as a Presbyterian minister after army service in 1945. He was educated at Glasgow University where he earned highest honors in philosophy and divinity, and his doctorate in divinity in 1954. He taught at Glasgow U. for a few years and moved to New York in 1962 where he converted to the Episcopal Church and joined the Union Theological Seminary as Professor of Systematic Theology. He returned to England in 1970 and became the Lady Margaret Professor of Divinity at Oxford University.

Macquarrie wrote many books including "Principles of Christian Theology" (1966) and "Paths of Spirituality" (1972) and became a major interpreter of Rudolph Bultmann.

As reported in his New York Times obituary, "One of his goals was to develop an accessible theology relevant to a world that after the Holocaust and World War 1I seemed to doubt divine guidance."..."The God in which Macquarrie believed was Being itself, a definition that to him made it meaningless to suggest that God was dead or did not exist. .... "Dr. Macquarrie wrote that all language about God was symbolic and not to be taken literally. But it must be taken seriously. .... "Faith's name for reality is God" "He said that the New Testament was misread to make Jesus seem divine; a view cemented into the church's early creeds. His Jesus was fully but not merely human, being the one human who most perfectly mirrored God's presence on earth." ... "In a speech in Richmond, Virginia

in 1993 he characterized Jesus as "a human being who was the bearer and revealer of a deity".

"As his systematic theology became ever more refined, Dr. Macquarrie's appreciation for the broad spectrum of Christian thought - from Quaker to Catholic to Baptist and beyond - grew. He propounded a view that some considered heresy: that religions other that Christianity can and do reveal ultimate truth." .... "that salvation was available to all, not just the chosen" ... "In the long run, the only effective answer to heresy, near heresy and errors of other kinds is for the church to show that she has a better theology than the person suspected of error," Dr. Macquarrie wrote.

Thus we have had in Dr. Macquarrie another believing Christian whose interpretation of the Bible and Christian theology made him what I call a "Religious Humanist".

(11.) Reverend Peter Gomes (1935 to present) Rev. Peter Gomes has been the Minister of the Memorial Church at Harvard University for many years and is the author of many excellent books interpreting religion for lay people. His book, "The Good Book, For the Mind and the Heart" (1996), is, in my opinion, the best book on Biblical interpretation for the modern American reader. Peter Gomes was ordained as a Baptist minister and is an eighth generation free black

American who was born, raised and still lives in Plymouth, Massachusetts. A truly "down home" Yankee. In "The Good Book" Gomes writes in plain, straightforward language about what the Bible says, and doesn't say, about a number of critical issues: Race, Anti-Semitism, Slavery, Women, Homosexuality, and Science. He also writes about the Bible as a contemporary resource for dealing with suffering, evil, temptation, wealth, joy and the mysteries of life. "The Good Book" is, in short, a handy and practical Biblical reference. While he is a Baptist minister, his generous heart and ecumenical spirit makes him a Humanist in my book.

(12.) James L. Kugel, emeritus professor of Hebrew literature at Harvard, and author of the recently published "How to Read the Bible, A Guide to Scripture, Then and Now" (2007, Free Press)

Professor Kugel's recent book about Biblical Old Testament interpretation illustrates how a modern scholar can carefully examine the Bible's complex historical origins; acknowledge its pre-Biblical sources; the laws of Hammurabi, the Epic of Gilgamesh, prophecies of Ezekiel from Middle Eastern temples and the Ten Commandments from ancient Hittite treaties; confront its obvious fictions of, for instance, Moses filling the Nile with blood, Joshua stopping the Sun

at noon, or Samson killing 1,000 men with the jawbone of an ass, and its many self contradictions such as the two Creation stories in Genesis, and the metamorphosis of the early God as one of many gods into the one God, YHWH; and still, as an orthodox Jew, maintain his belief in Judaism. In short, Kugel separates scholarship and belief. He illustrates why simplistic literalist interpretations of the Bible are wrong, but he also illustrates that the variety of myths and plagiarized law codes don't eliminate its sense of "holiness." It is a masterful and well-written book.

Kugel has also written two other books that show his knowledge and appreciation of Biblical poetry, perhaps the basis of his sense of the Bible's holiness. They are: "The Idea of Biblical Poetry: Parallelism and Its History", and "The Great Poem of the Bible: A Reader's Companion with New Translations". Kugel's works are certainly a wonderful example of belief as Poetry and knowledge as Prose.

c. Fundamentalism
(1.) Fundamentalism According to Karen Armstrong
Karen Armstrong, a former Roman Catholic nun, who left the church and has become a prolific author of books about various aspects of reli-

gion, has written an excellent book, "The Battle for God – A History of Fundamentalism", Ballantine (2001) The book is a masterful review of the history of modern fundamentalist movements in Judaism, Christianity and Islam. It is the frightening story of the reaction of many modern-day people who see the world in terms of an apocalyptic contest; between the forces of evil in modern life and the literal truths of their sacred religions texts. They see the contest in starkly Armageddon-like terms as a war between spiritualism and materialism. Fundamentalism is therefore not a throwback to some ancient form of religion, but a modern response to what is seen as the spiritual crisis of the modern world...And some recent world events, such as the war in Iraq and the suppression of "feminism", i.e., women, are evidence of the reality of these fundamentalist beliefs. Very much worth reading.

(2.) Fundamentalism According to Bishop John Shelby Spong
Bishop Spong is the retired Episcopal Bishop of New Jersey. He is also the author of many books, relevant to this discussion, such as: "Rescuing the Bible from Fundamentalism - a Bishop Rethinks the Meaning of Scripture", "Why Christianity Must Change or Die - a Bishop Speaks to Believers in Exile", and "This Hebrew Lord - A Bishop's Search for the

Authentic Jesus". His autobiography, "Here I Stand" provides an excellent opportunity to see how someone born into the segregated South of North Carolina in 1931 could grow up into a leading voice for reform in his Episcopal Church. Spong, like Crossan, is also quite controversial, but because of the issues he raises, and the intelligent way he discusses them, well worth reading.

(3.) Fundamentalism According to President Jimmy Carter
Jimmy Carter's recent book, "Our Endangered Values", Simon & Schuster (2005) is another excellent and thoughtful book discussing the rise of religious fundamentalism. Carter speaks from his perspective as a life-long active traditional Baptist. He also includes good discussions of science and religion and the separation of church and state. He sees the intrusion of fundamentalism in government, the illegal and unnecessary war against Iraq, and the fundamentalist distortion of American foreign policy, as very clear and present dangers.

(4.) Fundamentalism according to the 1994 Pontifical Report of the Roman Catholic Church:
"The fundamentalist approach is dangerous, for it is attractive to people who look to the Bible for ready answers to the problems of life. It can deceive these people, offering

them interpretations that are pious, but illusory, instead of telling them that the Bible does not necessarily contain an immediate answer to each and every problem. Without saying as much in so many words, fundamentalism actually invites people to a kind of intellectual suicide. It injects into life a false certitude" for it unwittingly confuses the divine substance of the biblical message with what are in fact its human limitations." (from the Pontifical Report as reprinted in "Bible Review", October, 1994)

(5.) *The Origin of Modern Fundamentalism*

Modern Fundamentalism began as a movement in North American Protestantism, specifically conservative Presbyterian academics and theologians at Princeton Theological Seminary, in the early part of the 20th century, that arose in reaction to modernism. Their reaction was against the "higher criticism" of historical-critical biblical interpretation and the Darwinian challenge to the Biblical story of the Creation.

This Modern Fundamentalism listed among the things it considered inimical to "Fundamentalist Faith"; Roman Catholicism, Socialism, modern philosophy, atheism, Christian Science, Mormonism, Spiritualism, Darwinism, and "liberal theology", all of which appeared to them to undermine the Bible's authority.

Modern Fundamentalism holds as essential to Christian faith five fundamental doctrines:

1. The literal inerrancy of the Bible

2. The Virgin birth.

3. The physical Resurrection of Jesus

4. Atonement by the sacrificial death of Christ, and

5. The Second Coming of Christ.

The concept of Modern Fundamentalism has since spread to other religions, typically as "anti-historical", opposed in principle to the application of historical or textual criticism of religion. So there are now Fundamentalists in most Christian sects, Islam, Buddhism, Hinduism, etc.

Modern Fundamentalists generally feel alienated in modern society, oppressed by the cultural hegemony of secular values, and they feel their very existence and personal autonomy is continuously subject to the gravest challenges. One of the results of this sense of being threatened is a propensity to violence, or at least suppression of contrary opinion.

This sense of conflict is usually incomprehensible to other moderns who are at ease with modern secularism and who are not necessarily un-religious, but are comfortable with the modern privatization of religion.

(6.) Christian Nationalism

One chilling example of Fundamentalist Christianity in action is "Christian Nationalism" as practiced currently in America. Christian Nationalists are extreme right-wing "Christians" who argue that the Constitution does not require the separation of church and state and that the best future course for America is a Christian theocracy. As described in Michelle Goldberg's "Kingdom Coming: The Rise of Christian Nationalism" these true believers live in a "parallel universe" where they have created their "own reality" which they have used successfully to virtually take over the Republican Party. Operating from this "base" and with the eager cooperation of the existing administration and many Republican Congressmen, they have set the legislative agenda, infiltrated many government agencies, obtained huge grants of Federal tax money for their use, influenced foreign policy, environmental policy and the selection of Supreme Court and lower court judges, and purport to accept or reject Republican nominees for the next presidency. They have become a powerful force in American politics. They are, to me, a very dark side of religion.

One of the profound ironies of the right -wing "Christian" churches' position against the separation of church and state is that their position is the opposite of the founder of the Baptist Church in America, Roger Williams (1603 - 1683). Williams was a Puritan in England, persecuted by the Church of England, and emigrated to America seeking freedom of religious worship. He was a Cambridge educated man schooled in theology and also an accomplished linguist. He became disenchanted by the ruling American Puritans, partly because they took Indian land without purchasing it, and partly because they asserted control over civil law to enforce Puritan doctrine. It was Williams who first wrote the phrase "a wall of separation between church and state" in his argument that the Puritans should not create a theocracy. This same phrase was repeated by Thomas Jefferson in support of the First Amendment proscription against the "establishment of religion". After Williams was banished from Massachusetts he settled in providence, Rhode Island and founded the Baptist Church.

See also the following books: "American Theocracy: the Peril and Politics of Radical Religion, Oil and Borrowed Money in the 21st Century" by Kevin Phillips; "Conservatives Without Conscience" by John Dean; "The Baptizing of America: The Religious Right's Plans for the Rest of

Us" by Rabbi James Rudin; "American Fascists: The Christian Right and the War on America" by Chris Hedges; "The Assault on Reason" by Al Gore; "The Myth of a Christian Nation: How the Quest for Political Power is Destroying the Church", by Gregory Boyd; "Why the Christian Right is Wrong: A Minister's Manifesto for Taking Back Your Faith, Your Flag, Your Future", by Robin Meyers; and "God's Politics: and Why the Right Gets it Wrong and the left Doesn't Get It", by Jim Wallis. Each of these books describes the threat of right-wing fundamentalist "Christians" to the Christian Church and to our American democracy.

In spite of the Roman Catholic Church's rule for Historical-Critical Biblical interpretation, and its condemnation of Fundamentalism as "intellectual suicide", it continues to state publicly that it is "the only true religion" because it alone can confer "true salvation through the apostolic succession." It also maintains its theological positions on the Trinity, the actuality of the Eucharist, the absolute prohibition of abortion, the celibacy of priests, the refusal to ordain nuns, prohibition of artificial birth controls, and the condemnation of homosexuality as a sin. These positions are also contrary to the beliefs and practices of a majority of American and European Roman Catholics. So, the Roman Catholic Church is struggling with what appears to be enormous self-contradictions in theology and in practice. Hopefully these self-contradictions will somehow be resolved to enable the Church to continue and increase its many good works.

FROM THE CHRISTIAN REFORMATION TO HUMANISM, COMPARED TO ISLAM

While many people believe that the Christian Reformation began with Martin Luther's nailing his "Ninety-Five Theses" to the church door at Wittenberg in 1517 in revolt against the Indulgences exacted by the corrupt medieval church, the actual Reformation began much earlier. (Thanks to my good friend Dick Higgins who passed on to me the course outline of Professor Andrew C. Fix's course on the Reformation at Roosevelt University, I will repeat parts of his excellent outline here to make the connection between Christianity and Humanism)

The prelude to the Reformation began in the 14th and 15th centuries when the royal and popular grievances against the church became significant. The French King Philip IV imprisoned Pope Boniface VII and then secured the election of his own Pope and moved him from Rome to Avignon, France. Thus began a Papal Schism, which lasted until 1415. The issues were moral, financial and spiritual and generated an upsurge in mystical piety, one of the most outspoken being Meister Johannes Eckhart (1260 -1327). The essence of Elkhart's teaching was that each individual could communicate directly with God, thereby threatening the priestly system of the organized church.

a. Wycliffe, Hus, Petrarch, Erasmus, Selestat, Luther, Calvin, Servetus
Another of the most outspoken reformers was John Wycliffe (1320 - 1384), an English priest educated at Oxford and a prolific writer. The explosive nature of his writings almost severed Britain from the Roman Church 155 years before Henry VIII and anticipated all the reform ideas of John Huss (1369 -1415) and Martin Luther (1483 - 1546). Wycliffe spoke out against the priesthood, indulgences, the Trinity, transubstantiation, and the Church's wealth. Wycliffe also made the first translation of the New Testament

into English in 1381. His students then translated the Old Testament into English after Wickliffe's death and thereby made the whole Bible available to the English free of priestly interpretation.

Jan Hus (1370 - 1415) was one of Wycliffe's students who carried on Wycliffe's teachings when he returned to his native Bohemia. He became a famous preacher and professor at the University of Prague. Hus was equally critical of the Church, calling Pope John XXIII the "Antichrist", which got him excommunicated and ultimately tried for heresy. Although he sought a reconciliation he refused to recant his charges and was burned at the stake in 1415.

Queen Isabella of Spain (1451- 1501) reformed the Church of Spain, bringing in scholars, introducing printing presses and producing and publishing a great multilingual edition of the Bible in 1520. But her reform was of form and not of tolerance - she and her husband Ferdinand took control of the Inquisition in Spain and forced the conversion of Jews and Muslims to Christianity. Over 200,000 Jews left, some of whom went to the Netherlands as "Sephardic" Jews, such as the family of Spinoza.

(For an excellent new book about Spinoza please see "Betraying Spinoza", by Rebecca Goldstein, Schocken Books, 2006)

"The Renaissance started in Italy with the vision of renewing society by returning to the golden age of antiquity: to make a clean break with the corrupt and depressing Middle Ages. The Renaissance fathered modern Humanism. Humanism shifted the focus of attention from God and the church to mankind. It stressed liberal arts education and devotion to the classics. It championed fresh ideas for education, rhetoric, history and a love for the classics." "The spread of Humanism to Northern Europe was a major influence on the intellectual climate of the times and rise of anti-clericalism. (extensive quotes below from Professor Andrew C. Fix's course at Roosevelt University)

"Petrarch (1304 - 1375) was a significant author and founder of the Literary Humanism, a branch concerned with ethics. He relied on classical Latin writings, not just Scriptures to teach moral lessons. He rejected the abstract nature of scholasticism and divided history into three periods: antiquity, Middle Ages, and the present. His principle thesis was that the proper study of man was man; the body, the mind and creativity. Humanism spread from Italy and Petrarch's teachings to Northern Europe, particularly Germany. Humanism was very concerned for church reform long before the Reformation. Humanists were sometimes called Christian Humanists, seeking a reform of the church to an earlier less corrupted time. The invention of movable type made the spread of knowledge and Humanism much more rapid. King Francis I was a patron of French Humanism.

Erasmus of Rotterdam (1469 -1536), was the principle advocate of Christian Humanism. He was, first of all, a great scholar, and an excellent, prolific writer. He was ordained as priest at an Augustinian monastery in 1492, but his extensive readings threatened the church's basic doctrines of Trinity and transubstantiation, leaving him however with a profound admiration for the ethics of Christ. He traveled extensively, to England in 1499, Paris in 1500, England again in 1505-6, Italy 1506 and again in 1509. He returned to England for five years in 1509 as a guest of Henry VIII and Thomas More. His "Praise of Folly" was written in seven days in England. It was published in Paris in 1511 and enjoyed forty editions and a dozen translations.

Erasmus left England for Basel with the manuscript of his most important work, a critical revision of the Greek text of the New Testament, with a Latin translation. This work, the first application of Humanistic learning to the early literature of Christianity, was published in 1516. He called into question one after another of the Christian usages of his time - indulgences, fasting, pilgrimages, auricular confession, monasticism, clerical celibacy, relic worship, prayers to the saints and the burning of heretics. He dreamed of replacing theology with "The philosophy of Christ". Erasmus was the greatest of the Northern Humanists.

Josie and I ran across Erasmus's trail when we visited the beautiful town of Selestat, in Alsace, France. There is a library there, "The Bibliotheque Humaniste", containing the magnificent collection of medieval books acquired by Beatus Rhenanus, a Humanist and great friend of Erasmus, who visited Selestat frequently. Very much worth a visit.

(For perhaps best story of the Renaissance and the Reformation, as well as most of human history, please see "The Story of Civilization", Volume V: "The Renaissance", and Volume VI: "The Reformation", by Will Durant (Simon and Schuster, 1953, 1957)

The Reformations in Germany and Switzerland were energetic and turned to violence. Martin Luther (1483 - 1546) was a very bright and energetic young man whose father was a strict, stern and harsh man. Martin's education as an Augustinian priest, and as Doctor of Divinity at the University of Wittenberg led him to act out his reaction against his father and the Church's unjust exercise of authority in very public and combative ways. The Church's persistence in aggressively selling indulgences through Johannes Tetzel, precipitated Luther's most well known protest. He posted his famous Ninety-Five Theses on the door of the church in Wittenberg in 1517 hoping to help make the church better, but the Pope's response was immediate and hostile.

After much conflict, involving the Augustinians, Frederick the Wise, Charles V, the German Nobility, and the "infallibility" of the Pope, Luther was excommunicated from the Church. Luther's response was to burn the bull of excommunication.

Luther continued his protests, rejecting virtually all the practices of Roman Catholicism, and eventually translating the Bible into vernacular German to make it available to all who could read. When the German peasants read Luther's revolutionary religious ideas they transformed them into a doctrine of social revolution and a massive Peasant Revolt broke out in Germany in 1525. Luther sided with the German nobility to stop the revolt which they did with brutal means, killing 100,000 peasants and one of the leaders, Thomas Muntzer, a Lutheran activist. Luther then turned to converting the German princes persuading them to convert the people by government decree, known as the Magisterial Reformation.

Lutheranism became a political movement and Lutheran churches became state churches. The German nation was divided between Lutheranism, adopted in the Northern German States, and Catholicism in the Southern States. Luther died in 1546, and the new Emperor, Ferdinand I, reversing Charles V's policy of toleration, oversaw the Thirty Year War between Protestants and Catholics as Protestantism continued to spread into new areas like Austria.

Ulrich Zwingli (1484 - 1531) was a Swiss philosophy student in Vienna and Basel and became a Catholic priest. He became an avid reader of Erasmus's books and his then new edition of the Greek New Testament, beginning his slow conversion to Protestantism. He also read Luther's writings, but he was more heavily influenced by the Humanistic ideas of Erasmus. He converted the Zurich city council to his Protestant views, seized all church property and set up a municipally controlled church. After Zurich was converted, other cities, like Bern, converted to Zwinglianism. Soon Switzerland was split between Catholic and Zwinglian churches. Failing to work out a compromise with Luther, Zwingli provoked a war with the Catholic alliance by imposing an economic blockage of Catholic cities. He personally led the Protestant forces into battle and was killed at the Battle of Kappel. The Catholics quartered his body and burned it on a pile of excrement. Luther, who viewed Zwingli as a rival, called his ghastly death "a triumph for us".

One terrible stain on the record of the Reformation was the virulent anti-Semitism of Martin Luther. He reiterated it until his dying days and only tempered his hatred and slander of the Jews by holding out hope that they might convert to Christianity. Unfortunately Luther's hateful anti-Semitism survived in the German culture long enough to become adopted and promulgated by the Nazis (and even a few leaders of the 20th century German Lutheran church) as a religious foundation for the monumental Nazi crime of the Holocaust.

The modern Lutheran church officially abhors and rejects Luther's anti-Semitic ravings, but still tries to temper its historical significance by speaking of Luther's hope for Jewish conversion to Christianity - the ultimate condescension!

Jean Calvin (1509 - 1564) was the son of a priest who studied law at the universities of Paris, Orleans and Bourges and entered a Humanist school in Paris started by Bude. This study caused Calvin to slowly convert to Protestantism. When his feelings became known he was forced to flee France and he went to Strasbourg and then Basel, where he wrote his own systematic theology, the "Institutes of the Christian Religion".

Calvin then set up his idea of civic reform into a theocratic Christian community in Geneva, Switzerland. Many people objected to his strict supervision of their lives and he was exiled in 1538. But in 1541 the Geneva city council recalled Calvin and he agreed to come on his own terms. Calvin ruled Geneva in a totalitarian manner. In effect it became a police state, making no distinction between religious and secular matters. They could summon anyone for questioning about anything, enter homes unannounced, specify the number of dishes to be served at a meal, and even dictate the color of garments to be worn. In Calvin's Orwellian theocracy, established in 1542,"acts of God" - earthquakes, lightning, flooding - were acts of Satan. Copernicus was branded a fraud, attendance at church was compulsory and refusal to take Eucharist was a crime. Abortion was not a political issue because any single woman discovered with child was drowned. Calvin's stepson was found in bed with another woman and both were executed. His daughter-in-law was found with another man and they were both executed. A man accused of putting up a poster accusing him of "Gross Hypocrisy" was tortured until he confessed, without any other evidence his feet were nailed to a stake and he was ultimately decapitated.

In 1553 Calvin arrested Michael Servetus, a renowned Unitarian and medical doctor, while he was worshiping in a Geneva church, tried him for blasphemy for denying the Trinity, and had him burned at the stake as a heretic. In his last nine years in Geneva he had no opposition. He believed that the church should guide and direct the state because "all power and authority is in the hands of God."

Calvin and Luther were not reformers, they were reactionaries. Their intolerant dogmatism, their predestination theology, their indifference to secular learning, their renewed emphasis of demons and hell, their concentration on personal salvation in a life beyond the grave- all these alienated the Humanist from the Reformation. Protestantism, as the Humanists saw it, was treason to the Renaissance, and was restoring all the supernaturalism, irrationalism, and diabolism that had darkened the medieval mind, a re-subjection of the emancipated mind to the primitive myths of the populace.

b. The Radical Reformation
"A number of radical reformers thought that Luther and Zwingli had not gone far enough . There were three branches of the radical reformation: the Anabaptist, the Radical Spiritualist, and the Evangelical Rationalists. Of the three the Anabaptists were the largest and most radical.

The Anabaptists
The Anabaptist sect began in Zwingli's Zurich church in 1523. They initially called themselves the "Brethren" and were influenced by the Humanist's call for a return to the apostolic church. They wanted to eradicate Catholicism "root and branch". They called for a perfect restitution of the first church as the Bible described it. Nothing not in the Bible could be a part of the restored church. They rejected infant baptism because in their view baptism was a sign of one's acceptance of the principles and ideas of the church and only conscious rational adults could understand and accept such principles. They held that pacifism is an essential element of Christianity. They refused service in the military. They refused to pay taxes. They refused to swear oaths, rejected the clergy and church ceremony.

They believed in a purely personal, inward, spiritual and individual faith, with little or no stress on doctrine or theology. They were egalitarians; women had the same rights as men. The Sermon on the Mount must be obeyed literally.

Their enemies called them Anabaptists, meaning "rebaptisers". Because of their radical beliefs, the Anabaptists were hated by all major religions: Catholic, Lutherans and Zwinglians alike. They were also considered subversives by most states and rulers. In 1526 Zurich issued a decree condemning all Anabaptists to execution. With cruel irony, many Anabaptists were drowned. They then began to leave the city and spread their message all over Europe. They became known as the Moravian Brethren after their founder Balthasar Hubmaier in Moravia and the Hutterites, after Jakob Hutter, in Moravia. Both Hubmaier and Hutter were arrested, tortured and executed, as was Michael Sattler who was burned at the stake. In 1534 Jan Matthys led a band of followers to Munster, Germany, took over the government, which called itself "The Anabaptist Kingdom of Munster" introducing polygamy and a communistic sharing of all property. The Catholic Bishop fled, organized an army, returned and besieged the city. Matthys and all his Anabaptist followers were arrested and executed.

Menno Simons hid in the Netherlands and led a large group, which practiced strict pacifism and succeeded in living in peace in Dutch communalities. They eventually became accepted as the Mennonites. The Amish sect broke off from the Mennonites. Both sects, together with the Hutterites, immigrated in large numbers to America and Canada where they thrive to this day.

The Radical Spiritualists
The Radical Spiritualists took the Protestant emphasis of individual religion to the extreme. They rejected all aspects of the religion that they felt were "external", meaning: No clergy, no ceremonies, no sacraments, no church institutions and no organized religion. They also rejected the central Protestant belief that the Bible was the source of religious truth: the Bible, too, was "external." True religion survived only in the truly inspired individual. The collection of these inspired individuals was called the "invisible church" by the Spiritualists, who were mostly the highly educated members of the middle or even upper class.

Among these Spiritualists were Kaspar von Schwenkenfeld (1489-1561), Sebastian Franck (1499-1542), Thomas Muntzer (1489-1525), Jacob Boelune (1575-1624) and George Fox (1624-1691). George Fox is best known as the founder of the Society of Friends, the "Quakers" who were joined by William Penn, the founder of Pennsylvania. (please see my book "Serendipity" which describes the Quakers and the founding of Pennsylvania, as well as the Anabaptists)

Evangelical Rationalists
The Evangelical Rationalists were Humanistic biblical scholars who used reason to interpret Scripture and, thus, rejected many fundamental Christian beliefs. This was not an organized group, but an isolated collection of individual scholars. While persecuted, the Evangelical Rationalists eventually grew into the Unitarian movement. They found the doctrine of the Trinity in partic-

ular to lack biblical foundation and to be absurd. They were, thus, anti-Trinitarians.

Among these Evangelical Rationalists were Laelius Socinus (1525-1562), and Michael Servetus (1511-1553) one of the better-known anti-Trinitarians. Born in Spain he studied law and medicine and traveled widely in Europe. In his biblical studies he came to see Christ as a historical person who was not divine. He rejected the Trinity as an absurd philosophical doctrine unrelated to living faith in his book "On the Errors of the Trinity". He was also a renowned physician who discovered and was the first to accurately describe the pulmonary circulatory system. His religious teachings contradicted John Calvin who personally had him arrested while he was attending church in Geneva, Switzerland where he was tried and convicted of blasphemy and burned at the stake in 1553.

Another Spiritualist, Francis David (1510-1572) was also a Unitarian who had converted from Catholicism to Lutheranism to Calvinism and finally to Unitarianism because he could find no biblical basis for the doctrine of the Trinity. He converted the King of Transylvania, John Sigismund, to Unitarianism, and was appointed minister to the royal court. King Sigismund issued the Edict of Toleration, which was the first in the history of Europe, protecting the right of all Christian churches to co-exist in peace. Francis David was arrested by a subsequent Catholic King and died in prison. Such was the birth of the Unitarian-Universalists who continue to exist and thrive, albeit in small numbers.

c. The Christian Counter-Reformation

The Church, feeling threatened by the Reformation, reacted by condemning many Reformation publications via its "Codex" and denying the truth of many scientific discoveries that appeared to contradict its Aristotelian based view of the natural world. This conflict continued until recent times when the Roman Catholic Church has at long last made peace with the scientific community. Unfortunately the "Counter-Reformation" continues as an expression of Christian Fundamentalism, which resists the teachings of science such as Evolution, etc. The reaction of Fundamentalists against modernity, clinging to a literalist interpretation of the Bible will probably always persist so long as there are people who are made insecure by the uncertain nature of science and are attracted to the apparent "certainty" of Fundamentalism.

One of the most profound effects of the Reformation and Humanism was the proliferation of various Protestant sects and the ultimate separation of Church and State. One dominant religious institution made unity with the state relatively easy, but it became impossible with many competing institutions. The ultimate expression of this separation occurred in America where the First Amendment to the Constitution prohibits the "establishment" of any religion by the state. Present-day Fundamentalists are trying to re-combine the state and religion, but have so far met with mostly successful resistance. Curiously, in countries where religion is still supported by the state, such as Germany and England, the private practice of religion has all but disappeared, while in America, where the church and state are separate, the private practice of religion is thriving! The unity of the state with religion is apparently bad for both the state and religion.

d. The Struggle for Reformation in Islam

The major divisions within Islam, Sunni and Shiite, have never undergone a reformation similar to Christianity. Over 85% of the 1.3 billion believers in Islam are Sunni with the remaining 15% concentrated mainly in Iran and Iraq. Most Sunnis and Shiites profess belief in the literal truth of Qur'an and so must be classified as Fundamentalists. This creates the possibility for extreme violence, which continues until the present in the Middle East.

Only one very small minority Islamic sect, the Ismaelis, created circa 1,000 CE, interprets the Qur'an as written by men and subject to rational, historical-critical understanding. The Ismaeli sect is very small, numbering just a few million, and very private, engaging mostly in doing good works such as building hospitals and schools. The inherited leader of the Ismaelis is the Agha Kahn who spreads his vast wealth around in many charitable works among Islamic countries. Another religious sect, which derived from Islam, the Bahai's, which professes a pan-religion belief, has been fiercely persecuted within Islam, and exists also as a very small group in various Western countries.

So, for all practical purposes, Islam has never undergone a Reformation and continues to function as it has since its founding in circa 600 CE as a Fundamentalist religion, which also sees itself as its own government, prescribing both the Shariah system of law and the personal behavior of its believers and their families.

One hopeful sign of possible long-term reformation of Islam is the present King Abdullah's personal commitment of $10 Billion to create a secular Science and Technology University in Saudi Arabia, free of any government or religious control, and open to men and women on a nondiscriminatory basis. This project is in fact already begun at on the shores of the Red Sea, but at some distance from existing Islamic cities. However, since it will be physically isolated and focused mainly on technical subjects it is not likely to be a center for Islamic cultural reformation.

HUMANISM

a. Humanism

Humanism is a broad category of ethical philosophies, generally affirming the dignity and worth of all people, based on the ability to determine right and wrong by appeal to universal human qualities - particularly rationalism. Typically, humanism rejects supernatural belief, although some forms of Christian "religious humanism" continue affiliation with Christian dogma. Humanistic Judaism, however, is more akin to "secular humanism" following Jewish traditions, but rejecting its supernatural theology. A number of religious humanists feel that secular humanism is too coldly logical and rejects the full emotional experience that makes humans human. (See Greg Epstein, Humanist Chaplain at Harvard, discussed later in this essay). From this comes the notion that secular humanism is inadequate in meeting the human need for a socially fulfilling philosophy of life. Disagreements over things of this nature have resulted in friction between secular and religious humanists, despite their similarities.

Some critics of secular humanism claim that it offers no eternal truths or a relationship with the divine. They comment that a philosophy without these beliefs leaves humanity adrift in a sea of "post-modern" cynicism. Humanists respond that such criticisms fail to look at the actual content of humanist philosophy, which, far from being cynical and post-modern, is rooted in optimistic, idealistic attitudes that trace back to the Enlightenment, the Renaissance, the pre-Socratic Greek philosophers, Buddhism and Chinese Confucianism.

Secular humanism has appeal to atheists, agnostics, freethinkers, rationalists, skeptics and materialists, as well as to some Buddhists, Hindus and Confucians. Christian fundamentalist opponents of humanism typically use the term "secular humanism" pejoratively to mean atheism or secularism or to lump together all monotheistic varieties of humanism. Humanists object to such usage, finding it misleading or overly broad. Thus, modern humanism can be said to be of two categories, religious and secular. Secular humanism rejects theistic and supernatural belief and is mostly associated with scientists and academics. Religious humanism is associated in America with Unitarian Universalism, liberal Christians, Humanistic Judaism, the Ethical Culture movement, and scholars in the liberal arts. In addition, many Dharmic religions like Hinduism, Buddhism, Taoism and other Asian belief systems like Confucianism have always been primarily humanistic. Christian Existential Humanism, based on the work of Soren Kierkegaard, features a humanistic perspective grounded in Christian religious belief. The radical theology of Rev. Don Cupitt, discussed later in this book, rejecting the supernatural, but staying within the boundaries of Christianity, is a form of religious humanism.

In short, you don't have to be a formal "Humanist" to be a religious humanist. To many religious people humanism provides a natural bridge between religion and science.

b. The Greeks, Indians and Chinese Philosophical Materialism

(1.) Modern Humanism traces its most ancient origins to 5th and 6th century Greek, Indian and Chinese philosophers. Each group developed its own form of "atomism". Philosophical Materialism coincided with the "Axial Age" (600 BCE - 200 BCE.) during which the world's great religions were conceived. In philosophy materialism is that form of physicalism, which holds that the only thing that can truly be said to exist is matter; that fundamentally, all things are composed of material and all phenomena are the result of material interactions; that matter is the only substance. It stands in sharp contrast to dualism or idealism and religions, which include the supernatural.

Philosophical Materialism is the oldest philosophical tradition in Western civilization. Originated in the West by a series of skeptical pre-Socratic Greek philosophers ; Thales of Miletus, Xenophobes of Colophon, Anaxagoras – "the first freethinker", Protegra's and Leukippos (450 - 420 BCE), it reached its full classical form in the "atomism" of Democritus and Epicurus in the 4th century BCE. Thucydides, "the first historian", was also a freethinker who espoused a scientific and rational approach to the study of history. None of these philosophers was actually a scientist in the modern sense of the word. They did not base their findings upon empirical evidence. They were, however, incredibly creative and imaginative thinkers trying their best to describe the world they observed.

(1.) Epicurus, Philosophical Materialism

Epicurus ((341 BCE - 270 BCE) was the founder of Epicureanism, a popular school of thought in Hellenistic Philosophy that spanned about 600 years. For Epicurus the purpose of philosophy was to obtain a happy, tranquil life, characterized by the absence of pain and fear, and by living a self-sufficient life surrounded by friends. He taught that pleasure and pain are the measures of what is good and bad, that death is the end of the body and soul and should therefore not be feared, that the gods do not reward or punish humans, that the universe is infinite and eternal, and that events in the world are ultimately based on the motions and interactions of atoms moving in empty space. Epicurus was often vilified as favoring the uninhibited pursuit of pleasure (hedonism); however, he invariably counseled restraint and temperance with respect to physical desires.

In many ways Epicurus was similar to Buddha whose "middle way" to gain enlightenment counseled a moderate, unselfish, peaceful and constructive way of life. Buddhism also did not recognize any gods and counseled people to rely on themselves to achieve enlightenment.

Epicurus' school, "The Garden", was located near Plato's "Academe" and lasted strongly through the later Roman Empire. In Rome, Lucretius (99 BCE - 55 B.C.) was the school's greatest proponent, composing "On the Nature of Things", an epic poem, in six books, designed to recruit new members. Lucretius did not believe in any kind of life after death or in any divinity concerned with man's welfare. The main purpose of the poem was to free men's minds of superstitious fear of gods and death.

After the official approval of Christianity by Emperor Constantine, Epicureanism was repressed. Epicurus' materialist theories that the gods were physical beings composed of atoms who were unconcerned with human affairs and had not created the universe, and the non-dualist idea that the human soul was mortal, were essentially irreconcilable with Christian teachings. The school then endured a long period of obscurity and decline until the 16th century during the Renaissance when the works of Lucretius were being printed in Europe. In the 17th century the French Franciscan priest, scientist and philosopher Pierre Gassendi wrote two books forcefully reviving Lucretius and Epicureanism. Influenced by Gassendi, Walter Charleton published several works on Epicureanism in English. Attacks by Christians continued, most forcefully by the Cambridge Platonists. In the following times there was a resurgence of Epicurean philosophy: in the Modern

Age, scientists adopted atomist theories, while materialist philosophers embraced Epicurus' ethics and restated his objections to natural theology.

(2.) *Socrates, Plato, Aristotle and Protagorus*

Although Christianity adopted Aristotle's static view of science, complete with its earth centered universe and its non-evolving catalog of living things, and also adopted Platonic "idealism", rejecting Philosophic Materialism, Socrates (470 - 399 BCE), Plato (428-348 BCE), Aristotle (384- 322 BCE) and Protagorus (480 -410 BCE) certainly advanced human thinking in extraordinary ways, ultimately adding to the base for modern Humanism. Their wisdom is also incredibly instructive for our present day lives. They also, however, made elaborate justification of the "soul", later adopted by Christianity.

Will Durant's "Story of Philosophy" includes the following summary of Plato's comments on what he calls the "keystone of the arch of Plato's thought":

"Justice would be a simple matter, says Plato, if men were simple; an anarchist communism would suffice. But men are not simple, because of greed and luxury. Men are not content with a simple life: they are acquisitive, ambitious, competitive, and jealous; they soon tire of what they have, and pine for what they have not; and they seldom desire anything unless it belongs to others. The result is the encroachment of one group upon the territory of another, the rivalry of groups for the resources of the soil, and then war. Trade and finance develop, and bring new class divisions. "

"Any ordinary city is in fact two cities, one the city of the poor, the other of the rich, each at war with the other; and in either division there are smaller ones - you would make a great mistake if you treated them as single states."

"A mercantile bourgeoisie arises, whose members seek social position through wealth and conspicuous consumption: "they will spend large sums of money on their wives." These changes in the distribution of wealth produce political changes: as the wealth of the merchant over-reaches that of the land owner, aristocracy gives way to a plutocratic oligarchy - wealthy traders and bankers rule the state. Then statesmanship, which is the coordination of social forces and the adjustment of policy to growth, is replaced by politics, which is the strategy of party and the lust for the spoils of office." (In present day America the so-called "political contribution" has become a blatant system of massive legal bribery.)

"Every form of government tends to perish by excess of its basic principle. Aristocracy ruins itself by limiting too narrowly the circle within which power is confined: oligarchy ruins itself by the incautious scramble for immediate wealth. (Or, as Aristotle said in his "Politics", "Oligarchy is when men of property have the government in their hands.") In either case the end is revolution. When revolution comes it may seem to arise from little causes and petty whims; but though it may spring from slight occasions, it is the precipitate result of grave and accumulated wrongs; when a body is weakened by neglected ills, the merest exposure may bring serious disease. Then democracy comes; the poor overcome their opponents, slaughtering some and banishing the rest; and give to the people an equal share of freedom and power."

"But even democracy ruins itself by excess -- of democracy. Its basic principle is the equal right of all to hold office and determine public policy. This is at first glance a delightful arrangement; it becomes disastrous because the people are not properly equipped by education to select the best rulers and wisest courses. "As to the people, they have no understanding, and only repeat what their rulers are pleased to tell them. " (Protagorus, who also said, "Man is the measure of all things: of things which are, that they are, and of things which are not, that they are not.")"

"Mob rule is a rough sea for the ship of state to ride: every wind of oratory stirs up the waters and deflects the course. The upshot of such a democracy is tyranny or autocracy; the crowd so loves flattery, it is so "hungry for honey", that at lasts the wiliest and most unscrupulous flatterer, calling himself the "protector of the people" rises to supreme power." (Consider the history of Rome)

"The more Plato thinks of it, the more astounded he is at the folly of leaving to mob caprice and gullibility the selection of political officials -- not to speak of leaving it to those shady and wealth-serving strategists who pull the oligarchic wires behind the democratic stage."

"But behind these political problems lies the nature of man; to understand politics, we must, unfortunately, understand psychology. "Like man, like state". -"governments vary as the characters of men vary; states are made out of the human natures which are in them" . -the state is what it is because its citizens are what they are. Therefore, we need not expect to have better states until we have better men; till then all changes will leave every essential thing unchanged. "How charming people are! - always doctoring, increasing and complicating their disorders, fancying they will be cured by some nostrum which somebody advises them to try, never getting better, but always growing worse …. Are they not as good as a play, trying their hand at legislation, and imagining that by reforms they will make an end to the dishonesties and rascalities of mankind - not knowing that in reality they are cutting away at the heads of a hydra?"

"Let us examine for a moment the human material with which political philosophy must deal.

"Human behavior, says Plato, flows from three main sources: desire, emotion, and knowledge. Desire, appetite, impulse, instinct - these are one; spirit, ambition, courage -- these are one; knowledge, thought, intellect, reason -- these are one. Desire has its seat in the loins; it is a bursting reservoir of energy fundamentally sexual. Emotion has its seat in the heart, in the flow and force of the blood; it is the organic resonance of experience and desire. Knowledge has its seat in the head;it is the eye of desire, and can become the pilot of the soul.

"These powers and qualities are all in all men, but in diverse degrees. Some men are but the embodiment of desire; restless and acquisitive souls, who are absorbed in material quests and quarrels, who burn with lust of luxuries and show, and who rate their gains always as naught compared with their ever-receding goals: these are the men who dominate and manipulate industry."

(Author's note - "It's not how much I have, it's how much more is out there"; famously said by Peter G. Peterson, (nee Petropolis), a contemporary and very rich Greek-American, born in 1926 of successful Greek immigrant parents. Once CEO of Bell & Howell Co., Peterson is now the retired Chairman and co-founder of Blackstone, one of the world's largest equity investment funds.)

Plato continues, "But there are others who are temples of feeling and courage, who care not so much what they fight for, as for victory "in and of itself"; they are pugnacious rather than acquisitive; their pride is in power rather than possession, their joy is on the battle-field rather than in the mart: these are the men who make the armies and navies of the world. "

"And last are the few whose delight is in meditation and understanding; who yearn not for goods, nor for victory, but for knowledge; who leave both market and battlefield to lose themselves in the quiet clarity of secluded thought; whose will is a light rather than a fire, whose haven is not power but truth: these are the men of wisdom, who stand aside unused by the world. "

"Unguided by knowledge, the people are a multitude without order, like desires in disarray; the people need the guidance of philosophers as desires need the enlightenment of knowledge. Ruin comes when the trader, whose heart is lifted up by wealth, becomes ruler; or when the general uses his army to establish a military dictatorship. The producer is at his best in the economic field, the warrior is at his best in battle; they are both at their worst in public office; and in their crude hands politics submerges statesmanship. For statesmanship is a science and an art; one must have lived for it and been long prepared. Only a philosopher-king is fit to guide a nation"… "Until philosophers are kings, or the kings and princes of this world have the spirit and power of philosophy, and wisdom and political leadership meet in the same man, cities will never cease from ill, nor the human race."

(3.) *The Italian Renaissance*
The European Renaissance began in Tuscany, centered in the cities of Florence and Siena, and later affecting Venice and Rome. It was truly the beginning of great cultural change, marking the transition between Medieval and Early Modern Europe. Dante Alighieri (1265-1321) predates, but informs the Renaissance. Francesco Petrarch (1304-1374), was a scholar, poet and early Renaissance Humanist, often called "The Father of Humanism". Giovanni Boccaccio (1313-1375) was a friend and correspondent of Petrarch and an important Humanist in his own right. His writings, particularly his poetry and

"The Decameron" had profound influence on subsequent generations of writers, such as Chaucer and Shakespeare. Nicola Machiavelli (1459-1527), a diplomat, political philosopher and the author of "The Prince", is still referred to for political advice today.

"These men, and others, represented a new method of scholarship, Renaissance Humanism, an optimistic philosophy that saw man as a rational and sentient being, with the ability to decide and think for himself. This was an implicit rejection of the Roman Catholic Church's vision of souls as the only absolute reality - then seen as mystical and imaginary. Humanism saw man as inherently good by nature, which was in tension with the Christian view of man as the original sinner needing redemption. It provoked fresh insight into the nature of reality, questioning beyond God and spirituality, and provided for knowledge about history beyond Christian history." (Wikepedia)

Northern Italy was also undergoing fundamental transitions in its culture. The plague reduced its population by one-third to one-half, thus raising the value of labor. The failure of the church to deal with the plague reduced its influence, and the business genius of the Italian merchants to develop new forms of finance and trade significantly enhanced their power. Simultaneously the Christian nations' successful overthrow of the Muslim occupations opened the door to the Greek and Roman writings, science and art objects preserved and developed by the Muslims. Thus, the northern Italian merchants and scholars were put in touch with pre-Christian Greek and Roman Classical antiquities.

The arts, in particular flourished. Painting, sculpture, architecture and the crafts were explored and developed into expressions of the new Humanist perspective. Giorgio Vasari (1511-1574), himself a famous painter and architect, wrote the story of these developments by publishing his "The Lives of the Artists" in 1550 and 1568. Vasari's dedication of these volumes to the Grand Duke Cosimo de'Medici was apt, "The example of so many able men and all the various details of all kinds collected by my labors in this book will be no little help to practicing artists as well as pleasing to all those who follow and delight in the arts." Vasari wrote over 200 short biographies of these artists, arranged in chronological order. Some of the most able and presently well-known are: Cimabue, Duccio, Ghiberti, Pisano, Luca della Robbia, Masaccio, Donatello, Giotto Uccello, Brunelleschi, Michelozzo, Alberti, Botticelli, Carpaccio, Peiro della Francesca Filippo Lippi, Verrocchio, Giusto

de'Menabuoi, Fra Angelico, Bellini, Mantegna, Signorelli, Leonardo da Vinci, Raphael, Titian, Giorgione, Giulio Romano, Correggio, Michelangelo and Tintoretto. Most of these men were polymath artists, accomplished as painters, sculptors and architects. The Italian Renaissance of the arts was an extraordinary explosion of creative energy and skill. It is well worth serious study, but it is too vast a subject to do more than mention in this book.

(4.) Hobbes, Locke, the Enlightenment and the Great Separation
Thomas Hobbes (1588-1679) was perhaps the most complete philosophical materialist of the 17th century.

He rejected Cartesian dualism and Aristotelian and scholastic philosophy in favor of the "new" philosophy of Galileo and Gassendi. His most famous work, "The Leviathan" states, "The universe is corporeal; all that is real is material, and what is not material is not real." During his full life his patron was the Earl of Devonshire; he met several times with Francis Bacon, translated Thucydides from the original Greek into English, became friends with Gassendi, met several times with Galileo, tutored the future Charles II in mathematics and continued a long life of writing many scientific, political and philosophic works. His "Leviathan" was one of the first scholarly works on Social

Contract theory. He stressed that life in a state of raw nature was "war of all against all" and that without a common social contract and a strong state life would be "solitary, poor, nasty, brutish and short."

John Locke (1632-1704) was a critic of Hobbes' "absolutist" political philosophy, but continued the theme of the Social Contract. He is considered the first of the British Empiricists and is widely regarded as one of the most influential philosophers for men such as Voltaire and Rousseau, many Scottish Enlightenment thinkers, as well as the American and French revolutionaries. Locke's theory of mind is often cited as the origin for modern conceptions of identity and "the self', figuring prominently in the later works of philosophers such as David Hume, and Kant. Thus, Philosophical Materialism was independently influential and also a stimulant to the later thinking of the Enlightenment.

As written by Professor Mark Lilla in his "The Stillborn God: Religion, Politics and the Modern West: "Hobbes planted a seed, a thought that it might be possible to build legitimate political institutions without grounding them on divine revelation ... The new political thinking would no longer concern itself with God's politics; it would concentrate on men as believers in God and try to keep them from harming one another. It would set its sights lower than Christian theology had, but secure what mattered most, which was peace."

"Hobbes was neither a liberal or a democrat. He thought that consolidating power in the hands of one man was the only way to relieve citizens of their mutual fears. But over the next few centuries, Western thinkers like John Locke, who adopted his approach, began to imagine a new kind of political order in which power would be limited, divided and widely shared; in which those in power at one moment would relinquish it peacefully at another, without fear of retribution; in which public law would govern relations among citizens and institutions; in which many different religions would be allowed to flourish, free from state interference; and in which individuals would have inalienable rights to protect them from government and their fellows. This liberal-democratic order is the only one we in the West recognize as legitimate today, and we owe it primarily to Hobbes. In order to escape the destructive passions of messianic faith, political theology centered on God was replaced by political philosophy centered on man. This was the "Great Separation". The separation of church and state." Ibid

Thus, there is an historical line, from early Greek: Epicurean Philosophical Materialism, followed by Lucretius, then through and in conjunction with Platonism, Buddhism, Judaism, Christianity, the Reformation, Islam, Deism, Hobbes, Locke and the Enlightenment, leading to our present-day Western separation of church and state. The separation of church and state provides a cultural and political context in which Humanism can thrive, giving people access to their different religions while also providing access to science and the freedom and safety to practice their religions.

Unfortunately, intolerant and violent fundamentalist religions and theocratic states still exist in many cultures, and continue to cause terrible strife for millions of people.

"Renaissance Humanism" has shaped modern humanism. It began in Florence at the end of the 14th century CE, reviving the study of Latin and Greek, thus reviving the study of science, philosophy, art and poetry of classical antiquity. This revival marked a great change from the contemplation of Biblical values. The crisis of Renaissance humanism came with the trial of Galileo, which forced the choice between religious teaching and scientific observations. The trial made the contradictions between humanism and traditional religion apparent to many and humanism was branded a "dangerous doctrine". Any challenge to religious teaching was seen as a challenge to religious authority - the same problem which continues today in the contest between fundamentalists and the teaching of evolution.

Great humanist scholars from the Renaissance include Desideratum Erasmus (who challenged the church), Thomas More (who defended the church but was learned in the classics), the French writer Rabelais, the Italian poet Francesco Petrarch and the Italian scholar Giovanni Pico della Mirandola.

During the French Revolution of 1793 the Cult of Reason, based on atheism, resulted in turning the cathedral Notre Dame de Paris into a "Temple of Reason" and for a time Lady Liberty replaced the Virgin Mary on several altars. In the 1850's Auguste Comte, the father of Sociology, founded Positivism, a "religion of humanity". Comte was a student and secretary for the Count de Saint-Simon, the father of French socialism. Comte coined the term "altruism".

During the Enlightenment of the 17th, 18th and 19th centuries CE philosophers like Spinoza, Hume, Priestley, Rush, Paine and Jefferson proclaimed "Deism" as their belief system, rejecting the supernatural and speaking out for what is now seen to be Humanism.

c. The Scientist as Humanist
Many scientists say that since we cannot and do not know about supernatural phenomena, we must simply deal with our lives and each other as we actually are, seeking meaning as part of the community of all life on

the planet earth. These scientists find that their awe of the majesty and infinite scale of the universe, and of the marvels and mysteries of nature can be an equivalent alternative to belief in supernatural events.

(1.) Albert Einstein, a "deeply religious unbeliever"

Albert Einstein (1879-1955), whose theory of General Relativity in 1905 provided the theoretical basis for modern post-Newtonian physics, including the "Big Bang", has often been misquoted about his presumed religious belief. Most often he is quoted as saying that "God does not play dice with the Universe" as if to show that Einstein believed in a personal God.

What Einstein actually said was: "It was, of course, a lie what you read about my religious convictions, a lie which is being systematically repeated. I do not believe in a personal God and I have never denied this, but have expressed it quite clearly. If there is something in me which can be called religious then it is the unbounded admiration for the structure of the world so far as science can reveal it." He also said; "I am a deeply religious unbeliever", and "My God is the God of Spinoza".

Einstein continued, in his essay entitled: "The Meaning of Life".

"The most beautiful experience we can have is the mysterious. It is the fundamental emotion, which stands at the cradle of true art and true science. Whoever does not know it and can longer wonder, nor longer marvel, is as good as dead, and his eyes are dimmed. It was the experience of mystery - even if mixed with fear - that engendered religion. A knowledge of the existence of something we cannot penetrate, our perceptions of the profoundest reason and the most radiant beauty, which only in their most primitive forms are accessible to our minds - it is this knowledge and this emotion that constitute true religiosity; in this sense, and in this alone, I am a deeply religious man. I cannot conceive of a God who rewards and punishes his creatures, or has a will of a kind that we experience in ourselves. Neither can I nor would I want to conceive of an individual that survives his physical death; let feeble souls, from fear or absurd egoism, cherish such thoughts. I am satisfied with the mystery of the eternity of life and with the awareness and a glimpse of the marvelous structure of the existing world, together with the devoted striving to comprehend a portion, be it ever so tiny, of the Reason that manifests itself in nature."

Thus, Einstein expressed in modern times the thoughts developed by Spinoza and the Enlightenment thinkers in the 17th, and 18th centuries. Philosophers like David Hume, scientists like Joseph Priestley, and political leaders like Thomas Paine, Benjamin Rush, James Madison and

Thomas Jefferson; men who were quite religious, but who defined themselves as Deists, and who believed that the separation of church and state, and science, was essential to American democracy.

(2.) Spinoza, Jefferson and Paine as Deists

For interesting historical background to these extraordinary thinkers' ideas, read Thomas Jefferson's "The Jefferson Bible", (Beacon Press, 1989); Eric Foner's "Tom Paine and Revolutionary America", Thomas Paine's "The Age of Reason", edited by Philip Foner (Citadel, 1974). This short list will lead you to many other related books.

Thomas Jefferson, J. B. Priestley and Thomas Paine, and many others of the "American Enlightenment" described themselves as "Deists" who believed in an immanent, but not Biblical, God and also professed their belief that Jesus was the world's greatest teacher of ethics, but was not "divine" in any supernatural sense. They were in this sense, followers of Baruch Spinoza (1632 -1677) the Dutch Sephardic Jewish philosopher who believed that "God is immanent in all things", but was not the mythical God taught by Judaism and Christianity. Spinoza was a peaceful, decent man, but was expelled by his Synagogue and was shunned by Dutch Christians for challenging the Judeo-Christian dogmas.

His many books, including "Ethics" have stood the test of time and he is now widely revered and praised as one of history's great philosophers.

Both Jefferson and Paine praised Jesus and professed their belief in a Deist God, but criticized the Judeo-Christian Bible for its inconsistencies, self-contradictions and descriptions of supernatural events and miracles. Jefferson avoided publishing his audaciously edited New Testament which he said "separated the diamonds from the dross", literally cutting out the miracles, until very late in his life to avoid political repercussions.

Thomas Paine was fiercely criticized for describing Biblical inconsistencies. Even though he had been a hero of both the American and French Revolutions the last years of his life were spent in poverty and as an object of bitter reproach as a supposed "atheist". 150 years after Paine's death president Theodore Roosevelt had the temerity to call him a "dirty little atheist" for having written "The Age of Reason". Paine was neither dirty, nor little, nor an atheist, but such was the cost for being openly critical of the Bible. When publicly challenged on the inaccuracy of his remark, Teddy Roosevelt refused to reply.

Thus, even though each of these great thinkers was a peaceful, constructive and reasonable person, profoundly concerned with ethics and morality, and deeply reverent in a basically religious sense, they were reviled and excoriated and punished for being critical of the existing religious traditions and institutions. So it was, and even still is by some; such as Darwinism, whose theory and mountain of facts confirming Evolution was seen as a direct challenge and contradiction to a literal interpretation of the Judeo-Christian Bible.

Some people, like Einstein, or the Deists such as Jefferson or Paine, or many modern day secular humanists, are satisfied with a science based system of "religious" belief but most people, particularly most American people, are not. They are only satisfied by a religious belief that incorporates a tangible, but supernatural, God with whom they believe they can communicate about human problems. This discussion of science and religion in relation to genealogy is not intended in any way to demean such religious belief.

(3.) Santayana, James and Dewey, Philosopher Humanists

George Santayana (1863 - 1952)

One of the joys of writing this book is the occasional discovery of the valuable teachings of someone whom I had known of only vaguely when I was younger. Such are the teachings of the great American philosopher, poet and novelist, George Santayana. He is of course mostly quoted for his famous, "Those who cannot remember the past are condemned to repeat it." But while doing research for this book I learned that he thought and wrote a great deal about religion and science, much of it about religion as "poetry" compared to the "prose" of science. His thinking and writings are also another example of the discovery that most of my own ideas are not original with me. They have been in fact well explored and expressed by many others before me, from the Greeks until today. I am frequently humbled by these discoveries, but also happy to find that I have long been an amateur traveler on a trail blazed by the great philosophers of history. Philosophy is, or should be, the stuff of ordinary life.

Santayana developed the idea of religion as poetry at some length. In his "Reason in Religion", published in 1913, he wrote: "Here, after all, is a remarkable phenomenon - that men everywhere have had religions; how can we understand man if we do not understand religion? Such studies would bring the skeptic face to face with the mystery and pathos of mortal existence. They would make him understand why religion is so profoundly moving and in a sense so profoundly just."

Santayana thought, with Lucretius, that it was fear which first made the gods. Santayana identified himself as a philosophical materialist and was a serious student of Democritus and Epicurus, Lucretius's philosophical mentors, and Spinoza. Thus Santayana was, in this larger sense, a Religious Humanist.

He said,

"Faith in the supernatural is a desperate wager made by man at the lowest ebb of his fortunes; ... Add to fear, imagination: man is an incorrigible animist, and interprets all things anthropomorphically; (in human form) he personifies and dramatizes nature, and fills it with a cloud of deities; The rainbow is taken ... for a trace left in the sky by the passage of some beautiful and elusive goddess."

"Not that people quite literally believe these splendid myths; but the poetry of them helps men to bear the prose of life. This mythic poetic tendency is weak today, and science has led to a violent and suspicious reaction against imagination; but in primitive peoples, and particularly in the near East, it was unchecked. The Old Testament abounds in poetry and metaphor; the Jews who composed it did not take their own figures literally; but when European peoples, more literal and less imaginative, mistook these poems for science, our Occidental theology was born. Christianity was at first a combination of Greek theology with Jewish morality; it was an unstable combination, in which one or the other element would eventually yield; in Catholicism the Greek and Pagan elements triumphed, in Protestantism, the stern Hebraic moral code did. The one had a Renaissance, the other a Reformation."

"Nothing would be so beautiful as Christianity", Santayana thought, "if it were not taken literally" ... "For taken literally, nothing could be so absurd as some of the dogmas, like the damnation of innocents, or the existence of evil in a world created by omnipotent benevolence. The principle of individual interpretation led naturally to a wild growth of sects among the people, and to a mild pantheism among the elite - pantheism being nothing more than "naturalism poetically expressed".

As Will Durant puts it in his "Story of Philosophy", "Santayana was by constitution and heredity incapable of sympathy with Protestantism; he prefers the color and incense of his youthful faith. He scolds the Protestants for abandoning the pretty legends of medieval Dom, and above all for neglecting the Virgin Mary, whom he considers, as Heine did, the "fairest flower of poesy." As a wit has put it, "Santayana believes that there is no God, and Mary is His mother". He adorns his room with pictures of the Virgin and the Saints. He likes the beauty of Catholicism more than the truth of any other faith, for the same reason that he prefers art to industry."

Quoting Santayana;

"There are two stages in the criticism of myths ... The first treats them angrily as superstitions; the second treats them smilingly as poetry .... Religion is human experience interpreted by human imagination ... The idea that religion contains a literal, not symbolic, representation of truth and life is simply an impossible idea. Whoever entertains it has not come within the region of profitable philosophizing on that subject. Matters of religion should never be matters of controversy ...we seek rather to honor the piety and understand the poetry embodied in these fables."

And, as a published poet, novelist and philosopher Santayana, knew whereof he spoke. He also taught an extraordinary range of students at Harvard: T.S. Eliot, Gertrude Stein, Wallace Stevens, Walter Lippmann, Conrad Aiken, Robert Frost, Max Eastman, Van Wyck Brooks, Samuel Eliot Morrison, Felix Frankfurter and James B. Conant. He was a student and colleague of William James and a friend of Henry James. He was born and lived until age eight in Spain, moved to Boston, Massachusetts where he attended the Boston Latin School and Harvard where he earned his undergraduate B.A. and Ph.D degrees (1889)) and taught there for many years. He spent forty years thus in Boston and then, tiring of the administrative aspects of academe,

retired early at age 48 in 1912 and lived the remaining years of his long life as an independent scholar and writer in Europe. His last years from 1941 to his death at age 89 in 1952 were spent living near Rome at Clinica delia Piccola Compagan di Marie, a hospital-clinic run by a Catholic order of nuns. (When my wife Josie was a student and traveling in Europe in 1950 her professor-travel mentor arranged for a meeting with Santayana which was unfortunately called off at the last minute because of his precarious health.) It is impossible to do more than make these short references here to the exceptional life and teachings of George Santayana. But he is certainly a thinker and writer to whom we commend our children and grandchildren to study.

Other great American philosophers who created the school of Pragmatism were part of the late 19th and early 20th century development of Humanism. They were William James (1842 - 1910) and John Dewey (1859 -1952). James was an MD who was an early student and professor of psychology, "Principles of Psychology" (1890) who also became deeply interested in religion, "The Varieties of Religious Experience" (1902), "A Pluralistic Universe" (1902) and later a professor of philosophy "Pragmatism" ((1907). Dewey was initially interested mainly in education, "Experience in Education" (1938) but was also a serious student of religion, "A Common Faith" (1934), a humanistic study of religion. Both James and Dewey were Humanists who based their observations about the human condition upon scientific phenomena, acknowledged the importance and power of religious experience, but set aside the supernatural and religious dogma. Their many books are well worth reading.

d. Religious Humanists
Greg Epstein, Humanist Chaplain
at Harvard University

Greg Epstein is the newly appointed Humanist Chaplain at Harvard University, following the retirement of Tom Ferrick, who founded the Harvard Humanist Chaplaincy in the 1970's. Greg has a BA (Religion and Chinese) and MA (Judaic Studies) from the University of Michigan and in 2005 was ordained as a humanist rabbi from the International Institute for Secular and Humanist Judaism. He was recently interviewed by David Niose of Humanist magazine and made a number of interesting comments about his view of humanism and, in part, on his view of the "culture wars" involving creationism, atheism and religion in general.

For instance, both Richard Dawkins and Sam Harris have written unusually popular books fiercely critical of religion, Christianity and Islam in particular. And Daniel Dennett, a professor at the Harvard Divinity School has also asserted that belief is simply part of our evolutionary nature. They seem to have struck a resilient chord in the American reading public's mind. They have also raised the ire of many dedicated Christians, both fundamentalists and mainstream. The obvious reason for both the popularity and controversy about these books is simply that they and present themselves aggressively as atheists.

As Greg Epstein, says; " Richard Dawkins, Daniel Dennett and Sam Harris are the "unholy trinity". Epstein also says that, "I have great respect for all three, and I agree with Dawkins and Dennett on their naturalistic, nontheistic view of the Universe. But I take an extremely different approach than they do to representing humanism." Epstein goes on to say that "The New Atheism", described as "No Heaven, No Hell. Just Science", raises the concern, often quite valid, that the new atheism is too cut off from emotion, from intuition, and from a spirit of generosity toward those who see the world differently. In short it represents the "head" of humanism, an over-intellectualized, disembodied approach. To be relevant in the twenty-first century we must also emphasize the "heart" of humanism."

Epstein continues,

"I do see a movement taking shape that is positive rather than negative, with the potential to reach millions of young people in the coming generation or two. In response to "The New Atheism" we should call this approach "The New Humanism." "The new humanism is noteworthy in three ways: it's multi-cultural, it's inclusive, and it's inspiring. Of course none of these notions are completely new, but one could argue that they haven't been emphasized enough by the organized humanist community."

"My humanism is not a proselytizing humanism. I don't go out trying to convince people to abandon belief in God, hoping that will somehow cure all ills. However, my humanism is not a silent humanism either. The difference is the approach; ours should be to educate anyone, everyone, about what humanists do believe in. Why we see God as a human creation, not vice-versa. Why we feel this life, this world, is the only one we have. And especially how such beliefs help us to live good, meaningful, productive, and joyous lives. This isn't an approach designed to make humanists the dominant majority, but it certainly will make us a strong and respected minority."

Rev. Don Cupitt, Life Fellow
Emmanuel College, Cambridge
Don Cupitt, born in 1934 in Lancashire, England, was educated at Charterhouse, Trinity Hall Cambridge, and Wescott House Cambridge where he studied successively, Natural Science, Theology and the Philosophy of Religion. He was ordained deacon in the Church of England, becoming a priest in 1960. He served briefly as curate in the north of England, was appointed Vice-Principal of Wescott House and was elected to a fellowship and appointed Dean at Emmanuel College in 1965, teaching the Philosophy of Religion until his retirement in 1996. He then proceeded to a Life Fellowship at Emmanuel, which remains his base today.

Cupitt's principal occupation for the past thirty years has been writing books which have been described as "radical Christian theology". His "The Myth of God Incarnate", three BBC television projects, "Open to Question", "Who Was Jesus" and "The Sea of Faith" were produced in the late 1970's and early 1980's. His notoriety peaked in 1980 with the publication of his "Taking Leave of God" which caused him to be labeled an "atheist" and "perhaps the most radical theologian in the world". He survived then because the then Archbishop of Canterbury and then Master of Emmanuel defended his right to put forward his ideas. Since then he has devoted all his energies to developing his ideas in a long line of books. He travels regularly, lecturing for the Sea of Faith networks, in Britain, Australia and New Zealand, for the Westar Institute of Santa Rosa, California (the Jesus Seminar), and for the Snowstar Institute of Southern Ontario, Canada.

The essence of his present thinking is that the world of religion is a mythical representation of the world of language. He sees God not as a transcendent reality, but as a reflection of human selfhood. Human beings themselves are the only source of meaning and value. Belief in God is a valuable and interesting form of consciousness. He has said "the entire supernatural world of religion is as mythical representation of the creative - and also powers of language". "This supernatural world, as the term implies, existed apart from yet corresponding to the natural one, but as historical investigation of the latter answered more questions that formerly had supernatural explanations, the real existence of the supernatural world - of God, demons, and angels - became ever more problematic. Cupitt asserts that no one can believe in an objectively real God anymore. But he also asserts that to give up religion would be a mistake and he proposes a new world religion based on "a non-realist reading of Christianity" in which God is a unifying symbol of common values, disinterested love is the highest value, and Jesus shows the possibility of exemplifying love as a living human."

One of Cupitt's admirers and friend is Bishop John Spong who mostly agrees with Cupitt, but disagrees specifically with Cupitt's assertion that there is no "real" God. Spong's says that "While I am certain the word "God" is a human attempt in admittedly human language, to describe a human experience, I affirm that the experience is real. We call the God experience "otherness", "transcendence', or even "the holy". We recognize that this reality is not capable of being defined, but that inability does not make this experience unreal... "So I stand before this undefined presence that I call God, in awe and wonder. God is real to me. I create my definitions of God, but I do not create the God experience. So I am theologically a "Realist" not a "non-Realist". I still admire and profit from Don Cupitt's work and I still claim him as a special friend.

Unitarian – Universalism,
Humanistic Religions
Both Unitarianism and Universalism are rooted in Christian Protestantism, but they have long since separated from its mainstream. Unitarianism was rebuffed by orthodox Christianity at the first Council of Nicea in 325 CE, but resurfaced subsequently in church history.

The Christian church was adopted and made the state religion by the Roman emperor Constantine (324-337 CE) and its varying doctrines and theologies were regulated into official dogma at the First Council of Nicea in 325 CE. One of the theological issues was the identity of God and Jesus. Some sects claimed that Jesus was both God and man, some said he was only a man and some said there was also the idea of the spirit separate from both God and Jesus. The decision was to declare the Trinity, that the "Godhead" consisted of "The Father, the Son, and the Holy Ghost", i.e. God, Jesus and the Holy Spirit. Although this decision makes no literal sense it resolved the controversies among the differing sects and became church dogma - still existing to this day. The Unitarians objected, declaring "God" as a singular entity, and were therefore declared "heretics". By making the abstract ideas of God and the Spirit and Jesus' divinity into concrete entities the Council of Nicea's decision to create the Trinity became a perfect example of the confusion that can result from Whitehead's "misplaced concretness" of the abstract.

Unitarians were formally established in Transylvania and Poland in the 16th century. Michael Servetus, a Spanish proto-Unitarian, and renowned medical scientist, espoused Unitarianism against Trinitarians, and was burned at the stake in Geneva, Switzerland on the orders of John Calvin in 1553.

In the United States the Unitarian movement began primarily in the Congregational parish churches of New England. They gained a key faculty position at Harvard in 1805. Their dispute with the Trinitarians culminated in the foundation of the American Unitarian Association as a separate denomination in 1825. Another liberal church, the United Church of Christ, also split off from the Congregational church. In the 19th century, under the influence of Ralph Waldo Emerson, who had been a Unitarian minister, and other Transcendentalists, Unitarianism began its long journey from liberal Protestantism to its present more pluralistic form. The Unitarians also claim Thomas Jefferson as a Kindred Spirit.

Universalism started as a separate Christian "heresy", with its own long history. It can be traced deep into Christian past, beginning with the earliest church scholars. Both Origen and St. Gregory preached its essentials. Universalism denies the doctrine of eternal damnation; instead it proclaims a loving God who will redeem all souls. In 1793 Universalism emerged as a separate denomination in the United States as the Universalist Church of America. Over time both the Unitarian and Universalist churches evolved into inclusive, tolerant religions. In 1961 they merged into the Unitarian Universalist Association.

In 1995 the UUA helped establish the International Council of Unitarians and Universalists to connect Unitarian and universalism faith traditions around the world. They number over 1,000 member congregations and 629,000 members in the United States. Most congregations attend church on Sunday, have sermons, bless marriages and have "coming of age" ceremonies.

Unitarian Universalism is a faith with no creedal requirements imposed on its members. Belief in a supernatural, transactional god with whom you can communicate is not required. A majority of the members consider themselves to be Humanists, with substantial minorities identifying themselves as Agnostics, Atheists, Buddhists, Christians, and even Pagans. Their commitment to social justice has led them from the abolition of slavery in the 19th century to women's suffrage, the civil rights movement, gay rights, and feminism in the 20th.

Susan B. Anthony, a Unitarian and a Quaker, was extremely influential in the women's suffrage movement. Unitarian Universalists and Quakers still share many principles, notably that they are creedless religions with a long-standing commitment to social justice. It is therefore common to see Unitarian Universalists and Quakers working together.

Although the UUA does not require a creed of its members, they have expressed their common values in a statement of principles in what has become known as "The Principles and Purposes", as follows:

The Principles of the Unitarian Universalist Association
"We, the member congregations of the Unitarian Universalist Association, covenant to affirm and promote":

The inherent worth and dignity of every person;

Justice, equity and compassion in human relations;

Acceptance of one another and encouragement to spiritual growth in our congregations;

A free and responsible search for truth and meaning;

The right of conscience and the use of the democratic process within our congregations and in society at large;

The goal of world community with peace, liberty, and justice for all;

Respect for the independent web of all existence of which we are a part.

"The living tradition which we share draws from many sources:"

Direct experience of that transcending mystery and wonder, affirmed in all cultures, which moves us to a renewal of the spirit and openness to the forces, which create and uphold our life;

Words and deeds of prophetic women and men which challenge us to confront powers and structures of evil with justice, compassion, and the transforming power of love; - Wisdom from the world's religions which inspires us in our ethical and spiritual life;

Jewish and Christian teachings, which call us to respond to God's love by loving our neighbors as ourselves;

Humanist teachings, which counsel us to heed the guidance of reason and the results of science, and warn us against idolatries of the mind and spirit;

Spiritual teachings of earth-centered traditions which celebrate the sacred circle of life and instruct us to live in harmony with the rhythms of nature."

"Grateful for the religious pluralism which enriches and ennobles our faith, we are inspired to deepen our understanding and expand our vision. As free congregations we enter into this covenant, promising to one another our mutual trust and support."

e. Carl Sagan (1934-1996)

Carl Sagan was an American astronomer and astrobiologist and a highly successful popularizer of astronomy. He wrote many popular books and co-wrote and presented the award winning 1980 television series COSMOS, A Personal Voyage which has been seen by more than 600 million people in over 60 countries, making it the most widely watched PBS program in history.

In his works he frequently advocated skeptical inquiry, humanism and the scientific method. He was a graduate of the University of Chicago where he earned his Bachelor of Science in 1955, his Master in Physics in 1956, and his PhD in Astrophysics in 1960. He became a full professor at Cornell and directed its laboratory for planetary studies there. He was also a leader in the American space program and an adviser to NASA from the 1950's until his death. He was a renowned astronomer and was awarded a Pulitzer Prize for general non-fiction in 1978. Sagan was a leader in the search for extraterrestrial life and was one of the founders of SETI. His skepticism also interested him in the search for Unidentified Flying Objects (UFO's), which he determined, had no basis in scientific fact.

Sagan identified himself as a skeptical agnostic, but he also wrote seriously about religion and the relationship between religion and science, expressing his skepticism about many conventional conceptualizations of God. He once said, "The idea that God is an oversized white male with a flowing beard, who sits in the sky and tallies the fall of every sparrow is ludicrous. But if by "God" one means the set of physical laws that govern the universe, then clearly there is such a God. This God is emotionally unsatisfying ... it does not make much sense to pray to the law of gravity."

Late in his life, Sagan's books developed his skeptical, naturalistic view of the world. His "Demon Haunted World; Science as a Candle in the Dark" advocated rules for detecting false arguments, the wider use of critical thinking, and the scientific method.

In 2006, Sagan's widow, Ann Druyan edited Sagan's 1985 Gifford Lectures into a new book, "The Varieties of Scientific Experience: A Personal View of the Search for God" in which he elaborated on his views of the boundary between science and religion. One of his lecture comments is, "I would suggest that science is, at least in part, informed worship." And he goes on to say; "The search for who we are does not lead to complacency or arrogance. It goes with a courageous intent to greet the universe as it really is, not to foist our emotional predispositions on it but to courageously accept what our explorations tell us."

Ann Druyan, who also produced the film "Contact" based on Carl Sagan's novel compares Sagan to Richard Dawkins, the author of "The Selfish Gene," "The God Delusion" and other works on our biological heritage, and says: People like Carl and Dawkins are more serious about God than people who just go through the motions. They are the real seekers."

f. Other Humanists – Paul Kurtz – Affirmations of Humanism

There are a number of publications articulating the secular humanist viewpoint on a responsible and well-informed basis. I believe the best is "Free Inquiry", a bimonthly magazine edited by Paul Kurtz, professor emeritus of philosophy at the State University of New York at Buffalo and the Chair of the Center For Inquiry. Free Inquiry is published by the "Council For Secular Humanism". The Council and the magazine can be reached for further information at their website: http://www.secularhumanism.org

Their "Affirmations of Humanism: A Standard of Principles"; by Paul Kurtz, are quire lengthy, but a few examples areas follows:

"We are committed to the application of reason and science, to the understanding of the universe, and to the solving of human problems.

We deplore efforts to denigrate human intelligence, to seek to explain the world in supernatural terms, and to look outside nature for salvation.

We believe in an open and pluralistic society and that democracy is the best guarantee of protecting human rights from authoritarian elites and repressive majorities.

We are committed to the principle of the separation of church and state.

We want to protect and enhance the earth, to preserve it for future generations, and to avoid inflicting needless suffering on other species.

We respect the right to privacy. Mature adults should be allowed to fulfill their aspirations, to express their sexual preferences, to exercise reproductive freedom, to have access to comprehensive and informed healthcare, and to die with dignity.

We believe in the common and moral decencies: altruism, integrity, honesty, truthfulness, responsibility. Humanist ethics is amenable to critical, rational guidance. There are normative standards that we discover together. Moral principles are tested by their consequences.

We are engaged by the arts no less than by the sciences.

We are skeptical of untested claims to knowledge, and we are open to novel ideas and seek new departures in our thinking.

We believe in optimism rather than pessimism, hope rather than despair, learning in the place of dogma, truth instead of ignorance, joy rather than guilt or sin, tolerance in the place of fear, love instead of hatred, compassion over selfishness, beauty instead of ugliness, and reason rather than blind faith or irrationality."

Josie's and My Personal Ethical Code
In addition to the principles set forth in the Humanist Principles, Josie and I subscribe to a more personal set of principles that can be briefly set forth as follows:

Always try to ascertain and speak the truth, to each other and to ourselves.

Speak truth to power, even when it costs you.

Say you are sorry - apologize - when it is clear you have made a mistake. Try to make amends.

Don't compound injury with insult.

Cultivate your empathy and sympathy for others. Try to understand how other people feel.

Make and keep serious commitments in life. They are the frameworks of life's meaning. Such as marriage and taking good care of children and other close relatives and friends. Do not make false promises.

Obey the Golden Rule; "Do unto others as you would have done to you". This rule has been professed by all religions since Hinduism, Buddhism, Confucianism, Judaism, Christianity and Islam. There is also evidence that it is a biologically and culturally inherited moral code that was practiced by prehistoric cultures. There are, however, limits to this rule when one's kindness is betrayed and you are threatened. So, always be on your guard. But be willing to risk trust and hope to earn trust in return.

Strive for peaceful, non-violent solutions to problems. Again, there are limits to this principle because it is possible that your trust will be betrayed. We are not total pacifists, but we try to be peaceful, non-violent citizens.

Do not be afraid to express your love to people who are worthy of it. Articulate your hopes and dreams. Even for those who do not believe in a supernatural deity, prayer can be a poetic expression of hopes and dreams.

Give of yourself to those who are not as fortunate. Some churches and many charities are worthy of regular financial and in-kind contributions. Obey Isaiah's admonition to take particular care of the widows and orphans.

Seek justice for yourself and others. The best civic organization we know for pursuing this principle is the American Civil Liberties Union.

g. Zygon, A Journal of Religion and Science

Founded 41 years ago by Ralph Wendell Burhoe (1911-1997) the Zygon Journal has become the premier quarterly academic journal providing a forum for the publication of the highest quality commentary on the connections between religion and science.

Zygon's long-standing editor is Philip Hefner, Professor of Systematic Theology at the Lutheran School of Theology at Chicago. An associate editor is Arthur Peacocke, Honorary Chaplain, Christ Church Cathedral, Oxford (a PhD physicist and an ordained Anglican priest).

Zygon's editorial board includes Ian G. Barbour, Bean Professor Emeritus of Science, Technology and Society, Carleton College, and Michael Ruse, author and Professor of Philosophy, Florida State University, and many others well known in the field of science and religion.

Another author of some of its articles is John Polkinghorne, K.B.E, E.R.S., is a fellow of Queen's College, Cambridge, and Canon Theologian of Liverpool, England. Polkinghorne has also written such books as "The Faith of a Physicist", "Scientists as Theologians", and "Belief in God in Age of Science". He is also a PhD physicist and an ordained Anglican priest.

Zygon's "Statement of Perspective" is as follows:

"The word "zygon" means the yoking of two entities or processes that must work together. It is related to "zygote" - meaning the union of genetic heritage from sperm and egg, a union, which is vital in higher species for the continuation of advancement of life. The journal Zygon provides a forum for exploring ways to unite what in modern times has been disconnected - values from knowledge, goodness from truth, religion from science."

"Traditional religions, which have transmitted wisdom about what is of essential value and ultimate meaning as a guide for human living, were expressed in terms of the best understandings of their times about human nature, society, and the world. Religious expression in our time, however, has not drawn similarly on modern science, which has superseded the ancient forms of understanding. As a result religions have lost credibility in the modern mind. Nevertheless some recent scientific studies of human evolution and development have indicated how long-standing religions have evolved well winnowed wisdom, still essential for the best life."

"Zygon's hypothesis is that, when long-evolved religious wisdom is yoked with significant, recent scientific discoveries about the world and human nature, there results credible expression of basic meaning, values, and moral conviction that provides valid and effective guidance for enhancing human life."

Other Publications about Science and Religion – The Zygon Center
The Zygon Center For Religion and Science has recently begun publication of an excellent newsletter, "News & Views", describing its various programs, such as the course schedule for "The Epic of Creation" and the Advanced Seminar in Religion and Science, and related events.

The December, 2005 issue, for instance, republishes the complete "Clergy Letter", signed by over 10,000 clergy of many Christian denominations. The letter was composed by a Wisconsin minister and the Clergy Letter Project has been created and coordinated by Dr. Michael Zimmerman, Dean of the College of Letters and Science and professor of biology at the University of Wisconsin, Oshkosh. The Letter states so concisely much of what we have been discussing in this book that it is worth republishing here.

An Open Letter Concerning Religion and Science
"Within the community of Christian believers there are areas of dispute and disagreement including the proper way to interpret Holy Scripture. While virtually all Christians take the Bible

seriously and hold it to be authoritative in matters of faith and practice, the overwhelming majority do not read the Bible literally, as they would a science textbook. Many of the beloved stories found in the Bible- the Creation, Adam and Eve, Noah and the Ark - convey timeless truths about God, human beings, and the proper relationship between Creator and creation expressed in the only form capable of expressing these truths from generation to generation. Religious truth is of a different order from scientific truth. Its purpose is not to convey scientific information but to transform hearts."

"We, the undersigned, Christian clergy from many different traditions, believe that the timeless truths of the Bible and the discoveries of modern science may comfortably coexist. We believe that the theory of evolution is a foundational scientific truth, one that has stood up to rigorous scrutiny and upon which much of human knowledge and achievement rest. To reject this truth or treat it as "one theory among others" is to deliberately embrace scientific ignorance and transmit such ignorance to our children. We believe that among God's good gifts are human minds capable of critical thought and that the failure to fully employ this gift is a rejection of the will of our Creator. To argue that God's loving plan of salvation

for humanity precludes the full employment of the God - given faculty of reason is to attempt to limit God, an act of hubris. We urge school board members to preserve the integrity of the science curriculum by affirming the teaching of the theory of evolution as a core component of human knowledge. We ask that science remain science and the religion remain religion, two very different but complimentary forms of truth."

The Zygon Center's address is:

Zygon Center
for Religion and Science
Lutheran School of Theology
1100 East 55th Street
Chicago, Illinois 60615,
Telephone: (773) 256-0670
Website: wwwczygoncenter.org

h. And some other
Humanist publications:
Freethought Today
Published by the "Freedom From Religion Foundation, Inc."
P.O. Box 750
Madison, Wisconsin 53701
Telephone:(608) 256-5800
Website: www.ffrf.org

This publication is a monthly subscription newspaper. It is a lively, obviously "irreverent" newspaper that includes many well-researched and well-written articles reporting on church-state separation questions, science and religion, and many other related topics. The publisher's Foundation also engages in litigation of church-state separation questions.

i. The Skeptical Inquirer
Published by the "Committee for the Scientific Investigation of Claims of the Paranormal.", an international organization. The Committee is chaired by Paul Kurtz who is also the editor of Free Inquiry. The Committee's headquarters are at the "Center for Inquiry - Transnational, located at:

Center For Inquiry
P.O. Box 741
Amherst, NY 14226-0741
(716) 636-4869
Website: www.centerforinquiry.net

This bimonthly magazine is responsibly written and edited and is full of interesting news about the endless paranormal scams that are regularly foisted upon a credulous world.

The Humanist Society –
The Humanist
The oldest Humanist group in the United States is the Humanist Society, founded in 1939. It has an extensive educational and publishing program. "Humanism is a progressive life stance that without supernaturalism, affirms our ability and responsibility to lead meaningful, ethical lives capable of adding to the greater good of humanity." - American Humanist

Society "Humanism is an approach to life based on reason and our common humanity, recognizing that moral values are properly founded on human nature and experience alone." The Bristol Humanist Group.

The American Humanist Association has a website: www. AmericanHumanist.org. and publishes a monthly magazine. Its brief statement of identity is:

"Humanism is a rational philosophy informed by science, inspired by art, and motivated by compassion. Affirming the dignity of each human being, it supports liberty and opportunity consonant with social and planetary responsibility. Free of theism and other supernatural beliefs, humanism thus derives the goals of life from human need and interest rather than from theological or ideological abstractions, and asserts that humanity must take responsibility for its own destiny."

They can be contacted at:

The Humanist Society
1777 T Street, NW
Washington, DC 20009-7125
Telephone: (202) 238-9088
Fax: (202) 238-9003
E-mail: info@ humanist-society.org

*(No list of Humanists would be complete without including Will Durant who, with his wife Ariel, wrote the great eleven volume "The story of Civilization" and "The Story of Philosophy".)

j. Separation of Church and State
Some Fundamentalist preachers keep trying to falsely claim that because the phrase "separation of church and state" does not appear verbatim in the U.S. Constitution there is no such constitutional principle. Their claim is outrageously fraudulent.

The principle is powerfully stated in the First Amendment of the Constitution:

"Congress shall make no law respecting an establishment of religion, or prohibiting the free exercise thereof; or abridging the freedom of speech, or of the press, or the right of the people peaceably to assemble, and to petition the government for a redress of grievances."

Court cases, including those decided by our recent "conservative" Supreme Court, have repeatedly confirmed this principle and referred to it as the separation of the church and state. The phrase is merely a shorthand reference to the First Amendment and the court cases. It was coined first by Roger Williams, and then later by Thomas Jefferson in a letter he wrote in support of the First Amendment. James Madison also articulated the same concerns as Thomas Jefferson when he prepared the final language of the Bill of Rights.

There are two private, non-profit organizations dedicated to preserving the separation of church and state and the freedom of religion. They are both directed by ordained ministers and are active in speaking, writing and litigating cases involving the separation of church and state.

They are:

1. **People For the American Way,**
2000 M Street, NW, Suite 400
Washington, DC 20036
Telephone: 202-367-4999
(www.PFAW.org)
Its director is: Rev. Barry Lynn

2. **Interfaith Alliance**
1331 H Street, NW
Washington, DC, 20005
Telephone: 202-639-6370
(www.interfaithalliance.org)
Its director is: Rev C. Weldon Gaddy

This organization is also prominently supported by Walter Cronkite.

The '"no religious test" clause of the United States Constitution is found in Article VI, section 3, and states that:

"... no religious test shall ever be required as a qualification to any office or public trust under the United States."

This has been interpreted to mean that no federal employee, whether elected or appointed, "career" or "political," can be required to adhere to or accept any religion or belief. This clause immediately follows one requiring all federal and state officers to take an oath of support to the Constitution. This implies that the requirement of an oath, even presumably one taken "So help me God" (not a part of the presidential oath, the only one spelled out in the Constitution but traditionally almost always added to it), does not imply any requirement by those so sworn to accept a particular religion or a particular doctrine.

The clause is cited by advocates of separation of church and state as an example of "original intent" of the Framers of the Constitution of avoiding any entanglement between church and state, or involving the government in any way as a determiner of religious beliefs or practices. This is important as this clause represents the words of the original Framers, even prior to the Establishment Clause of the First Amendment.

THE DARK SIDE OF RELIGION, WILLIAM YEATS, DR. STEVEN WEINBERG, RICHARD DAWKINS, AND SAM HARRIS

a. Yeats "The Second Coming"

A great poet, the Irishman William Butler Yeats (1865 - 1939), who wrote a vast canon of lyrical, narrative and dramatic poetry, wrote one particular poem that speaks directly to the frightening capacity of mankind to destroy itself in the name of religion.

THE SECOND COMING

Turning and turning in the widening gyre

The falcon cannot hear the falconer;

Things fall apart; the center cannot hold;

Mere anarchy is loosed upon the world,

The blood-dimmed tide is loosed, and everywhere

The ceremony of innocence is drowned;

The best lack all conviction, while the worst are full of passionate intensity.

Surely some revelation is at hand;

Surely the Second Coming is at hand.

The Second Coming! Hardly are these words out

When a vast image out of Spiritus Mundi

Troubles my sight: somewhere in sands of the desert a shape with a lion's body and the head of a man,

A gaze blank and pitiless as the sun, is moving its slow thighs, while all about it reel shadows of the indignant desert birds. The darkness drops again; but now I know

That twenty centuries of stony sleep

Were vexed to nightmare by a rocking cradle, And what rough beast, its hour come round at last,

Slouches toward Bethlehem to be born?

Thus, poetry speaks to us in ways that science cannot.

b. Dr. Steven Weinberg, "Secular Rationalist"...

Steven Weinberg (1933 -) is a Nobel Laureate (1979- Physics) and a very outspoken person on the subject of religion and science. Although some of his comments about organized religion are quite acerbic, I include him in this book because I believe he is a very decent and humane man whose commitment to historic and scientific truth is so strong that he is willing to suffer criticism for stating his opinions very succinctly. He was educated at Cornell, Copenhagen and Princeton, is the author of many books and has held a number of significant academic posts. In 1982 he moved to the University of Texas (Austin) as the founder of the Theory Group. He also holds its Josey Regental Chair of Science and is Professor of Physics and Astronomy.

He is a self-described "secular rationalist" who sees the pursuit of scientific inquiry as uplifting. In his excellent book," The First Three Minutes", about the beginning three minutes of the universe, he argues that the search for scientific truth can give meaning to life: "the effort to understand the universe is one of the very few things that lifts human life above the level of farce, and gives it some of the grace of tragedy." ... and "Nothing in the last five hundred years has had so great an effect on the human spirit as the discoveries of modern science." Weinberg can also wax a bit poetic saying, "the night sky is as beautiful as ever".

Weinberg is an outspoken critic of religion. Following are some selected quotes from just a few of his writings and speeches: (many more are available through Google)

"Religious people have grappled for millennia with the theodicy, the problem posed by the existence of suffering in a world that is supposed to be ruled by a good God. They have found ingenious solutions in terms of various supposed divine plans: I will not try to argue with these solutions, much less to add one of my own. Remembrance of the Holocaust leaves me unsympathetic to attempts to justify the ways of God to man. If there is a God that has special plans for humans, then He has taken great pains to hide his concern for us. To me it would seem impolite if not impious to bother such a God with our prayers." (Dreams of a Final Theory)

"The whole history of the last thousands of years has been a history of religious persecutions and wars, pogroms, jihads, crusades. I find it very regrettable, to say the least." (Physicist Ponders God, Truth and a Final Theory, Glanz, New York Times,

2000) "I can hope that this long sad story, the progression of priests and ministers and rabbis and ulamas and imams and bonzes and bodhisattvas, will come to an end. I hope this is something to which science can contribute ... it may be the most important contribution that we can make. This is one of the great social functions of science - to free people from superstition."... (Freethought Today, April, 2000)

"The prestige of religion seems today to derive from what people take to be its moral influence, rather than from what they may think has been its success in accounting for what we see in nature. Conversely, I have to admit that, although I really don't believe in a cosmic designer, the reason that I am taking the trouble to argue about it is that I think that on balance the moral influence of religion has been awful-" "A Designer Universe?", 1999.

"On the one side, I could point out the endless examples of the harm done by religious enthusiasm, through a long history of pogroms, crusades, and jihads. In our own century it was Muslim zealot who killed Sadat, a Jewish zealot who killed Rabin, and Hindu zealot who killed Gandhi. No one would say that Hitler was a Christian zealot but it is hard to imagine Nazism taking the form it did

without the foundation provided by centuries of Christian anti-Semitism. On the other side, many admirers of religion would set countless examples of the good done by religion. For instance, in his recent book "Imagined Worlds", the distinguished physicist Freeman Dyson has emphasized the role of religious belief in the suppression of slavery. I'd like to comment briefly on this point, not to try to prove anything with one example, but just to illustrate what I think about the moral influence of religion."

"It is certainly true that the campaign against slavery and the slave trade was greatly strengthened by devout Christians, including the Evangelical layman William Wilberforce* in England and the Unitarian minister William Ellery Channing in America. But Christianity, like other great world religions, lived comfortably with slavery for many centuries, and slavery was endorsed in the New Testament. So what was different for anti-slavery Christians like Wilberforce and Channing? There had been no discovery of new sacred scriptures, and neither Wilberforce nor Channing claimed to have received any supernatural revelations. Rather, the eighteenth century had seen a widespread increase in rationality and humanitarianism that led others - for instance, Adam Smith, Jeremy Bentham, and Richard Brinsley Sheridan - also opposed to slavery, on grounds having nothing to do with religion. Lord Mansfield, the author of the decision in Somerset's case, which ended slavery in England (though not its colonies), was no more than conventionally religious, and his decision did not mention religious arguments. Although Wilberforce was the leader of the campaign against the slave trade in the 1790's, this movement had essential support from many in Parliament like Fox and Pitt, who were not known for their piety. As far as I can tell, the moral tone of religion benefited more from the spirit of the times than the spirit of the times benefited from religion."

"Where religion did make a difference, it was more in support of slavery than in opposition to it. Religious arguments were used in Parliament to defend the slave trade. Frederick Douglass told in his Narrative how his condition as a slave became worse when his master underwent a religious conversion that allowed him to justify slavery as the punishment of the children of Ham. Mark Twain described his mother as a genuinely good person, whose soft heart pitied even Satan, but who had no doubt about the legitimacy of slavery, because in years of living in antebellum Missouri she had never heard any sermon opposing slavery, but only countless sermons preaching that slavery was God's will. With or without religion, good people can behave well and bad people can do evil; but for good people to do evil - that takes religion." "A Designer Universe?", Weinberg, 1999

"I am all in favor of a dialogue between science and religion, but not a constructive dialogue. One of the great achievements of science has been, if not to make it impossible for intelligent people to be religious, then at least to make it possible for them not be religious. We should not retreat from this accomplishment." (American Assn. for the Advancement of Science,1999)

*(Wilberforce was in fact the British parliamentary leader, but the original impetus for the anti-slavery movement in England began in London in 1787 with the first grass-roots human rights campaign begun and sustained for over thirty years by Thomas Clarkson, a lay Englishman who became imbued with the anti-slavery cause as a young student debater at Cambridge. For the complete story see "Bury the Chains", by Adam Hochschild, (Houghton Mifflin, 2001)

c. Sam Harris, Author

For two incisive, carefully researched and well written critiques of the self-contradictions and dangers inherent in the Judeo-Christian-Islamic religions, Sam Harris's two books are required reading. Although they are hard-hitting they are not written out of spite, but are each a passionate call to reason and to an end of religious strife. They do, however, focus on the self-contradictions and historical sins of the Judeo-Christian-Islamic religions.

"Letter to a Christian Nation", Alfred A. Knopf (2006) Sam Harris

"The End of Faith", "Religion, Terror and Future of Reason", W.W. Norton (2005)

d. Richard Dawkins

Clinton Richard Dawkins (born 1941) is a British ethologist, evolutionary biologist and popular science writer who holds the Charles Simotiyi Chair for the Public Understanding of Science at Oxford University.

Dawkins first came to prominence with his 1975 book "The Selfish Gene", which popularized the gene-centered view of evolution and introduced the term "meme" into the lexicon, helping found "memetics." In 1982, he made a major contribution to the science of evolution with the theory, presented in his widely cited book ,"The Extended Phenotype", that phenotypic effects are not limited to an organism's body, but can stretch far into the environment, including into the bodies of other organisms. He has since written several best-selling popular books, and appeared in a number of television and radio programs, concerning evolutionary biology, creationism, and religion.

Dawkins is an outspoken atheist, humanist, and skeptic, and is a prominent member of the "Brights" movement. In a play on Thomas Huxley's epithet "Darwin's bulldog", Dawkins impassioned defense of evolution has earned the appellation "Darwin's Rottweiler".

Dawkins is an ardent and outspoken atheist, an Honorary Associate of the National Secular Society, vice-president of the British Humanist Association and a Distinguished Supporter of the Humanist Society of Scotland.

Dawkins continues to be a prominent figure in contemporary public debate on issues relating to science and religion. He sees education and con-sciousness-raising as the primary tools in opposing what he considers to be religious dogma.

Following the September 11, 2001 attacks on the New York City World Trade Towers, when asked how the world might have changed, Dawkins responded:

"Many of us saw religion as harmless nonsense. Beliefs might lack all supporting evidence but, we thought, if people needed a crutch for consolation, where's the harm? September 11th changed all that. Revealed faith is not harmless nonsense, it can be lethally dangerous. Dangerous because it gives people unshakable confidence in their own righteousness. Dangerous because it gives them false courage to kill themselves, which automatically removes normal barriers to killing others. Dangerous because it teaches enmity to others labeled only by a difference of inherited tradition. And dangerous because we have all bought into a weird respect, which uniquely protects religion from normal criticism. Let's now stop being so damned respectful!"

Of "good scientists who are sincerely religious" he mentions Arthur Peacocke, Russell Stannard, John Polkinghome, and Francis Collins, but he says "I remain baffled .... by their belief in the details of Christian religion." The biologist Steven Ross considers that: "Richard's view about belief is too simplistic, and so hostile that as a committed secularist myself I am uneasy about it".

e. Atheists, Agnostics, Evolutionary Humanists

Richard Dawkins and Sam Harris identify themselves as "atheists". Many other secular humanists also identify themselves as atheists, or agnostics. I find both terms inadequate because they are merely negative expressions. They really only identify what they do not believe. "Atheist" should more accurately be "Non-theist", which seems to me to be less pejorative. And "Agnostic" speaks only about not knowing - we do know a lot about religion and science so to identify one's self as someone who doesn't know seems inappropriately negative.

On the other hand, "The Atheist Centre" in south-central India (Vijayawada) "is one of the more remarkable free thought institutions in the world. Its long track record of service in humanist social and educational work has earned it the goodwill of the state government and other nongovernmental organizations, and it can always attract senior public figures to its events. The Sixth World Atheist Conference, held in January, 2007, was no exception." (April/May, 2007 Free Inquiry)

India, is of course still plagued by endemic poverty, caste, and "godmen" who practice "magic" exploiting the ignorance and fear of the poor. The Atheistic Centre offers a wide range of practical, free, public lectures on medical, sex and hygiene knowledge. The Centre is, therefore, a very positive expression of atheism. (See also, "the Dictionary of Atheism, Skepticism and Humanism" authored by Bill Cooke, the Asia-Pacific Coordinator for the Center For Inquiry/Transnational.)

I still much prefer the term "scientific humanist", "evolutionary humanist", or even "scientific/religious humanist" as more complete and accurate identification. The terms, "scientific", "evolutionary", or "religious humanist" stress the knowledge of science, evolution and the great humanist tradition.

POETRY AND PROSE,
HOW CAN ANYONE BE RELIGIOUS
AND RATIONAL AT THE SAME TIME?

a. The Scientist As Poet
How Can Anyone Be Religious and
Rational At the Same Time?
Dr. Ursula Goodenough - Religious,
Naturalist, Humanist
One beautifully written book by an
accomplished biologist expressing this
point of view is "The Sacred Depths
of Nature" (Oxford Press, 1998), by
Ursula Goodenough. Dr. Goodenough
describes a biological view of the ori-
gin and processes of life, and its
meaning, in very profound and poetic
ways. This 200 page book covers, in
very readable language, the entire
story of the Origins of the Earth, the
Origins of Life, How Life Works, How
an Organism Works, How Evolution
Works, The Evolution of Biodiversity,
Awareness, Emotions and Meaning,
Sex, Sexuality, Multicellularity and
Death, and Speciation. The Afterward
is a thoughtful exposition of Emergent
Religious Principles.

Dr Goodenough describes herself
as a "Religious Naturalist", which is
another way of saying "Scientific/
Religious Humanist", but stressing
the poetic and religious aspects of a
system of thought.

Quoting Dr. Goodenough directly:

"Reverence:

Our story tells us of the sacredness
of life, of the astonishing complexity
of cells and organisms, of the vast
lengths of time it took to generate
their splendid diversity, of the enormous improbability that any of it
happened at all. Reverence is the
religious emotion elicited when we
perceive the sacred. We are called to
revere the whole enterprise of planetary existence, the whole and all of
its myriad parts as they catalyze
and secrete and replicate and mutate
and evolve."

"Ralph Waldo Emerson invites us to express our reverence in the form of prayer.

"Prayer", he writes, "is the contemplation of the facts of life from the highest point of view. It is the soliloquy of a beholding and jubilant soul"

Dr. Goodenough continues:

"And so, I profess my Faith. For me, the existence of all this complexity and awareness and intent and beauty, and my ability to apprehend it serves as the ultimate meaning and the ultimate value. The continuation of life reaches around, grabs its own tail, and forms a sacred circle that requires no further justification, no Creator, no super-ordinate meaning of meaning, no purpose other than that the continuation continue until the sun collapses or the final meteor collides. I confess a credo of continuation."

"And in so doing, I confess as well a credo of human continuation ..... We, whether we like it or not, are the dominant species and the stewards of this planet. If we can revere how things are, and can find a way to express gratitude for our existence, then we should be able to figure out, with a great deal of work and good will, how to share the Earth with one another and with other creatures, how to restore and preserve its elegance and grace, and how to commit ourselves to love and joy and laughter and hope."

It goes back in the end to my father's favorite metaphor. "Life is a coral reef. We each leave behind the best, the strongest deposit we can so that the reef can grow. But what's important is the reef."

"I love traditional religions. Whenever I wander into distinctive churches or mosques or temples, or visit museums of religious art, or hear performances of sacred music, I am enthralled by the beauty and solemnity and power they offer. Once we have our feelings about Nature in place, then I believe that we can also find important ways to call ourselves Jews, or Muslims, or Taoists, or Hopi, or Hindus, or Christians, or Buddhists. Or some of each. The words in the traditional texts may sound different to us than they did to their authors, but they continue to resonate with our religious selves. We know what they are intended to mean."

"Humans need stories - grand, compelling stories - that help to orient us in our lives and in the cosmos. The Epic of Evolution is such a story, beautifully suited to anchor our search for planetary consensus, telling us of our nature, our place, our context. Moreover, responses to this story - what we are calling religious naturalism - can yield deep and abiding spiritual experiences. "

With Dr. Ursula Goodenough we have an extraordinary example of the scientist as poet.

b.- Gerard Manley Hopkins

We have just seen how an accomplished scientist can also express her religious belief very poetically. The metaphor of Religion as Poetry and Science as Prose is one that I think best describes the difference and yet the relationship between Science and Religion. With the Poetry and Prose metaphor in mind I would like to introduce here the poet whom I think best exemplifies a religious person's poetic approach to religion and nature, creating powerfully evocative concrete images.

Gerard Manley Hopkins (1844 - 1889) was an extraordinary English poet who, in his all too brief life, converted from being an ordained Anglican priest to the Jesuit Order of the Roman Catholic church. Only a small group of his close friends even knew that he wrote poetry and it was not until thirty years after his death that a collection of his poems was published by the poet laureate Robert Bridges. His technical innovations in meter and sprung rhythm, his especially sensitive use of language, and the intensity of his religious and philosophical convictions made a great impact on the young poets of the 1920's and 30's, and his influence is still considered seminal to the development of modern poetry in general. (see Gerard Manley Hopkins, Bergonzi, Collier, 1927)

A few of my favorites are:

"GOD'S GRANDEUR
The world is charged with
the grandeur of God

It will flame out, like shining
from shook foil;

It gathers to greatness, like the
ooze of oil

Crushed. Why do men then now
not reck his rod?

Generations have trod, have trod,
have trod;

And all is seared with trade;
bleared, smeared with toil;

And wears man's smudged and
shares man's smell: the soil

Is bare now, nor can foot feel,
being shod.

And, for all this, nature is never spent;

There lives the dearest freshness
deep down things;

And though the last lights off the
black West went

Oh, morning, at the brown pink:
eastward, springs

Because the Holy Ghost over the bent

World broods with warm breast
and with ah! bright wings."

"SPRING

Nothing is so beautiful as Spring-

When weeds, in wheels, shoot long
and lovely and lush;

Thrush's eggs look little low heavens,
and thrush

Through the echoing timber does so
rinse and wring

The ear, it strikes like lightning's to
hear him sing;

The glassy pear tree leaves and
blooms, they brush

The descending blue; that blue is
all in a rush

With richness; the racing lambs too
have fair their fling.

What is all this juice and all this joy?

A strain of the earth's sweet being
in the beginning.

In Eden garden. – Have, get, before
it cloy,

Before it cloud, Christ, lord, and
sour with sinning,

Innocent mind and Mayday in
girl and boy,

Most, O maid's child, thy choice
and worthy the winning."

"PIED BEAUTY

Glory to be to God for dappled
things –

For skies of couple-color as
a branded cow;

For rose-moles all in stipple upon
trout that swim

Fresh- fire coal chestnut-falls;
finches' wings;

Landscape plotted and pieced –
fold, fallow, and plow;

And all trades, their gear and tackle
and trim.

All things counter, original,
spare, strange;

Whatever is fickle, freckled
(who knows how?)

With swift, slow; sweet, sour;
a dazzle, dim;

He fathers-forth whose beauty
is past change:

Praise him."

c. Emily Dickinson (1830-1886)

"The Belle of Amherst", Emily Dickinson was also scarcely published during her lifetime. Only 10 of her total 1,700 poems were published before she died. Although she was well read and enjoyed gardening and music she lived a life of increasing, self-imposed seclusion, broken only by letter correspondence with a few friends. She is one of America's truly "immortal" literary figures. Many good biographies are available.

(Although Emily Dickinson did not label her poems with titles I have done so to help in remembering them.)

"What of that?

I reason, Earth is short-

And Anguish--absolute--

And many hurt,

But, what of that?

I reason, we could die--

The best Vitality

Cannot excel Decay,

But, what of that?

I reason, that in Heaven--

Somehow, it will be even--

Some new Equation, given--

But, what of that?"

"The Brain

The Brain--is wider than the Sky-

For--put them side by side—

The one the other will contain

With ease-and You--beside—

The Brain is deeper than the sea-

For--hold them--Blue to Blue-

The one the other will absorb-

As Sponges--Buckets--do—

The Brain is just the weight of God

For--Heft them--Pound for Pound-

And they will differ--if they do-

As Syllable from Sound-"

"Death

Because I could not stop for

Death--He kindly stopped for me

The Carriage held but just Ourselves-

And Immortality.

We slowly drove--He knew no haste

And I had put away

My labor and my leisure too,

For his Civility-

We passed the School,
where Children strove

At Recess-in the Ring-

We passed the Fields of Gazing Grain-

We passed the Setting Sun-

Or rather--He passed Us-

The Dews grew quivering and chill-

For only Gossamer, my Gown-

My Tippet--only Tulle-

We paused before a House that
seemed

A Swelling of the Ground-

The Roof was scarcely visible-

The Cornice--in the Ground-

Since then—'tis Centuries--and yet

Feels shorter than the Day

I first surmised the Horses' Heads

Were toward Eternity-"

Also, on the subject of death, Dickinson once wrote; "Unable are the loved to die, for love is immortality."

d. Biblical Poetry

The Old Testament contains many poetic writings, some of which were not intended as poetry, but which centuries of common usage have elevated from prose to poetry. "The Song of Solomon" which was intended as poetry, is one of the most beautifully sensuous poems in literature: It begins;

"O that you would kiss me with the kisses of your mouth!

For your love is better than wine" your anointing oils are fragrant, your name is oil poured out;"

The Psalms are also very poetic. My mother's favorite, and a constant source of comfort and solace for her, and many others, is the Twenty-third Psalm:

"The Lord is my shepherd, I shall not want;

He makes me lie down in green pastures. He leads me beside still waters; he restores my soul.

He leads me in paths of righteousness for his names sake.

Even though I walk through the valley of the shadow of death, I fear no evil; for thou art with me; thy rod and thy staff they comfort me.

Thou prepares a table before me
in the presence of my enemies;

Thou anointest my head with oil,
my cup overflows.

Surely goodness and mercy shall
follow me all the days of my life;

And I shall dwell in the house
of the Lord forever."

And, beyond these, the books of
the Bible commonly referred to as
the "Wisdom books", such as
Proverbs and Ecclesiastes, are well
worth reading.

Also, Isaiah, Chapter 1, as the Old
Testament prophet who admonished
Israelis to put an end to sacrifices,
saying, "I have had enough of burnt
offerings or rams and the fat of fed
cattle. I do not delight in the blood
of bulls, or of lambs or goats" ...
and "Incense is an abomination to
me."..."Put away the evil of your
doings from before my eyes. Cease to
do evil. Learn to do good: Seek justice,
Rebuke the oppressor; defend the
fatherless, Plead for the widow."

And, "Come now, let us reason
together, saith the Lord". And, "The
word of Lord from Jerusalem. He shall
rebuke many people: They shall beat
their swords into plowshares, and
their spears into pruning hooks;
Nations shall not lift up sword
against nation, Neither shall they
learn war anymore."

Isaiah also prophesied the coming
of a "Prince of Peace", and was the
voice of compassion for Judaism.

The Protestant Affirmation of Faith,
"The Apostles' Creed", while certainly
not credible as a statement of scientific
fact, is just as certainly a profound
and poetic statement of faith and
hope, shared by millions of Protestant
and Catholic Christians.

"I believe in God the Father Almighty,
maker of heaven and earth;

And in Jesus Christ his only Son
our Lord:

Who was conceived by the Holy
Spirit, born of the Virgin Mary,
suffered under Pontius Pilate, was
crucified, died, and was buried;

He descended into Hell, the third
day he rose from the dead;

he ascended into heaven, and sitteth
at the right hand of God the Father
Almighty;

from thence he shall come to judge
the quick and the dead.

I believe in the Holy Sprit, the holy
Catholic Church, the communion
of saints, the forgiveness of sins,
the resurrection of the body, and the
life everlasting ..

Amen."

United Methodist Hymnal, 1989

SOME REMARKABLE RELIGIOUS PEOPLE I HAVE KNOWN

Let me turn now to telling you of some remarkable religious people I have known and whose lives illustrate other ways to relate lives of faith and rational thought. The first is:

a. Reverend Philip L Blackwell

Reverend Phil Blackwell has been the best guide for my last twenty-two years of searching for answers to the relationship between science and religion. He is now the senior pastor of the First United Methodist Church, "The Chicago Temple", located (since 1834!) at Clark and Washington Streets in downtown Chicago, Illinois.

Phil and his wonderfully independent, bright and thoughtful wife, Sally, have become good and close friends of my wife Josie and mine during the twenty-two years we have known them. Phil is an extraordinary Christian, living his faith in every way, and providing leadership to an urban congregation in a time of turmoil. His church invites all comers without regard to race, gender, homelessness, sexual orientation, poverty or wealth, or creed. His church has a full program of educational and social service programs, great music, and a staff of ethnically diverse clergy and service people. Phil is a gifted preacher and writer who has a thorough knowledge of Christian theology and has long-standing relationships with the Jewish and Muslim communities in Chicago. Phil also has an unquenchable sense of humor, which permeates all that he does. He can certainly be serious and presses many serious community and church issues, but he does everything in a spirit of joy and heartfelt good humor.

We met Phil and Sally first in 1985 when he became the pastor at Trinity United Methodist Church in Wilmette, Illinois. Prior to Wilmette Phil had served as the United Methodist minister at the University of Chicago. He had also served churches in Rockford

Left to right, Reverend Philip Blackwell and his wife Sally with Josie and me at their place in Wisconsin.

and Apple River, Illinois and Wolverhampton, England. From 1997 to 2001 he served as the assistant to Bishop Sprague for the Northern District of Illinois. Phil has a B.S. degree from the University of Wisconsin, a B.D. from the Yale Divinity School and a Doctor of Divinity from the Divinity School of the University of Chicago. Phil and Sally have two children, Elizabeth and Peter and three grandchildren.

During Phil's thirteen-year tenure in Wilmette he organized a number of educational programs, one of which was a Science and Religion book study group, which was the genesis of my science and religion library, which I subsequently donated to Phil's present church,"The Temple" in Chicago. We also organized the "Clampitt Lecture Series" (named after its sponsor), which offered public lectures on topics of religious or com-

munity interest. Such topics as "Creationism on Trial" by Dr. Langdon Gilkey, "The Holocaust: Its Meaning for Christians" by Dr. Franklin Littell, "Mind, Illness, Hope and Health" by Dr. Barry Amazon, "A Liberal Arts Education: Is It Still Worth the Price?" by Dr Arnold Weber, "Fundamentalism Around the World", by Dr. Martin Marty, "Spirituality and the Chicago Bulls", by Coach Phil Jackson, and "Faith or Frenzy, Living Contemplation in World of Action", by Dr. Parker Palmer. I published most of these talks in bound pamphlet form for free public distribution.

The essential idea that Phil, and the other group participants, taught me during these thirteen years was that skepticism and faith can live vigorously side-by-side. They can be integrated. In fact they must be for a full life. Phil was always able to translate the meaning of Christianity from its scriptural and historical language into credible lessons for today's world without denying or avoiding modern scientific knowledge.

In his preface to one of the Clampitt Lectures, Phil quoted Rev. John Wesley, the principal founder of Methodism: "It is a fundamental principle with Methodists that to renounce reason is renounce religion, that religion and reason go hand in hand, and that all irrational religion is false religion." Phil also quoted Rev. Charles Wesley, John's hymn writing brother, "Unite the pair so long disjoined, Knowledge and Vital piety: Learning and holiness combined, and truth and love let all men see." And lastly, Alfred Tennyson, "There lives more faith in honest doubt, Believe me, than in half the creeds."

Phil also wrote, in a review of "Contact", a film about science and religion:

"Now there are wise people around ... These are the people who record the truths of life with a pencil because it feels too arrogant to them to write their conclusions with a pen. These are the people who are willing to change answers they thought they had, and they even are content sometimes just live with the questions, aware that answers are beyond their grasp. The sages in our midst know that they do not know it all.

That is why wisdom is best sought in community, not alone. Because no one possesses all the truth, the wisest people meet together to share what they know. In that way, even the sages can risk being wrong, because there is a collective obligation to protect and correct one another."

"There is no short-cut to wisdom. Maybe that is why it comes late in life, after gathering information, after attaining knowledge. And, even then, it is not automatic. It requires maintaining a sense of awe, wonder, and mystery in an age that brags that it can reduce everything to bytes of data. Or, in the old language, we must "fear the Lord" in order to find wisdom."

We are blessed to count Phil and Sally Blackwell among our closest friends.

b. Reverend Ivan Illich; S.J. (1926 - 2002) and Father Gerry Morris
This most extraordinary man, who was a controversial Vatican educated priest and Monsignor, thought and spoke and wrote about the role of religious and most other institutions in original and insightful ways. His conflicts with authority of the Roman Catholic Church eventually led to his being tried for heresy in Rome - where he successfully defended himself! - but caused him to voluntarily resign his offices as a priest (but keeping his

Reverend Ivan Illich

help themselves. He was a modern-day "Don Quixote", tilting at modern windmills.

I met Ivan at CIDOC in Cuernavaca and at Northwestern University during the late 1960's and early 1970's, corresponded with him and donated various samples of photographic and audiovisual equipment to him for his use with students. I also met and corresponded with his priest colleague, his "Sancho Panza", Brooklyn born and bred Father Gerry Morris, in Oaxaca, Mexico where be was helping Mexican Indian children learn Spanish and useful trades. My wife Josie and I also had the good fortune to entertain Gerry for dinner and a stay at our home in Wilmette, Illinois a few years later.

Ivan's teachings were so novel for his time that he was considered a radical. Many of his ideas have since become accepted wisdom. He was also such a ferociously brilliant thinker and communicator that he frightened many people. I found that his ferocity was not aggression, but was simply an indication of the intensity of his belief.

Illich wrote a number of short, polemical books on the major institutions of the world: "Deschooling Society", "Tools for Conviviality", "Energy and Equity", "Medical Nemesis", "The Right to Useful Unemployment and its Professional Enemies", and "Shadow Work".

vows) and to found CIDOC (Centro Intercultural de Documentation) at Cuernavaca, Mexico. His experience as a priest in New York City and as Vice-Rector of the Catholic University of Puerto Rico, gave him the insight that educational institutions could cause the very problems they were intended to cure. He also saw that the agents of other institutions; teachers, priests, doctors, lawyers, social workers, customers, etc., could become more interested in protecting their jobs and status, and defining the world in terms of their "clients" that they were interested in helping the students, patients, etc. learn how to

Francine du Plessix Gray wrote an excellent biography of Illich in "Divine Disobedience". (KNOPF, 1969)

Although Illich resigned his offices as a priest he maintained his vows of chastity and poverty all his life, and considered himself primarily a theologian. He once told me in conversation that he would, always love the Church as "She", but not as "It". Whenever I think of how a man can combine a brilliant creative intellect and a profound religious faith, I think of Ivan Illich.

c. "Brother" Bill Tomes (1933–present)

A completely different but profoundly believing Roman Catholic man is "Brother" Bill Tomes who lives in Evanston, Illinois. His combined qualities of loving naiveté, physical bravery and committed Christian belief are unique in my experience.

I met Bill when I called him because I saw a "For Sale" sign on the front lawn of his house on Ridge Boulevard and, I wanted to talk with him about his genealogy before he moved away. There are very few Tomeses anywhere and I had known that a Wylie Tomes lived at Bill's address, but had never contacted him.

When I called Bill and told him I was interested in Tomes genealogy and wanted to talk with him before he moved I was surprised to learn that his house was not actually for sale. I asked why he had the sign out and he told me he put the sign up as a favor to a neighbor down the side street, because there was more traffic on Ridge than on the side street! He said he wished he hadn't because of all the people who rang his doorbell! How naive, and yet how friendly to his neighbor.

Brother Bill Tomes on the streets of Chicago.

I then said by way of conversation that there was another Bill Tomes in Chicago, known as "Brother Bill", who was risking his life interceding between gangs on the west side of Chicago. The Bill I was talking to on the phone then said, "That's me". I was amazed and said I would like to meet him if he had the time. I added that I would also be pleased to give him what information I had on the Tomes genealogy and he said he would like that.

We did meet at his house a few weeks later and I learned the even more amazing story of how he became "Brother Bill". When I asked him to tell me his story, the first thing he said was, "You won't believe it". I said "I'm sure I'll believe that you believe what you are telling me, so please proceed."

What he told me was incredible, but believable in that I'm sure he experienced what he told me. He said that a few years, before, while he was looking for a job, he visited a chapel in a Ukrainian Catholic church near O'Hare field for some peace and quiet to consider his job offers. He said that while he was sitting in a pew in the chapel a picture of Jesus Christ on the wall "spoke to me". He said Jesus told him to "Never be afraid, I will protect you."

Brother Bill said he was afraid of the vision he saw and he went to his priest at his church. The priest advised him to pray and go back to work, "knowing that Jesus would protect him." He did, but he had a second vision which made him go back to his priest, asking him "Why me, I'm just an ordinary man?" The priest said that "God calls on many ordinary men to do his work". He advised Bill to offer his help to a west side Convent of the Sisters of Charity. Brother Bill did just that and they put him to work doing odd jobs around the Convent. In this way he began to meet some gang members from the neighborhood who then invited him to meet other street friends of theirs. After a few weeks of these encounters, the leader of one of the gang's leaders told him, "We decided we ain't going to kill you".

I asked Bill what he did with the gangs and he said he "really didn't do anything, he just befriended them. They treat me like a father. They trust me." I asked him if he preached to them and he said, "Oh, no they have a lot of local ministers preaching to them, so they know they are bad." He did say he tried to make peace between warring gangs and they began to seek him out for peace making.

During this period of time he kept in touch with his priest who told his church about the work Bill was doing. They in turn contacted the Catholic Diocese, then under Cardinal Bernardin, and they were sympathetic. The Cardinal authorized Bill to wear a kind of Franciscan robe tied around the middle with a rope belt, and to call himself "Brother Bill". Over time he became well known and was interviewed by the press, which was where I had heard of him.

The amazing thing all during this time that even though Brother Bill was on the street every night in the midst of gang warfare, he was never once hurt.

I continued to ask him what he did when he was with the gangs and he finally said, "I go to a lot of funerals" I asked what he did at the funerals, did he preach there? He said "No, I'm not a priest, I'm only an ex-social worker who went to Notre Dame." So I asked, what do you do at the funerals? His answer was one that I will never forget as an image, of the extraordinary love of one man for his fellow forgotten, and even despised, men. Brother Bill said that "Sometimes I recite The Beatitudes."

The image of this middle aged, rather chubby man, dressed in a Franciscan robe, standing among a crowd of grieving relatives and gang members at the funeral of a recently killed gang member, reciting The Beatitudes, is almost too much to bear. Surely, if the Christian belief in the return of Jesus ever occurs, He will be standing among the grieving friends and families of the dispossessed and despised.

Brother Bill continued his dangerous work for many years, even traveling once to Palestine to try to make peace there by walking among those warring tribes, and he retired in 2003 turning his work over to another dedicated brave "Brother".

So, as much as I like to think I am a rational, science-trained, person, I have actually met a man who has had a vision of Jesus and acted upon it risking his life repeatedly for the peace of others. And his name is "Brother" Bill Tomes.

d. Dr. Langdon Gilkey (1919-2004)

Dr. Gilkey was the author of "Creationism on Trial, Evolution and God at Little Rock" (Harper & Row, 1985), the story of his appearance as a principal witness in 1981 on behalf of the ACLU and mainstream Protestant, Catholic and Jewish religion plaintiffs who challenged an Arkansas law mandating the teaching Creationism as an alternative to evolution. The case; McLean v. Arkansas, was decided in favor of the plaintiffs and the Arkansas law was held unconstitutional in violation of the Federal Constitution's First Amendment prohibition against the establishment of religion.

I was introduced to Dr. Gilkey by Phil Blackwell when we invited him to be our first Clampitt Lecture speaker at Trinity United Methodist Church in Wilmette, Illinois in April of 1988. I personally published a transcript of his talk among the other Clampitt Lectures for the years 1988-1989. We found Dr. Gilkey to be a most interesting, brilliant and engaging man with a marvelous sense of humor.

When we met Dr. Gilkey he was a professor at the University of Chicago Divinity School, where his father had previously been head of the school. He was a graduate of the University of Chicago and Union Theological Seminary and an ordained Baptist minister. Gilkey's professional life was dedicated mostly to teaching, both as a professor (from 1963 to 1989) and as the author of many books. He was a prominent Protestant theologian who argued publicly for "a rational, even satisfying, coexistence between science and faith in the modern secular age".

Dr. Martin Marty, another famed University of Chicago theologian and Lutheran minister, said at Gilkey's memorial service; "He was a leader in the generation that followed the 20th Century titans; Reinhold Niebuhr; H. Richard Niebuhr, his brother; and Paul Tillich. They were the first generation that could be really at home with Catholicism, and they had a more open embrace of popular culture."

Dr. Gilkey maintained that "Christian thought could profitably inform and be informed, by a world that contained science, secularism and an abundance of other faiths."

Gilkey's first book was "Shantung Compound: The Story of Men and Women Under Pressure" which was the story of his internment as a prisoner of war by the Japanese during World War II after he was captured while teaching in China before the war. His fifteen other books, are all about theology and religion and culture, are in print and readily available in bookstores and on the Internet. He is an excellent and even entertaining writer who translates religious subjects and concerns into real life language.

SACRED PLACES:
CHURCHES, CATHEDRALS AND ABBEYS
IN ENGLAND AND FRANCE

Although I am not a believer in any particular religion I have frequently visited and revisited many Christian cathedrals and churches, and some Buddhist and Shinto shrines. I find I am drawn to them as places of contemplation, history, community and beauty. Most people have such sacred places where they seek refuge, solace, sanctuary, and peace, and celebrate the common human rites of passage; birth, puberty, marriage and death, and contemplate the mysteries of life.

a. England, My Ancestral Churches

The churches of my ancestors are Anglican, typically built over the foundations of Anglo-Saxon, then Norman churches. The grandest of them is St. James in Chipping Camden in the Cotswold's in England. My great-great grandfather, Francis Tomes, was baptized there in 1780, as were all his siblings as they were born. It is a beautiful Cotswold stone church, built in the "Perpendicular" style, and standing on a high promontory overlooking the town. It is now bounded on one side by the road to Shipston-on-Stour, where my great great great grandfather, Richard Tomes, walked or rode to court his bride, Sarah Hawks. On the other side is the church cemetery where Richard and Sarah are buried, and beyond is now an empty meadow where cattle grazed but once was the site of a large manor house, the gatehouse of which is all that remains. It is a lovely site, both externally and inside the church.

Another ancestral church is St. Eadburgha, in Broadway, also in the Cotswold's. It is now called the "old church" because it is located a mile or so from the town center and has been superceded in use by a Victorian church built in the town in the 19th century. St. Eadburgha dates from the 1100's when it was built on the site of an even older Anglo-Saxon church. It is located in an open field between a flowing stream and the narrow road

Top left, St. Eadburgha, in Broadway, Top right, St. James in Chipping Camden. Middle, St. Laurence in Bidford-on-Avon. Bottom right, St. Michael in Buckland.

from Broadway to the nearby town of Snowshill. Because it is in a very rural setting and has an un-embellished interior (thanks to the Victorian church) it is a simple and exceptionally beautiful church. Local townspeople have kept it open as a church and continue to have services during the summer months.

Also, nearby, in the town of Bidford-on-Avon, is the ancient church of St. Laurence. It is situated on the highest hill of the town, overlooking the Avon. Other ancestors of mine are buried in its cemetery, beginning with Benjamin Tomes, the Sadler of Bidford", in 1786 at age 75. His father, also named Benjamin, was also buried there, as well as others we have not yet identified. His son Richard was baptized there in 1745. Visiting these village churches, sitting in the pews, walking in their cemeteries, and thinking about my ancestors who attended these churches during the past three hundred years, gives me a tangible connection with the past that is unlike any other. Many generations of my ancestors prayed in these churches, thanking their God for their blessings, hoping for relief from their sufferings, baptizing their children, marrying their sons and daughters, and burying their dead. These churches are intimate witnesses to their lives.

England has thousands of these village churches. We have visited many of them and attended services in some of them most recently at Christmas Eve service on December 24th, 2005 in the 14th century church of St. Michael in Buckland, near Broadway. We have been staying at Buckland Manor, next to the church for many years. Each one of these churches also bears sad witness to the terrible cost of war with long lists of the names of those who have died in the service of England. The longest lists are for those killed in World War I, with shorter but still significant lists for World War II and other conflicts.

Another Norman Church of St. James is in Long Marston, the ancestral home of Major Ian Tomes and the "King's Lodge" where prince Charles stayed for one night in 1651 escaping from Cromwell at the battle of Worcester. Ian's branch of the Tomes family has been in Long Marston since at least the 16th century, and probably before, so they have been worshiping at St. James for many generations. The church stands with its Norman porch, and baptismal font, in an open field next to the King's Lodge. It has a memorial on the wall for Capt Geoffrey Tomes who was killed at Gallipolis in 1915. The church Sexton, Harold Newman, and his wife Irene, the parents of our good friend Linda Newman Rigler, are buried in its cemetery. The village of Long Marston is so small and "undeveloped" that it is easy to close one's eyes and imagine how it has been over the centuries, with its Norman font and porch, and with local church-goers coming and going for over 900 years.

Having belonged to the Methodist Church for many years we have also visited the two principal Methodist sites in England First is the New Room, the oldest Methodist chapel in England, built by John Wesley in Bristol in 1739. It is still very actively in use and also houses a Methodist museum, with a statue of Wesley out front. The other well-known site is the City Road church in London, also still an active church. Wesley's example of his lifetime devotion to the needs of the poor, and his commitment to the idea that "to renounce reason is to renounce religion, and that all irrational religion is false religion", still reverberates today.

English Cathedrals and Abbeys
England is of course also the land of many cathedrals, and many ruins of cathedrals and abbeys, torn down and dispersed during the Dissolution of Roman Catholicism by King Henry VIII in the 1560's. Fortunately, many of the cathedrals still exist and many of the ruins are still wonderful to see as evidence of what once was.

The mother church of Anglican Christianity is Canterbury Cathedral in Kent, southeastern England. Its origin dates to 597 C.E. when Pope Gregory sent "St. Augustine The Less" to "recover" England for Christianity.

St. Augustine The Less built a Benedictine abbey and then a church on the site of a nearby Roman temple. A subsequent Saxon cathedral was burned in 1067 and replaced by William the Conqueror in 1070, Archbishop Thomas Beckett was murdered in the cathedral by knights loyal to King Henry II in 1170, and Beckett was consecrated a Saint in 1173. Canterbury is still the seat of English Christendom, but has been Anglican instead of Roman Catholic since Henry VIII took over the church in 1532. It is, of course, the destination of the pilgrims in Chaucer's Canterbury Tales.

Westminster Abbey in London is equally famous as the crowning and burial place for most English sovereigns and many of its literary and other historic greats. It too dates from about 600 C.E. as the site of a Saxon church; supplanted in 1065 by Edward the Confessor. It stands next to the Houses of Parliament on the Thames and is one of the most frequently visited tourist sites in England. St. Paul's Cathedral, rebuilt after the fire that bummed down most of London in 1666, but withstood the worst incendiary bombing the Nazis could throw at England in 1940, is a remarkable landmark and symbol of England's courage.

There are many other lesser, but still grand cathedrals and abbeys throughout England, most with similar histories, built by Normans during the 11th century on the site of Saxon churches dating from the 7th century. Visiting these great sacred spaces is always inspiring and full of English history. Lincoln Cathedral in Lincolnshire is one, where Josie and I woke up to the pealing of the great bells that we could see out of our window after arriving late at the next-door White Hart Inn on the night before. The following day we also had tour of Lincoln cathedral, which included a walk over the top of the nave under the roof, looking out through the open windows down the buttresses to the ground way below. There is no better way to get a sense of the enormous scale of these cathedrals than to climb up to the top and take the stairs all the way down into the Crypts. They are all awesome examples of architecture. They are each extraordinary reminders of how puny each of us individual human beings are, and how vast the ideas of religion and the universe are. And they usually all have beautiful examples of statuary and stained glass windows. They were of course designed to teach the Christian stories to a largely illiterate population.

Ely Cathedral in Cambridgeshire, Salisbury Cathedral in the town of Salisbury, and Durham Cathedral in the north near Newcastle, are other examples of truly grand architecture and history. Durham, for instance is the burial site of the Venerable Bede (673-735 C.E.), who wrote the earliest known history of England.

Other exceptional cathedrals, on a somewhat smaller scale, are Tewkesbury in Gloucester shire, Glastonbury in Somerset, Wells in Somerset and Winchester in Hampshire. Each of these has its own particular beauty and history and must be visited to appreciate. Traveling through England from cathedrals to abbeys, both still standing and some in ruins, is a powerful lesson in the connection between religion and English history. For instance, in the very small village of Deer Hurst, near Tewkesbury, is Odda's Chapel, a Saxon church, built in 1056 and now attached to a half-timbered house. It is a single nave, about twenty feet high and forty feet long, with a simple stone altar and a few high windows. To stand in a house of worship that was made by hand by relatively primitive people, and yet is still standing, almost one thousand years later, is profound testimony to the faith of those who built it.

Three English abbeys, which must be mentioned, are first, Tintern Abbey in southeastern Wales, along the banks of the Wye River. It is a glorious ruin, well kept by the National Trust which also manages an excellent exhibition center with good guidebooks; and second, Hailes Abbey in Gloucestershire, nearby Broadway. It was a Cistercian monastery, founded in 1246 and possessed, until it was dissolved in 1539, a relic reputed to be "the blood of Christ", which made the abbey a very popular pilgrim site. When the abbey was dissolved the relic was declared false, but it had become quite famous in the meantime and is mentioned in Chaucer's Pardoner's Tale of the Canterbury Tales. Third is Bury St. Edmunds Abbey and Church in Suffolk, another "must see." The ruins of the abbey and the church and grounds are vast and well marked. Just walking around the ruins of these abbeys is a reminder of the power and influence held by religion during most of England's history.

b. – France, Cathedrals and Abbeys in France.

For me, and many others, the greatest cathedral in France is the Cathedral of Notre Dame in the town of Chartres, about an hour's drive west of Paris on the Autoroute. The cathedral stands on the highest ground in the town, which is encircled by the river Eure. Its twin spires, dating from the 11th and 12th centuries, on its west front soar up over 330 feet above its base. They are visible from afar for all the surrounding countryside. The cathedral was built on ground previously held sacred by Druids. It was repeatedly burned and rebuilt through the 13th and 14th centuries, but amazingly was not damaged by the Religious wars, the Revolution or the

Second World War. Its most striking features, apart from its sheer size and long history, are its stained glass and three rose windows, with their deep Chartres" blue color. Josie and I once hired an expert Chartres guide who gave us a full tour, from the crypt to the roof of the nave.

We had friends who lived in a chateau north of Chartres, which gave us many opportunities to visit.

And, during the years when I traveled frequently to France and had an office in Paris, I spent a few Sundays driving to Chartres, just sitting alone in the cathedral, absorbing its beauty and watching the flow of humanity, celebrating and coming and going.

Chartres Cathedral, west facade with the Royal Portals

I learned later that I was, intuitively, following the advice given by Henry Adams, over 100 years ago. Adams said in his classic "Mont Saint Michel and Chartres", "If you want to know what Churches were made for, come down here (to Chartres) on some great festival of the Virgin, and give yourself up to it; but come alone! That kind of knowledge cannot be taught and can seldom be shared. We are not now seeking religion; indeed, true religion generally comes unsought. We are trying only to feel gothic art. For us, the world is not a schoolroom or a pulpit, but a stage, and the stage is the highest yet seen on earth. In this church the old Romanesque leaps into the gothic under our eyes; of a sudden, between the portal and the shrine, the infinite rises into a new expression, always a rare and excellent miracle in thought."

And Thomas Goldstein's "Dawn of Modern Science" (Houghton Mifflin, 1980) states unequivocally: "For it was at the School of Chartres that the philosophical groundwork was laid for the rise of Medieval and early modern science. Here the study of nature was established as a discipline in its own right, unhampered by older doctrinaire restrictions; here a conceptual seed was sown, from which the plant of Western science was to sprout forth into its full-blown growth and into all the branches of modern specialization."

12th century artists depict music and grammer.

"At Chartres during the twelfth century the study of science was first given priority over the teaching of the liberal arts, and professors advocated bold reforms for higher education as a whole centering the curriculum on the natural sciences of the quadrivium - arithmetic, music taught largely as a mathematical discipline, geometry, and astronomy - rather than on the traditional humanities of the tritium - subjects then called grammar, rhetoric, and logic. Here the exponents of the new, scientific view of the world had to face the outraged denunciations of their more conservative colleagues at the great cathedral schools of

Sculpture depicting Aristotle

Orleans, St. Victor of Paris, and Laon. At Chartres the writings of ancients scientists were systematically collected into a first library of science for the Western world, a basic book of knowledge from which the masters of Chartres could draw their inspiration and develop their original thoughts, which future generations were able to expand:"

"The enormous spadework of medieval science, the West's first vigorous steps toward the conquest of nature, was initiated at the School of Chartres in the twelfth century."

"The wrath of the religious conservatives, which the pioneers of Chartres attracted upon their heads, had its understandable reasons. For a good seven hundred years, nature had been presented as the passive object of God's creation, devoid of any innate power to create by itself. Now the masters of Chartres were asserting that nature possesses intrinsic creative

powers that were unfolding according to inherent laws or patterns of their own and whose investigation they insisted was a perfectly worthy subject for the human mind. Seven centuries of Christian laws about the place of nature in the scheme of God were being challenged at the School of Chartres."

Evidently, these early discords contained the seeds of the historic war between theology and science, which was to plague the growth of Western science through the later Middle Ages to the Scientific Revolution, through the trial of Galileo into our time… "What may look in retrospect like an irreconcilable dichotomy between "science" and "faith" (or "reason" and "religion") began as a mere conflict between two ways of understanding the religious universe."

"Nor did it occur to the masters of Chartres to sever the natural universe from God's world. In their vision the laws of nature, the perceptions of the mind - as much as the contributions of the ancient philosophers to scientific understanding -were all encompassed within the divine universe and its design. Chartres cathedral and its statuary stand as a visual manifestation of an abiding conception of the universe, spanning the past and the future, nature as well as faith, Christian religion and scientific thought, the world of the Bible and the ancient world of Greece and Rome, the teaching of the liberal arts and the teaching of science - a tangible embodiment of the spirit that pervaded the School of Chartres. Ptolemy the cosmologist, Pythagoras the mathematician, Aristotle the teacher of exact rational thought and of the systematic order of the scientific disciplines - all sit beside Christ and the saints, together with the founders of the liberal disciplines, on the beautiful tympanum of Chartres Royal Portal."

"It was not the spirit of newly born science that rebelled against faith. "It was the timorous pedantry of conservative theologians, committed to a more limited view of God and the world, that eventually forced science on the defensive: the universe of these traditionalists was simply not large enough to contain both science and faith, nature and the Good Lord. Conservative theologians from Paris, Orleans, and Laon, prodded by St. Bernard, that ubiquitous Medieval conservative, were hounding the masters of Chartres, summoning them to appear in tribunal, denouncing their science as heresy, branding the teachers of science as rebels. And, from that moment, the conflict was on."

Other notable French cathedrals and churches.
There are so many churches and cathedrals in France it is difficult to select a few to mention in this short essay. Perhaps most obvious is Mont St. Michel situated on top of a 240 foot high granite cone just off the mainland on the north coast of France. It was crowned by a church, cloister and refectory beginning about the year 1040 and it has stood and withstood many sieges over the nearly one thousand years since. It is accessible only via a causeway, which was always subject to being flooded by the surging tides of the sea. In recent years the access is by a permanent causeway, which has had the effect of silting up the surrounding waterways.

It is one of the magnificent sites of Europe, and, as such, has long been a destination for religious pilgrims. The town that has grown up on its steep slopes is of course dedicated entirely to serving the few pilgrims and the very many tourists who now visit all year round. It is very much worth a visit. Josie and I stayed in the town in 1978 at the Mere Pollard hotel when we visited with our four children. One of ironic experiences of that trip occurred when we left Mt. St. Michel by car and stopped at a World War II German Military Cemetery

Mt. St. Michel

built on the flat marshy plain on the mainland. It was labeled "Cimiterie Militaire Allemand" so I turned in and found a circular fort-like building entered through a courtyard leading into its center. There was a walkway, around the circular perimeter on top of the "fort", from which you could see Mt. St. Michel in full view, standing up out of the sea. The view was spectacular. The irony was that there were Christian crosses mounted all around the perimeter walk, so that it was impossible to see the great Christian pilgrimage church without also seeing the crosses on top of the German Cemetery. The juxtaposition of these two Christian symbols, caused by the tragedy of World War II was, for us, very poignant.

Other pilgrimage churches well worth visiting are Vezelay, Autun, Auxerre, Moissac, and the Church of St. Foy in Concques. Each church has its own style and story and should be visited at leisure so you can absorb its history and spirit. The church of St. Foy is quite unique, located as it is in a remote valley in Languedoc in south central France. It is, like most of the others, very ancient, having been built in 1150 CE. and left mostly unrestored and un-embellished since then. The

Top left, Church of St. Foy Surrounded by the mountain village of Conques. Top right, the west facade of the church. Bottom left, the Romanesque tympanum. Bottom right, the shrine of St. Foy.

massive columns surrounding its nave are stunning and its tympanum representing the Last Judgment still has some of its original coloring. Most important for this pilgrimage church is its "Tresor", its Treasury, where its collection of remarkable relics is kept and available for visitor to see. Its principal relic the gold covered reliquary statue of St. Foy, the young Christian girl martyr after whom the church is named. Very much worth a serious visit.

Reims, the Cathedral Notre-Dame
Reims was a prehistoric and then a Gallic tribe capitol. After the Roman conquest it became an important Roman outpost, with some of its public buildings surviving until today. Then came the conversion of Clovis, the king of the Franks, circa 500 CE, and his baptism by the Bishop of Reims, Remi (440-533), on Christmas day, 499 CE. There is a legend of a dove bringing a vial of holy oil which Remi used to anoint Clovis, and which has been used subsequently to anoint the coronation of every subsequent King of France from the 11th century to 1825. The most famous was the coronation of King Charles VII in 1429, during the hundred years war, in the presence of Joan of Arc.

So, Reims has been an important religious, political and artistic center for France from its earliest days. One of its Archbishops, Gerbert, became Pope in 999 CE. During the 11th, 12th and 13th centuries the town expanded

Notre-Dame Cathedral, Rheims, France.

and built its Cathedral Notre-Dame and its Basilique St. Remi. Both of these sacred places are spectacular and are well worth visiting. Their architecture, stained glass and sculpture is extraordinary. The Cathedral was badly damaged, as was the whole town, during the 1914-1918 World War, but all has been carefully restored. There are also many museums, such as the Palais du Tau and the Musee St. Remi, and many other architectural gems to see in the town.

Josie and I visited Reims for the first time in the 1970's after we discovered that my great-grandfather, Dr. Robert Tomes, had been the U.S. Consul there in 1866-67. Robert wrote a book, "The Champagne Country" about his stay in Reims, describing the Cathedral and the Basilique in great detail, and also the champagne industry in Reims and surrounding countryside. He tells, for instance, about meeting the original "Veuve Cliquot" (the widow Cliquot) and riding by carriage to the neighboring towns of Sillery, Dizy, and Hauteville, where champagne was developed by Dom Perignon (1638-1715). Robert stayed in a hotel on the cathedral square during his time there and became friends with the Bishop in charge of the Basilique. The site of Robert's hotel is now a modern, glass walled town library with excellent views of the cathedral. The nearby towns of Epernay and Chalons sur Champagne are also worth visiting for more local history and excellent champagne.

The Benedictine Abbey of Mont Majur
In Province, near Arles, the ancient Greek-Roman-Gallic city built around its ruined temples, theatres and amphitheater, now used as a bull fight ring, is the Benedictine Abbey of Mont Majur. Mont Majur was begun in 949 CE and substantially enlarged in the 1200's, then restored beginning in the 1870's until the present. It consists of an unfinished yellow-stone church with a broad aisle-free Nave, with Transepts, a Crypt, a Cloister and an adjoining fortified Donjon with a rock-hewn Chapel.

One day when Josie and I were touring nearby we stopped for second visit. We entered via the Crypt and while there heard singing from the Nave above. We thought it might be a recording, which churches sometimes play to enliven the tours. But when we got to the top of the stone steps at the rear of the Nave we saw and

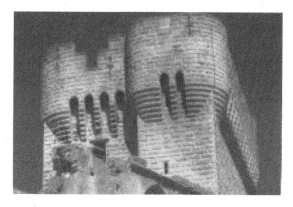

Above, shots of Mont Majur near Arles, France.

heard that the singing was the beautiful tenor voice of a young man standing alone in the sun-lit Nave. He was dressed in a shirt and shorts and was singing, a Capella, "Ave Maria". His rendition was so simple and clear, and the setting was so unadorned, that it brought us and the few other tourists to a standstill in silence until he finished. It was certainly a gift from the young man to all of us who were fortunate to be there. It was as if we were hearing "Ave Maria" for the first time. When he finished singing a young boy came running to his outstretched arms and was carried away among the tourists. It was truly a "sacred moment", touching the poetic "souls" of everyone there.

Notre Dame, Sainte Chapelle, St. Denis, Cluny, Abbaye de Fontenay
Also, in Paris, no visit is complete without seeing Notre Dame where many kings of France were crowned, and where Napoleon I crowned himself Emperor in 1804. It is a vast, busy place, which happily now faces a large open plaza under which are the excavated "Crypts Archeologic" and the ruins of Roman temples that preceded it. And, nearby Notre Dame is Sainte Chapelle, the remarkable shrine built in 1243-48 by Louis IX to house relics. It has "lofty and luminous stained glass windows" unlike any others, which fill its vast space with glorious varieties of color. Hard to believe that such beauty was created so long ago and has survived all the troubles Paris

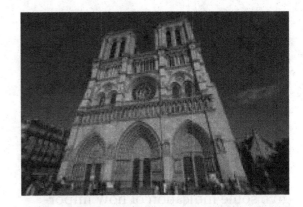

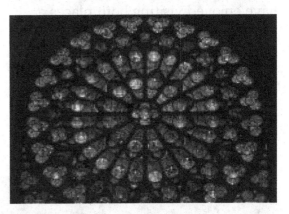

Above Notre Dame in Paris, with a close up of its three west portal and beautiful rose windows.

has seen since then. And, at the northern perimeter of Paris, is the Abbey of St. Denis, which houses the tombs of most of the kings of France. There are of course so many other sites in France that can and should be considered "sacred", but cannot even be listed in this relatively short essay. Places like Cluny, in central France, now a magnificent ruin, but once the site of the most powerful Cistercian Abbey in French history, until it was dismantled for use as building materials after the French Revolution. Another, Abbaye de Fontenay, near Dijon, beautifully restored, with its vast nave, scriptorium and refectory. These few samples should at least give some indication of how important the history of religion is to the history of France.

Modern French Religious Architecture
Notre Dame du Haut in Ronchamp is one of the most beautiful examples of religious architecture in the 20th century, an honor it shares with the Matisse Chapel in Vence. Josie and I have enjoyed visiting both places a few times over the years.

Ronchamp, completed in 1954, is considered the finest example of the French/Swiss architect LeCorbusier's (1877-1965) work. It stands alone on a high hill at Ronchamp, near Belfort in eastern France, on the site of sacred religious buildings which have come and gone since pre-Roman times. It is a very imposing structure, but not very large, intended primarily as a pilgrim site. It contains a beautiful inside chapel and also has an outdoor pulpit, accessible from the chapel, to reach larger crowds assembled on the large lawn space outside. The sweeping shape of its roof evokes the image of a nun's bonnet. Its walls are concrete set at angles and pierced by many openings, which contain stained glass to admit sunlight. It is a warm and welcoming building.

For us it symbolizes the capacity of modern Christianity to carry its central messages of love, charity and forgiveness into the 20th century.

Henri Matisse (1869-1954) designed the Chappell du Saint-Marie du

Notre Dame du Haut in Ronchamp

Above photos, Chappell du Saint-Marie du Rosaire in Vence, France

Rosaire located in Vence, a small town which calls itself "The City of Art", near Nice. The genesis of the chapel began when Matisse was cared for by a young woman in 1941 in Nice while he was recovering from cancer surgery. The young nurse later entered the Dominican convent at Vence, becoming Sister Jacques-Marie.

Matisse subsequently bought a home near the convent in Vence. Sister Jacques asked if he would help with the design of a chapel the convent wanted to build next to its school. Matisse of course said he would and began in 1947, at age 77, the greatest project of his life. He spent more than 4 years working on the chapel, designing its architecture, its stained glass windows, its interior furnishings, its murals, and the vestments for the priests and nuns. Matisse himself regarded it as his "masterpiece".

Although Matisse had been baptized as a Catholic he undertook the chapel work as an artistic challenge. It illustrates for us the universally poetic themes of all religions. As a "Religious Humanist" I am a hopeful, but realistic, optimist. I find these modern sacred places supportive of optimism, even in our modern, strife-ridden times.

French War Memorials as Sacred Places

There are other places in France and Belgium which, although not religious shrines, are profound memorials to the almost countless young men sacrificed in World Wars I and II. In France there are memorials at Ypres, Belgium recording the names of the tens of thousands of British and Commonwealth soldiers whose remains were either never found or identified. There are 55,000 names inscribed at the Menin Gate in Ypres and 35,000 more names at "Tyne Cotte" at Passchendale nearby. There are also over 150 smaller French and German cemeteries within ten square miles of Ypres where over 800,000 British, French and German soldiers were killed during WW I. And each small town in France has its monument to the many French "Poilus", infantry soldiers who died for France during WW I.

At Verdun in eastern France the entire battlefield is preserved as a memorial, some of which is still off-limits because of unexploded ordnance lying beneath the surface of the earth. Seven villages were totally destroyed during the battle and over 750,000 French and German soldiers were killed there during World War I. The Verdun cemetery has 15,000 graves and the "Ossuaire" contains the bones of another 175,000! One little known fact about Verdun is that it is where Charles De Gaul was wounded for the third time leading his men in an attack, after which he was captured and held for the remainder of the war as a prisoner.

In the Somme in north-central France there are also hundreds of cemeteries honoring the fallen French, British and German soldiers of World War I. At Thiepval there is a very large monument honoring over 73,000 missing British soldiers. And at Poziers nearby there are the names of 14,690 missing, and at Loos another 2,000 missing. My father's 27th Division is also honored at the cemetery at Bony where over 2,000 Americans were buried after they successfully breached the German defensive positions at the St. Quentin Tunnel of the Hindenburg Line in October, 1918.

And, most famously now, there is the huge American cemetery at Omaha Beach in Normandy where 9,385 of the American soldiers killed there during the June, 1944 invasion of France are buried. Each of these memorials, and many more throughout Europe, are shrines and stand in mute testimony to the enormous tragedy of war.

It is estimated that over one-half of the millions of soldiers killed during World War I were either unidentifiable or never found. They were doomed to be classified as "missing in action." After the war the governments of France, England, Germany and America each built and dedicated monuments to their "Unknown Soldiers". The French at the Etoile in Paris, the British at the Cenotaph and Westminster Cathedral in London, the Germans in Berlin, and America at the Tomb of the Unknown Soldier in Arlington Cemetery in Washington, D.C. Each of these monuments is a sacred place.

c. Austria and Germany

There are of course many great cathedrals in the great cities of Austria and Germany, but I will leave the description of most of those for the travel guides. A few of the abbeys and churches on the Danube are worth a short mention here. On the south side of the Danube, in the area known as the Wachau, are Melk and Gottweig. Melk is the elaborately embellished church that stands on a high promontory overlooking the river, painted in bright yellow and commanding an incredible view. Its interior is a jumbled array of encrusted religious decoration rivaling anything I have ever seen. It is still worth a visit. Gottweig is an abbey also on the south side of the Danube, across from the town of Krebs, where it also sits on top of a very high hill with a commanding view. It continues to function as an abbey where one evening, quite serendipitously, Josie and I and our daughter Julia happened to open the door of its huge church just in time to hear the monks chanting evening mass. We were the only ones in the church so it was quite a stirring experience. On the other side of the Danube, further west, is the town and church of Durnstein, also overlooking the river. The town is ancient and beautiful and the church is painted blue with white trim and therefore a memorable sight. The town of Durnstein sits at the foot of a very high hill, on top of which is a ruined castle, which was used as the prison for King Richard before he was ransomed back to France in the 1100's. It is a very steep, but worthwhile climb which I made one day with our daughter Betsy.

What I also want to note here is the existence of two other places that should be recognized as "sacred" for reasons other than religious. They are two Nazi concentration camps, preserved and restored after World War II as memorials to the thousands of innocent people imprisoned and murdered there. They are sacred because they stand as powerful testimony to the barbarity of the Nazis and the courage and sacrifice of their victims. The first is Dachau, a few miles north of Munich, Germany. Dachau was the first of the Nazi concentration camps, established in 1933 immediately after Hitler came to power, and used initially to imprison those who had opposed his power. Austrians and Germans who had resisted and criticized Hitler were quickly incarcerated at Dachau, which had been an old, disused army facility. During World War II Dachau became a full-fledged Nazi concentration camp with gallows, gas chambers and crematoria - incinerating ovens. Dachau was the preferred prison for

Christian Roman Catholic priests, Protestant ministers and Jehovah's Witnesses who protested Naziism. It was liberated by the American 45th Division in 1945 so it was one of the last camps to be freed. It has since been turned into a shrine to memorialize its victims. It is well worth a serious visit.

The second is Mauthausen, near Linz, Austria. This camp was built specifically as a concentration camp, designed by Albert Speer, Hitler's favorite architect. Prisoners were used to build the camp using rock cut out of the nearby quarry and carried by hand up the punishing stone steps, also built by the prisoners, to the camp site at the top of the hill. This camp was used to imprison and murder many Russian prisoners of war, and some British, French, and even American prisoners of war, and many political prisoners and many racial and other prisoners, such as Jews and Gypsies and homosexuals. It is a brutal looking place - truly the cruelest architectural expression possible of a concentration camp, with gas chambers and crematoria. It was also liberated by American troops in 1945 and has been preserved as a memorial to its victims. It is also worth a serious visit.

d. Japan - Shinto and Buddhist Shrines
Shinto Shrines

The root Japanese historical and spiritual sense of what we in the West call religion is Shinto. In Japanese it was simply "the way of life" before it became called "Shinto" to distinguish it from Buddhism which was imported to Japan from China and Korea in about 600 C.E. Shinto was the Japanese way of understanding the natural world around them and their relationship to it and to one another. To them nature was wondrous and bountiful. They were awed by its fertility and beauty. They felt a oneness with nature seeking to merge with it rather than struggling to overcome it. That which was particularly wondrous, whether in nature or among people, they accepted as a superior object of worship, called Kami. In fact, they traced their origin to the manifold Kami of nature, as in the case of the imperial family, descended from the supreme Sun Goddess. Thus, there are Shinto shrines, some very large and attended by many people, and some quite small and tucked away in surprisingly modest places all over Japan, in both rural and urban areas.

Subsequent waves of imported systems of spiritual or ethical thought have become very important in Japan; first, Confucianism, then Buddhism, and then more recently, Christianity.

Each new wave has left its mark on Japanese culture, but Shinto remains the root "religion" of Japan. So, in Japan, many people consider themselves both Shinto and Buddhist, and some also Christian, all with a background of Confucian ethics - and without any sense of conflict!

The greatest Shinto shrine in Japan is the Meiji Shrine in Tokyo. Its main entry is via the Omote Sando to the principal Torii, or gate, then on to the main buildings. The buildings are attended by Shinto priests who administer the shrine and perform various rites, such as purification. The most important effect of worship at a Shinto shrine is a sense of renewal. The many acts of worship in Shinto are usually associated with festivals, called Matsuri, celebrated throughout the calendar year in very colorful ways. A great many weddings are celebrated at Shinto shrines and are also very colorful.

I have found visiting Shinto shrines in Japan similar in some ways to visiting European or American cathedrals, and yet also quite different. There are, in both settings, many people seeking some form of religious experience, but the different underlying assumptions between Shinto and Christianity create a different mood for the visitor. Judaism, Christianity and Islam were each founded in the harsh deserts of the Middle East, where mankind had to struggle with a hostile environment. The Japanese, in contrast, consider themselves to be blessed by nature. There is in Shinto no equivalent to the Western philosophical distinction between man and nature, as drawn by the classical Greeks and heightened by Christianity. Nor is there the notion of man's sinful nature in need of discipline by religion. In contrast to the myths of the Garden of Eden, from which man emerges corrupted and radically evil, in the Japanese mythology human nature remains innocent, although people may perform actions unworthy of themselves. The Kami know of sexuality and therefore anxiety about the more intimate aspects of life is not felt so intensely by the Japanese. There is no shame in being what is human. Rather it should be appreciated and fulfilled. There is no apparent expiation of guilt to be seen in most Shinto shrines, but rather a celebration and appreciation of life.

Another aspect of Shinto is found in the various "Hachiman" shrines, particularly the great one in Kamakura. Hachiman is the Shinto "God of War", but the Hachiman shrines are quite beautiful places. The Shinto Yasukuni in Tokyo is a well-known, and sometimes politically controversial, memorial venerating Japan's war dead. The late Emperor Hirohito of Japan publicly stated that he would not worship there because many of those memorialized were convicted of World War II war crimes. Subsequently Prime Minister Koizumi of Japan decided otherwise and repeatedly visited Yasukuni, probably in deference to Japan's right-wing politicians, but over the objections of many Japanese and the Chinese government.

The huge Shinto shrine of Ise on Shukoku Island is a remarkable phenomenon, which is intentionally taken down and rebuilt in total every 20 years. It is handcrafted out of special wood and will be rebuilt for the 62nd time again in 2013. (1,240 years of regular rebuilding!)

Lastly, the great Shinto shrine in Nikko, memorializing the Emperor Tokugawa Ieyasu. One of the popular sayings in Japan is that "you haven't seen beauty until you have seen Nikko:"

Buddhist Temples

Buddhism, on the other hand, serves different functions than Shinto in Japan. First of all, it is not indigenous to Japan, but was imported from India, via China and Korea in about 600 C.E. It has since undergone various transformations in Japan, having begun as a philosophy, but now practiced as a religion. The original precepts of Buddhism were, basically, that life is full of suffering; the cause

of suffering is desire, and cessation of suffering can only be achieved by the cessation of desire. Then Buddhism teaches that the way of the "Eightfold Path" ends desire. The Eightfold Path is a straightforward set of rules of behavior to be followed by the person seeking Buddhist "enlightenment", or "nirvana", i.e. liberation from the cycle of birth and rebirth. And, since Buddha was a mortal man who eschewed all metaphysics and urged his followers to undertake their own paths to Enlightenment, Buddhism is devoid of references to the supernatural or divinity. (There are, however, modern varieties of Buddhism that deal with Buddha as if he were a divine god, and his "Bodhisattvas" as if they were Saints)

But, based on the original precepts, Buddhism is, in Western terms, a grand plan for self-help to avoid suffering in life. The Eightfold Path is, in short: Right outlook; Right resolve; Right speech; Right conduct; Right livelihood; Right effort; Right mindfulness; and Right concentration. There are many excellent books filling out the meaning of each of these principles. The first two and the last two refer to achieving a state of mind and the middle four to the correct conduct of one's life. The fourth principle that of non-violence has proved particularly attractive to many people from Western cultures.

So, since Buddhism is a kind of self-help system of thought, it is not the simple animistic and joyous celebration of life of Shinto, but it is rather more like the Christian way of trying to emulate a code of conduct. In this way it is also Comparable to Confucianism, which is basically an ethical and aesthetic code of conduct and appreciation. Some modern forms of Buddhism also stress faith as its basis, similar to Christianity, but without its supernatural gods and miracles.

Thus Buddhist temples are more concerned with education and welfare and the celebration of weddings and funerals. Buddhism is pervasive in Japan with over 30,000 "Jodo-Shin" Buddhist temples out of a total of 73,000, including other versions. Some of the most venerated Buddhist sites in Japan are the 900-year-old cast-bronze statue of the "Amida" Buddha in Kamakura, the "Dai-Buhtsu", housed in the world's largest wooden building in Kyoto. Another aspect of Buddhism that has fascinated the West is Zen Buddhism imported to Japan from China in 1200 CE. It is a contemplative form of religious practice, expressed in some remarkable physical ways, such as magnificent gardens, botanical and stone, and in the tea ceremony. To read about and see Buddhism in action in Japan is to begin to get an insight into the mysterious and wonderful workings of the Japanese culture.

So Buddhist Temples in Japan are quite different from Shinto Shrines, but both are interwoven and combined into a unified Japanese culture.

Some Buddhist parables.
As mentioned previously Buddha was a mortal man who professed his ideas of Enlightenment as a perambulating teacher. He based his thinking on the premise that all things were "impermanent" ("pattiscamapuddha"), and that the best way to cope with the natural suffering of mortal life was to follow The Eightfold Path. Right Outlook, right resolve, right speech, right conduct, right livelihood, right effort, right mindfulness and right concentration.

Two of the parables he used to teach his thinking that I have found particularly good, are:

The parable of the ownership of a gift.
One day, when Buddha was an old man and walking along a well-traveled path, he was met by an aggressive, angry man who challenged him and abused him verbally. After listening for a short while, Buddha raised his hand to ask the man a question. The man said, "Yes, but be quick about it". Buddha then asked, "If one man offers another a gift, but it is refused, who owns the gift?" The man quickly replied, "Obviously, if the gift is refused it is still owned by the person offering it." To which Buddha

replied, "So it is with abuse. Good day sir." And the Buddha walked on, leaving the abuser stunned and silent.

This parable is for me a much more credible piece of advice than the Christian admonition to "turn the other cheek" when one is abused. Turning the other cheek implies the acceptance and forgiveness of the abuse, which rarely happens in the real world. Abuse usually begets a combative, abusive reply. But by leaving the abuse with the abuser, as Buddha teaches, you can stop the abuser in his tracks and allow the target of the abuse free to go on his way unperturbed.

"Living well is the best revenge". This phrase was intended by Buddha to mean that if one followed the Eightfold Path, thus becoming Enlightened - free of worldly desires - one could "get revenge" against the suffering of mortal life. Thus the phrase meant that if one lived an enlightened life one could avoid the normal sufferings of life.

The irony of the phrase is that the phrase has been adopted by some western culture advertisers of very expensive consumer goods, completely inverting its meaning. In the advertising meaning the consumer is urged to "get revenge" on the feeling of not having something expensive by purchasing it. The ad man has turned Buddha upside down!

There are many other instructive parables attributed to Buddha. They are very helpful guides to leading a meaningful life. There are many English translations of Buddhist teachings. They are worth finding and studying.

e. American Sacred Places
There are of course many sacred places in America. Since they are readily accessible to Americans I will only list a few that have particular meaning for Josie and me.

The Frank B. Howes Memorial Chapel, on the campus of Northwestern University, in front of Garrett-Evangelical Theological Seminary, in Evanston, Illinois. Josie and I were married in this small chapel on June 26, 1954. There is a garden behind the chapel, and nearby is the Shakespeare Garden, in which are planted all of the flowers mentioned by Shakespeare in his many Sonnets and plays.

Howes Memorial Chapel

The National Cathedral in Washington, D.C. is an Episcopal cathedral. It is the official seat of both the Presiding Bishop of the Episcopal Church in the United States and the Episcopal Diocese in Washington. A truly magnificent cathedral, as grand as most European cathedrals, it was begun in 1903 and finished in 1990. It is America's sacred national place in which celebrations, commemorations, prayers and gatherings for worship at times of national significance take place. It is well worth a visit for anyone visiting Washington, D.C.

Rockefeller Chapel,
at the University of Chicago
in Hyde Park, Chicago, Illinois
This non-denominational, cathedral like building was built by the Rockefeller family and donated to the University of Chicago. The Rockefellers were Baptists, but the Chapel has become completely inter-denominational. It is an integral part of the life of the University, hosting its many graduation ceremonies and religious worship functions. The University has an active Divinity School and its campus houses various seminaries, including the Lutheran Theological Seminary, the McCormick Theological Seminary, The Catholic Theological union, the Chicago Theological Seminary and the Meadville/Lombard Theological Seminary. These seminaries are also part of The Association of Chicago Theological Schools, comprised of twelve theological seminaries in the Chicago area.

Reverend Phil Blackwell's church, The First United Methodist Church of Chicago, also known as "The Temple" is located at the intersection of Clark and Washington Streets in downtown Chicago. It is the oldest church in Chicago, founded in 1824 and moved to its present location in 1834 where it has been rebuilt many times, most recently in 1926 when it became the tallest "skyscraper" building in Chicago. Phil is the senior pastor here and has rededicated the church to its urban ministry serving everyone who wants to attend - rich and poor, all genders, the homeless, and all races. It has a strong educational program, houses my religion and science library, and recently became the site of the "Silk Road Theatre".

SUMMARY

Since we have covered a great deal of ground in just a few pages, billions of years in 200 plus pages, it seems appropriate to provide ourselves with a brief summary. We began by asking ourselves the age-old questions: Where do we come from? What are we? and Where are going? We finally come to see that we are all made of the same basic stuff-our basic DNA is interchangeable, and all living organisms have their own DNA. We are embedded in Nature and related to all of it. Our wide diversity of appearance in skin color, physiognomy, stature, etc., has developed over many tens of thousands of years by the natural process of biological evolution. We and all other living organisms evolve in response to mutations of our DNA and the competitive advantages conferred by them, and natural selection of those most fit to survive.

We began by considering the basic fact of human mortality, and some of the conceits and perspectives of genealogy.

Next, we considered the major categories of worldviews, or belief systems:

First, the polytheistic religions, such as Hinduism, and the Greek and Roman pantheon. And the animistic, "spirit" religions, such as Shintoism, Pacific Island, Aboriginal, North and South American Indian, and others, which also have multiple gods who are believed to have designed the universe and humanity and can be entreated to intervene in human affairs. There is also considerable archeological evidence of prehistoric burials of the dead with personal artifacts, indicating a belief in life after death.

Second, the Abrahamic monotheistic religions of Judaism (900 BCE), Christianity (100 CE) and Islam (600 CE), which see humanity as a creation of a single God, who brought humanity into being and guides it as father, judge and friend. God's will is interpreted from sacred scriptures and the wisdom of ecclesiastical authorities; each of these religions has a spectrum from moderate to intensely fundamentalist, and sometimes violent, believers, and theocratic governments.

Third, Buddhism (600 BCE), while known as a religion, is fundamentally different than most religions because it is not god-centered, is not "revealed" by any supernatural being, and does not have a creation myth, or metaphysics. Buddha himself was a mortal man who taught his students to follow a system of self-taught "Enlightenment". The central concern of Buddhism is the alleviation of suffering, similar to the goals of most religions, but through the reduction of Desire (seen as the cause of suffering) by rational thought and meditation and not by sacrifice, prayer, or other attempts to secure divine intervention. However, some modern forms of Buddhism have taken on many aspects of revealed religions. Confucianism (600BCE), as an organized system of prescribed behavior, is also sometimes regarded as a religion, but it has no gods or metaphysics.

Fourth, the 20th Century political behaviorism of the rapidly fading and mostly dysfunctional Communist states, which see humanity as a blank-slate molded by an atheistic, communistic political system. Some modern historians have identified Communism as a "pseudo-religion",

and the police states of Soviet, Chinese and North Korean Communism and German Naziism as mimicking the functions of religion, as secular or "surrogate religions", worshiping nation, class and race. They are examples of mankind's capacity, as compulsive believers, to believe in secular as well as supernatural gods. These systems have each been marked by extreme violence. The intensity of some of these fanatic secular believers, and the murderous self-righteousness of their causes, creating the Soviet Gulags and the Nazi Holocaust death camps, makes them even worse than the Christian Crusades, the Islamic Jihads and Anti-Semitic Pogroms of the past. When believers claim God, or even secular self-righteousness "on-their-side" they are capable of overruling their ethical as well as their rational minds, and committing unspeakable cruelty.

Fifth, Scientific Humanism, which Prof. Edwin G. Wilson says, "considers humanity to be a biological species that evolved over millions of years in a biological world, acquiring unprecedented intelligence yet still guided by complex inherited emotions and biased channels of learning. In scientific humanism, human nature exits, and it was self-assembled. It is the commonality of the heredity responses and propensities that define our species. Having arisen by evolution during the far simpler conditions in which humanity lived during more than 99 percent of its existence, it forms the behavioral part what, in the "Descent of Man", Darwin called "the indelible stamp of our lowly origin". Quotes from "So Simple a Beginning" edited by E.G. Wilson (Norton, 2005) According to Scientific Humanism we are the product of our biological evolution, modified by our cultural evolution, including the effects of our scientific knowledge and our religious beliefs.

Next we considered my own views of Humanism as "Scientific/Religious Humanism" as an extension of Scientific Humanism. This form of Humanism embraces the whole of mankind's experience in religious belief and practice as simply a profound category of human behavior. Humanity needs and has always had "sacred" gods, ideas of "life after death", "transcendence", sacred places, rituals and sacraments. Religious Humanism recognizes that all of these "supernatural" gods and many other elements of religious belief and practice have been created by mankind's fertile imagination. This is not to demean religious belief. To the contrary, such practices are usually the expression of mankind's highest hopes and aspirations, as well as his greatest fears.

So, a Scientific/Religious Humanist can participate in his or her religious tradition without accepting the supernatural and without conflict. Thus Religion is seen as "Poetic truth" and Science as "Prose truth".

I also comment that in my view "atheism" and "agnosticism" are rather empty and negative identifications. They only express a non-belief in the supernatural aspects of religion, and they are usually accompanied by attacks on organized religions.

In my view Scientific/Religious Humanism combines the best of science, religion and humanism into a credible and wonderful story of humanity.

We then considered the types of evidence upon which people base their beliefs. We described the "relatively objective" kinds of evidence, such as legal and scientific evidence, and the "subjective" kinds of evidence, such as emotional and religious evidence. We described scientific evidence as "organized skepticism", and religious evidence as "organized certainty".

We acknowledged that subjective evidence can many times overrule objective evidence because of its powerful emotional basis. We noted that scientific evidence is limited to observance and description of measurable natural phenomena, and that religious evidence also includes the description of perceived supernatural events. We also observed that there does not appear to be any "rational editor" in our minds, that "no fuses blow" when there are logical or ethical inconsistencies in our minds. We can easily hold onto beliefs that are contradicted by the "rational part" of our minds.

We then reviewed the long history of how the great variety of religions have answered the questions of where we come from and who we are. Most religions have what can be called "transactional gods", who people believe are aware of and care about human needs and who can and have intervened in human affairs, to either reward or punish, and to provide life after death, and with whom believers can communicate by prayer or otherwise. People have always sought gods and have always found them, and hold onto them tenaciously. Believing in Gods is a pervasive and persistent human trait. As one author said, "God didn't go away after the Enlightenment. "

We also observed that the wide variety and number of historical religions beginning with written language in Mesopotamia around 5,000 B.C.E. and throughout history, compels a pluralistic view of religion. (The Dictionary of Gods and Goddesses identifies 2,500 major deities in history) Although there are religions that claim to be "exclusively true" by their adherents, there is no one religion believed to be "exclusively true" by everyone.

We then reviewed the genealogical histories of many cultures and religions, particularly the Egyptian genealogies (20 years/generation since 3,950 B.C.E. yields 290 generations), and the Judeo-Christian genealogies in the Bible; Genesis and Chronicles in the Old Testament and Matthew and Luke in the New Testament - an average life-span of 900 years per life and 500 years per generation among the Old Testament Prophets. Luke lists 41 generations from Jesus to King David, plus 15 to Abraham, then 20 more to Adam totaling 76 generations. Matthew lists 42 generations from Jesus to David. And many of the people in the lines of descent are different. The main point of agreement seems to be to validate the descent of Jesus as the Messiah from the house of David, as told by the Prophet Isaiah. At 20 yrs/gen, it is 100 generations since Jesus and at 15 yrs/gen it is 133 generations.

And then we considered the scientific history of the universe - the almost unimaginable span of Deep Astronomical Time, from the 14 Billion years ago "Big Bang", to the formation of the earth 3.7 Billion years ago, through the origin and development of life on earth, and mankind's place in it, (all plant and animal life reproducing through DNA) - finally to the present age of "Homo Sapiens". We saw how the proto-human species evolved over millions of years, and how "Homo-Erectus" evolved in Africa about 1.8 million years ago, emigrated and populated many parts of the earth. He could make fire and some crude stone tools and probably was the ancestor of Neanderthal man (300,000 to 30,000 yrs ago) who made more sophisticated stone tools and buried his dead with artifacts, indicating a belief in life after death. (At 15yrs/gen 1.8 million years ago is 120,000 gens. and 270,000 yrs is 18,000 generations)

And then we saw how "Homo Sapiens" evolved independently in Africa about 200,000 years ago and also emigrated from Africa about 60,000 years ago, and ultimately populated the whole world. We saw how the art and burial practices of early Neanderthals and Homo-Sapiens left the first archeological evidence of our capacity for spiritual thought, feeling and expression. At an average generational age of 15 years, 60,000 years would be 4,000 generations. The extraordinary 18,000 years old art of the Lascaux caves was made 1,200 generations ago, and the 33,000 year old art of the Chauvet caves was made 2,200 generations ago.

We then reviewed the history of the theory and facts of Evolution, the resistance of some American fundamentalist churches to its teachings, and the repeated determinations by American courts that alternative theories, such as "Creationism" and "Intelligent Design", are simply not science. The scientific community holds the view, best summarized by

Theodorus Dobzhansky, "Nothing makes sense in biology, except in light of Evolution."

We also reviewed the acceptance of the teachings of Evolution by most American Protestant, Jewish and Roman Catholic religious institutions, and its recent reaffirmation by the Vatican.

We reviewed the primatologist's view of primate behavior, our evolutionary behavioral base, and our cultural evolution. We considered our American culture, our Founding Father's design in our Constitution and our Bill of Rights, our Civil Rights movement, Women's Rights, and the history of our many and still continuing wars.

We considered many aspects of our cultural evolution and also the unique "time bubble" of our freedom, affluence, and relative safety. We also considered the consequences of living recklessly in an age of non-renewable fossil fuels and global warming.

Then we looked at brain science and the biology of belief, and how we create "transactional", supernatural gods and goddesses. And we considered the neurological basis for the fact that our brains are wired first for survival, and second, for reproduction, and that "no fuses blow" when we hold contradictory beliefs or even contradictory facts. We are not "hardwired" for "truth" or "ethical behavior", although we can learn to discern both and behave ethically and truthfully. And we concluded that God, or gods, are certainly not dead, for the simple reason that many humans need or "create" gods and find them comforting and strengthening in times of stress. We considered the process of Alfred North Whitehead's "misplaced concreteness" and how it can lead to confusion between what happens in external reality and what happens only inside our brains.

We next considered Biblical interpretation, by both the mainstream Christian religions and the Fundamentalists. And we considered the connections between the Christian Reformation and Humanism, and the Counter-Reformation. And we also considered the fact that Islam has never undergone a similarly significant Reformation.

We then considered the scientist as a Secular Humanist; Spinoza, Jefferson and Paine as Deists, Einstein, Carl Sagan, George Santayana and other contemporary secular Humanists. And we gave examples of Religious Humanists who maintain the traditions of their founding faiths, but do not accept supernatural or other unscientific explanations of religious practice. For instance, Humanistic Judaism, Liberal Christian Humanism and Unitarian Universalist humanitarianism.

We then discussed the metaphor of religion as "poetry" and science as "prose", and gave examples of the scientist as poet, and some poets with extraordinary insights into nature.

We considered the lives of some scientists who express themselves poetically, and some formally religious people who have a profound understanding of nature and science; for example, Dr. Ursula Goodenough, Gerard Manley Hopkins, Emily Dickinson, and some Biblical poetry. We considered the metaphor for the relationship between religion and science that religion is POETRY, and science is PROSE. In this metaphor, both are readily accessible to everyone, and each has its own realm of truth, "literal or rational truth" for prose science, and "profound or emotional truth" for poetic religion. Each has its own language, so believers in both can simply consider themselves "multi-lingual", speaking and understanding both prose and poetry.

And while it is important to avoid confusing the two "languages" by confusing their evidentiary roots, it is possible to resolve differences by referring to the relevant evidence. It is also important for everyone to remember that we are all capable of appreciating both prose and poetry, and to enter into our discussions of science and religion with compassion, patience and kindness.

We then considered William Butler Yeats's poetic view of the dark side of religion, and quoted Dr. Steven

Weinberg as a Secular Rationalist, and Richard Dawkins and Sam Harris, as "atheists", each of whom recites the profoundly disturbing side of religion.

We then considered a few remarkable religious people I have known, namely; Rev. Philip Blackwell, Rev. Ivan Illich, "Brother" Bill Tomes, and Dr. Langdon Gilkey.

Then we described a number of sacred places; churches, cathedrals, abbeys and war memorials, that Josie and I have visited repeatedly in England and France. The Cathedral at Chartres, in particular, is a remarkable example of the historical connection between religion and science, with its Royal Portal depicting Ptolemy, Pythagoras and Aristotle. We also described some other sacred places in America, Japan, Austria and Germany, including some Holocaust memorials.

Who We Are and Where We Come From

We concluded with some profound lessons to be learned from the serious study of genealogy, telling us who we are and where we come from, namely:

1. The lesson of our individual mortality, implicit in each of us as living biological organisms. Each of us is born and each of us eventually dies.

2. Science teaches us that we are the product of both biological and cultural evolution and that our DNA makes us brothers and sisters with all mankind, most closely with our immediate families and ancestors. Our DNA also connects us with all other living things, from the present to the beginning of life on earth, three and one-half billion years ago.

3. Among all the different worldviews, both secular and religious, I personally believe the most tolerant is Humanism, a Scientific/Religious democratic, ethical way of life, which relies mainly upon reason, without the supernatural, but appreciates the poetry of religion. Its basic rule, in common with many religions, is, simply: "Doing unto others as we would have done unto ourselves." I believe that trying to live an ethical life is the highest and best expression of our humanity. Scientific/Religious Humanism also recognizes that we humans are capable of creating and appreciating both the art and "poetry" of myths and religion and the "prose" of science. Science and religion can thus be compatible, as human expressions of both poetry and prose.

4. The lesson of our existence inside of the vast environs of Nature, and our responsibility to conserve it, whose very origin remains an inscrutable mystery, to both science and religion. The fundamental mysteries of Being and Time. Thus, genealogy has taken us on a long journey through the history of science and religion, illustrating the mysteries, complexities and beauties of humanity's existence.

POSTSCRIPT

As much as I hope that a metaphor of "Poetry and Prose" may help mediate some of the conflicts between religion and science, I must be realistic and realize that it may only help a few people rationalize their religious belief, or a few other people feel less uncertain about being simultaneously religious and scientific.

We should be able to hope at least for tolerance among the world's religions. But even that minimal hope seems to be dashed every day by reports of violent strife between groups professing their religion, or even their different sects within the same religion, as the justification for their violence. And this hope is made even more forlorn since most religions profess their belief in peace and love and compassion.

I am afraid that my studies of the world tell me that mankind, as said by David Hume over 200 years ago, is ruled by his emotions, and that we are more tribal than rational. Or, as Charles Darwin said, 150 years ago, in his "Descent of Man", that man's behavior is still marked by the "indelible stamp of his lowly origin".

As Edward O. Wilson has also said, "To understand biological human nature in depth is to drain the swamps of religious and blank-state dogma. But it also imposes the heavy burden of individual choice that goes with total intellectual freedom."

Perhaps someday our children or grandchildren will see a time when humanity actually lives by the Golden Rule that all religions profess. Do unto others, as you would have them do unto you.